Digging the Days of the Dead

Digging the Days of the Dead

A Reading of Mexico's
Días de muertos

Juanita Garciagodoy

UNIVERSITY PRESS OF COLORADO

Copyright © 1998 by the University Press of Colorado

Published by the University Press of Colorado
5589 Arapahoe Avenue, Suite 206C
Boulder, Colorado 80303

Printed in the United States of America.

The University Press of Colorado is a cooperative publishing enterprise supported, in part, by Adams State College, Colorado State University, Fort Lewis College, Mesa State College, Metropolitan State College of Denver, University of Colorado, University of Northern Colorado, University of Southern Colorado, and Western State College of Colorado.

The paper used in this publication meets the minimum requirements of the American National Standard for Information Sciences — Permanence of Paper for Printed Library Materials. ANSI Z39.48-1984

Library of Congress Cataloging-in-Publication Data

Garciagodoy, Juanita, 1952–
    Digging the Days of the Dead : a reading of Mexico's días de muertos / Juanita Garciagodoy.
        p.   cm.
    Includes bibliographical references and index.
    ISBN 0-87081-499-0 (alk. paper). — 0-87081-590-3 (pbk. : alk. paper)
    1. All Souls' Day—Mexico.   2. Mexico—Social life and customs.
    I. Title.
GT4995.A4G37   1998
394.266—dc21   98-28489
                                                                        CIP

 The color signature in this book was funded in part by a grant from the Minnesota Humanities Commission in cooperation with the National Endowment for the Humanities and the Minnesota State Legislature.

MINNESOTA
HUMANITIES
COMMISSION

Illustrations on blank pages and section openings are taken from Posada's drawings.

This book was designed and typeset in Sabon and Papryus by Stephen Adams, Aspen.

07 06 05 04 03 02 01 00   10 9 8 7 6 5 4 3 2

Per a en Jordi Rabasa, el meu maco marit

For my parents, Jorge Garciagodoy and Marilyn Wiese de Garciagodoy

Para mis ánimas y el ánima sola

0.1 Para mis ánimas. Sugar figures,
San Miguel de Allende, Guanajuato

Contents

Illustrations

All photographs were taken by Juanita Garciagodoy except Dos catrinas, Fig. 2.1, taken by Jorge Garciagodoy.

Color Plates

Acknowledgments

The words *gracias* and *thanks* convey a shadowy suggestion of what I feel toward the people who, directly or indirectly, have helped me to write this book.

René Jara and John Fiske helped me learn to work in semiotics and popular culture; from 1988 to 1994, other scholars from the University of Minnesota's Department of Hispanic and Luso-Brasilian Languages and Literatures provided instruction and block grants; *merci,* Professor Tom Conley, Harvard University. Thanks for the support of Macalester College, in particular the Department of Spanish where María Elena Doleman, Fabiola Franco, and Galo González traded classes so I could attend Días de muertos guiltlessly. Anna Meigs, Anne Sutherland, and Jack Weatherford gave me interviewing tips. Faculty Travel and Research grants partially funded my research in Mexico.

My students at Macalester College helped me to refine my theories on Días de muertos, particularly Brian Berkopec, Felecia Bartow, and Katrina Olds. Érika Figueroa provided valuable editorial assistance.

Jonis Agee, Rina Epelstein, Al Greenberg, Tony Hainault, Greg Hewett, Janet Holmes, Pepe Jéssurun, and Jen Patti heartened me through these studious years.

Marilyn, Eduardo, and Terry Garciagodoy, Verónica Cervantes, and Jeanne Behn Smith helped me feel capable. Jorge Garciagodoy provided hours of cruising for calaveras and marathon drives to Mixquic and Cuetzalan.

Thanks, Rosalind Rosoff Beimler, for conversations in the D.F. and Mixquic; Hellen Plaschinksi and Ricardo Finkler for a day in Toluca; Carolyn Valero for trips to Toluca, Xochimilco, and Mixquic, complete with discussions of history and architecture.

Patricia y Rosa Patricia Rodríguez Ortiz, *gracias por compartir sus ideas sobre esta fiesta. Gracias monumentales a* Rosa Ortiz Torres *por sus anécdotas y sabiduría sobre Días de muertos y la vida como por su cariño—descansa en paz.*

George Rabasa, for reading and advising, for accompanying me, for wisdom, love, and delight, "thanks" is a pale witness to the gratitude I feel.

The Dead as Guests of Honor

A Family Reunion, National Affirmation

"For all eternity," muses an old man, "my descendants
will remember me and, on the eve of every second of
November, I will come back to them. I will find the house filled
with food, incense, the light of candles, and warmth. And I
will come in and, forever and ever, that one night of the year,
I will be among my own."
—Horcasitas 137

Every human group has a way to remember the dead. Many people
offer food to the souls of their departed. In the United States, Hallowe'en shows vestiges of such a memorial. On October 31 children dress up as grotesque corpses (the Frankensteins and the monstrously
masked), as spirits (the myriad, sheeted ghosts), as those who communicate
with the dead (the Count Draculas, the witches), or as someone or something of some totemistic value to the child (Bart or Lisa Simpson, Alice in
Wonderland, et cetera). They take to the streets, traditionally at the anoma-
lous time of dusk or shortly thereafter, when the liminality*[1] of the hour

---

[1] Words marked with an asterisk appear in the Glossary.

1.1 Sugar and chocolate calaveritas. Feria del Alfeñique, Toluca, Estado de México

itself—neither night nor day—seems to permit intercourse between the worlds of the living and the dead. The children knock on neighbors' doors and demand treats or threaten tricks. They do not remember deceased individuals through this activity and probably do not realize they are acting as the spirits for whom the treats were originally intended, who were believed to "trick" those who failed to proffer the requested goods.[2]

In Mexico *Días de muertos,*[3] Days of the Dead, is not primarily for children, although they have a role in it (see Plate 1) and are traditionally given candy skulls with their names on them (see Figure 1.1). If they are dead, they are among the honored guests. Whether they died as children or as adults, what Philippe Ariès wrote about the Christians of the first eight or nine centuries can also be said of those who celebrate Días de muertos: "Generally speaking, the dead are not regarded as separate from the living.

---

[2] For an interesting analysis of Hallowe'en as an example of age-role reversal, see Turner 172ff.

[3] I italicize non-English words only at their first appearance in the book. Thereafter, if I use them frequently I will mark them with an asterisk the first time they occur in a section to indicate they can be found in the Glossary.

They belong to the same unbroken family" (Ariès 151). They are not forgotten or excluded from recollections, prayers, or holidays because they are no longer visible.

Although some expectation exists that treating the dead well will result in a smoother year—good health, economic stability—and some fear exists that not doing so will result in problems during the year, relatively little emphasis is given to this expectation. Still, I have heard and read variations of a story about not caring for the dead; one version goes like this.

A woman married a man and went to live in his community. He did not believe the dead return once a year, and when his wife asked him for money to purchase the goods necessary for an ofrenda* for their deceased parents, he refused, laughing at her for being superstitious. On November 2 she insisted, and again he refused her angrily, and, annoyed at her persistence, said, "Offer them shit!" He left, slamming the door, and went to a bar to drink. The wife wept bitterly and set up a poor offering consisting of the little there was in the house.[4]

The husband left the bar so drunk that he passed out on his way home. He awoke at midnight and saw a procession of the happy dead carrying off beautiful fruits, flowers, and *ollas** (earthenware pots) of their favorite foods and wearing the new clothes that had been offered to them. Toward the end of the procession he saw his parents-in-law carrying the minimal offering his wife had managed to scrape together, wearing the threadbare clothes from the year before. The very last were his own dead parents who walked weeping, carrying a dish of their son's feces. The man repented and apologized to his wife and to both sets of parents, vowing never to disregard the dead again, but it was too late. That year, after losing everything he had, he suffered an accident and died.

The story is much more serious in its didactic, tragic tenor than the most ghoulish U.S. children could imagine in the worst ghost story, much less in the alliterative, hopeful shout, *Trick or treat*. The Mexican tale reveals the fear of traditions being lost because of the economic power wielded by an outsider; the miserly husband was not from the wife's community. It carries the heavy knowledge many celebrants of Días de muertos have that whereas at one time their ancestors determined and managed the

---

[4] A family does not have to be poor for there to be little in the house since, in traditional households, daily trips are made to the market to buy the freshest available groceries to be consumed that day.

order of society according to their own philosophy and needs, more recent forebears were conquered and colonized by outsiders who withheld the means of production, who subordinated them as a wife to a cruel and irresponsible husband. The tale has a bitter subtext that reminds the teller and the listener that things have not changed: The descendants and allies of the colonizers continue to dominate, exploit, and humiliate the descendants of the conquered. Ultimately, there is a triumphant note, for the husband dies a violent death as a consequence of his lack of solidarity with both the dead and his wife. But I dare say that such a revenge bears cold comfort.

Some versions of the story are less drastic. In them the husband has a terrible year in which he suffers losses and ill health, but he lives to budget for as magnificent an ofrenda as he can afford. His parents and parents-in-law are mollified, and in the future things go much better for him. These versions accomplish what the celebration of the fiesta* accomplishes: It restores hope and faith that by recalling and returning some part of the gifts received, they may be received again. Also, by remembering and reembodying traditions, order is restored in the family and in the universe.

Días de muertos is a great family reunion that especially honors those who no longer have bodies (see Plates 1 and 2). Marta Turok calls it a great, collective communion (Turok 40). Jésus Angel Ochoa Zazueta finds it comforting to know the dead are alive because such knowledge assuages the fear of death and recognizes that this celebration, by revitalizing the celebrating community's oldest traditions and institutions, provides solidarity for "un grupo que cada día necesita más cohesión y más elementos contra las fuerzas de desintegración que lo acechan" (Ochoa Zazueta 8) [a group that daily is in greater need of more cohesion and more elements against the forces of disintegration that threaten it].[5]

Días de muertos can be considered the coronation of the harvest and an expression of gratitude to God and the spirits of the deceased for their blessings on that which is reaped;[6] it also entails a sharing of those goods (see Figure 1.5). Piña Chan identified a pre-Hispanic cult to the dead that paralleled a fertility cult, both of which were tied to agriculture and to

---

[5] All translations in this book are mine. I always present the original Spanish; when no Spanish is given, the source was in English.

[6] José Camacho of Cocula, Jalisco, pointed out to me in an interview that "En Días de muertos, todo [lo que se ofrenda] es maduro—por eso creo que tiene que ver con la cosecha" [For Días de muertos, everything that is offered is ripe—that's why I think it has to do with the harvest.]

anthropogenesis (quoted in Ochoa Zazueta 32f). This aspect is most likely to be felt in agricultural areas, although I would venture that a majority of the urban people who continue to celebrate the fiesta are still tied in important ways to the rural communities in which they or their parents were born. They may not think literally about the harvest during the Days of the Dead, but they might take stock and give thanks for the good they experienced in the previous year. This is also a time at which uprooted villagers or country folk who cannot return to their communities of origin—something those who have had to seek work outside often do—feel reconnected to those communities by keeping the tradition alive and honoring the same dead that are being honored *en su tierra* (at home). For example, Esperanza Martínez—octogenarian, retired teacher, and lifelong inhabitant of Teloloapan, Guerrero—has said, "Lo bonito es que aunque nuestros hijos van y vienen a la ciudad siguen manteniendo nuestras costumbres, y se sienten muy satisfechos de ser distintos a los otros pueblos" (Garduño Espinosa). [What's nice is that even though our children come and go to the city, they continue to uphold our traditions, and they feel very happy to be different from other people.]

Néstor García Canclini considers fiestas *campesinas* (peasant fiestas) movements of communal unification through which people celebrate and give expression to their material experience of events or beliefs that have arisen from their daily contact with nature and society. Because fiestas are often associated with agricultural cycles, he thinks they are a way of symbolically—and sometimes materially—appropriating what nature or an unjust society has denied the celebrants. By formally recognizing the gifts and remembering and reliving how they received them, the people hope to receive them in the future (García Canclini 79).

More poetically and less politically, Elizabeth Carmichael and Chloë Sayer have written that

> The whole ritual cycle . . . is concerned with agricultural success. . . . An offering is made to the dead—to death—of the things that have been . . . harvested. . . . *Todos Santos* [All Saints] exercises and perpetrates the non-medianised bond between life and death . . . between human activity and the agricultural cycle by means of the essential coincidence between the time of harvest—the resurgence of the seed as fruit—and that of honouring the dead—who also return and issue out of the afterworld. . . .

It is evidently a collective force of an economic and social nature, which demands a family and group event as an obligation. (Carmichael and Sayer 66)

To some extent—especially among government officials, public school educators, and certain intellectuals including some artists, writers, and a few other members of the bourgeoisie—it is a celebration of national affirmation, encouraged sometimes in contrast or opposition to Hallowe'en, which merchants in the most cosmopolitan areas of the country's most cosmopolitan cities market, along with the products that reproduce its typical icons: jack-o'-lanterns, witches, and ghosts. This group latches onto Días de muertos with its own agendas: a populist one, a nationalistic anti-U.S. one, an exoticizing Orientalist one, a nostalgic one.

The Mexican interest in ancient history and in Indigenous[7] and popular cultures and traditions grew dramatically during the 1920s, partly in reaction against the francophile tastes of the dominant classes during the Porfiriato (1884–1911). Popular celebrations received a great impetus from the concern with forging a national consciousness in a young nation-state, as discussed in Chapter 3. A relatively successful attempt was made to establish Mexico's identity on the basis of its Indian past and its idiosyncratic syncretism. These were considered distinctive enough to separate Mexico from both Spain, from which it had gained its independence in 1821, and the United States, whose massive presence had—and has—sometimes made it a culturally fearsome neighbor.

The ruling classes have their own reasons for preserving and promoting traditions such as Días de muertos, as García Canclini has noted. He sees the belief in popular culture as the authentic seat of what is most human in Mexico and of the nation's pure essence as sentimental and ill founded. Those who hold this view consider the people the repository of biological and irrational racial virtues such as love of the land, religion, and ancestral beliefs. This conservative hyper-valuation had a useful function: It allowed bourgeois national populism to identify its interests with those of the entire nation and to hide its state of dependency, as well as internal class interests that might threaten its privileges. Based on this idea of folklore as a fossilized, apolitical museum, a populist politics could be promoted under the

---

[7] I capitalize the words Indian, Indigenous, Native, Pagan, and Aboriginal to give them the respect accorded to recognized and named nationalities and religions.

pretense of giving the people what they like without considering giving the people the power to choose and to create politics and economics out of their own vision (García Canclini 65).

When those who thus essentialized the popular read enough positivist philology to realize that popular culture had "degraded" high culture by mixing the latter with its own knowledge, wisdom, and culture, disappointment ensued (García Canclini 64). The realization left in its wake some resentment toward those who had disappointed the sentimentalists, as well as a nostalgia for the myth. The *desengaño*, the recognition of their self-deception, did not lead to a willingness to know the object of their nostalgia, which continues to inspire members of the bourgeoisie to seek *lo mexicano* (that which is Mexican) in the traditions and the *artesanía* of las clases populares.[8]

How People Celebrate

Estas [tumbas] son las de 'los muertos', como dicen de los que nadie visita. Quizá ya no hubo descendientes que acudan a plantar arbustos; a revivir jardineras con margaritas . . . ni, menos, a dialogar con ellos en una noche así.

—Quoted in Herrera

These (tombs) belong to "the dead," as they call those whom no one visits. Maybe there were no more descendants to come and plant bushes, to revive the pots with daisies . . . not to mention to dialogue with them on a night like this.

More than anything, Días de muertos are holidays during which the dead dear to the celebrants are remembered. For weeks beforehand, in preparation for the fiesta, merchants sell goods in the markets for the offerings to the dead. Booths, stands, or shops sell *copal,* the incense that has been used for centuries in Mexico; votive, wax, and tallow brown, yellow, and white candles of various lengths and thicknesses; new incense burners and candleholders; vegetables and fruits of the season; and seasonal flowers, especially the ubiquitous (and variously spelled) *cempoaxóchitl** (see Plate 1). Some of these items and others will have been collected during the previous year, according to the availability of funds and goods. Shortly

---

[8] For an example of this exercise in essentialization, see Octavio Paz, "Todos santos, día de muertos," *El laberinto de la soledad* (*The Labyrinth of Solitude*).

before the day on which families set up their offerings, they acquire the fresh items necessary for a worthy ofrenda, for which they will have planned a budget and toward which many will have saved all year long.[9]

La Ofrenda

Calaverita de dulce,	Little candy skull,
mi panecito de muerto,	my little bread of the dead,
detener quisiera el tiempo	I wish I could stop time
tan incierto, tan incierto.	so uncertain, so uncertain.

—Traditional (Quoted in Martel)

At home, an altar[10] is improvised, usually near the permanent altar many traditional and humble families keep in a hallway or corner of their living room or bedroom for devotions to their special saints. The altar for the dead may consist of stacked boxes or a box on a table. It may be a new *petate** (a reed mat). It may be suspended from a roof beam, as in Veracruz. It may be enormous and very elaborate or humble and very simple. The altar is usually covered by a clean white cloth, but paper, cut paper, or plastic sheeting can also be used, according to the tastes, traditions, and purse of the community or family. The altar may have a photograph of the deceased and some sacred images such as prints of Mary, Jesus, or other saints favored by the family or by the one being recognized. For the *angelitos,** those who died as children, there may be toys or miniature sugar figures of animals and foods. For adults there may be favorite or new full-sized or miniature work implements. For everyone there may be new or favorite clothing. There will probably be a candle for each spirit, as well as

---

[9] The regional market in Tlaxcala, according to journalist Juan Hernández of *Novedades,* receives thirty tons of thirty varieties of flowers, ten thousand candles, twenty tons of oranges, fifteen tons of guayaba, twenty-five tons of tangerines, and forty tons of wheat flour. Demand for eggs, sugar, and butter, used in *pan de muerto* (bread of the dead), rises 300 percent during this period. One family, buying a typical ten bunches of cempoaxóchitl, spends $40 (U.S.) for them. An ofrenda can cost a family 4 million old pesos,* for which they sometimes sell animals or part of their harvest.

[10] Artist Felipe Ehrenberg and Víctor Fosado Vázquez have expressed concern about the interchangeable use of the words *altar* and *ofrenda*. In my experience and usage, the distinction is drawn between the altar, which holds the ofrenda, and the ofrenda, which is everything offered on the altar. There seems little reason to distinguish between the two when the whole is meant, especially as people who set ofrendas tend to make no distinction between the two words.

sugar calaveras and the pan de muerto* traditional for that community (see Plates 3–6).

The food for the ofrenda is always the most labor-intensive, expensive holiday fare, which may take several days to prepare, as is the case with *moles*.[11] There will usually be traditional Mexican sweets like candied pumpkin and a fruit called *tejocote,* plus soft drinks, sweet drinks, alcoholic beverages, cocoa or *atole,** water, and a little plate of salt.

In Mixquic, the oldest settlement in Delegación Tláhuac, D.F.,* a town well-known for its faithfulness to Días de muertos and whose 21,000 residents had 2 million visitors for the celebration in 1993, the ofrenda is to consist of nine elements. The significance of each is explained thus: (1) Water slakes the thirst of the spirits and represents purity and the source of life; (2) salt, with its purifying qualities, is an invitation to the banquet, an element that retards the corruption of the body, and a symbol of wisdom; (3) candles, symbols of eternal love, faith, and hope, signify triumph for having passed into immortality; (4) copal, incense, is an offering to the gods and to transmit praises and prayers; (5) flowers stand for love and the sun; (6) a petate is for rest, as that is where the spirit stops to enjoy the ofrenda; (7) toys are for the angelitos; (8) an image of an *itzcuintli** will help the deceased cross the River Chiconauapan; (9) bread/tamales*/an *itacate* (traveler's provisions) are fraternal gifts (Guillén Peralta; Guarneros).

In their chapter on Mixquic, Elizabeth Carmichael and Chloë Sayer say that as part of an offering, salt symbolizes Christian baptism and "the savour of life," among other things they do not specify (Carmichael and Sayer 141). Their superb informant, María Antonieta Sánchez de Escamilla of Puebla, Estado* de Puebla, elaborates on what salt as part of an offering means to her: "When we share sugar and salt with the dead, we are symbolically sharing the sweet and bitter things of life. . . . Salt, so it is said, is especially important for children who die before baptism" (Carmichael and Sayer 121). Sugar and salt are also basic condiments on any table.

Journalist Juan Hernández garnered this explanation of the altars in the state of Tlaxcala:

---

[11] *Mole* (singular); literally, ground food. Rich, spiced stews containing vegetables and meats. The sauces of vegetables, chiles, chocolate, spices, and seeds are ground on a *metate,* stone mortar, with a *mano,* stone pestle.

El altar tiene tres niveles. En el primero el muerto saluda a sus familiares; en el segundo goza del banquete; el tercero es "el lugar sagrado de lo divino."

En la ofrenda tlaxcalteca se incluyen dos calaveras de barro las cuales simbolizan a la muerte, "pero no como algo terrorífico, sino la muerte como una dimensión diferente de la propia vida." (Hernández, "Tlaxcalles")

The altar has three levels. On the first one the dead greet their relatives; on the second one they enjoy the banquet; the third level is "the holy place of the divine."

On the Tlaxcalteca offering two earthenware skulls are included to symbolize death, "but not like something terrifying, rather death as a different dimension of life itself."

Once the souls of the dead have arrived at the altar, the living are warned against taking anything from the offering because the dead "en la noche les jalarán los pies" [will pull their feet during the night] (Hernández, "Tlaxcalles"). This last belief is not unique to Tlaxcaltecas.

When I was a child, my nana* Rosa Ortiz Torres told me an anecdote from her childhood in the hamlet of San Mateo where night was deeply dark, far from city lampposts and lights. She related that she and her sister, known for their sweet tooth, had been admonished not to touch the ofrenda. The family went to bed, she with her grandmother. Tempted by the sweets on the altar, she waited until her grandmother was asleep. Then she slipped quietly out of bed and tiptoed to the altar. She reached for a pan de muerto, and the whole household was awakened by the shriek, ¡Mamá! ¡Un muerto! [Mom! A dead person!] Rosita's hand had encountered her sister's, reaching for the same bread at the same instant. The children were spanked and scolded, and they never again violated an ofrenda.

When the ofrendas are in place, on the appropriate day according to the community and according to the ways they died but typically between October 28 and November 4, the dead are called home and welcomed to many hours of the companionship of their living relatives and friends. In a number of places, they are called or welcomed with firecrackers. In most, church bells toll in certain patterns depending on whether it is el Día de los angelitos—literally, the Day of the Little Angels—usually November 1, or el Día de los muertos, the Day of the Dead, those who died as adults, usually November 2. In and around Mérida, Yucatán, at midnight on October 31, an elaborate banquet is served for the bodiless guests of honor and their living relatives. It is called Hanal Pixan, which means dinner of the dead.

1.2 Ofrenda for the lone soul. Museo Nacional de Culturas Populares, México, D.F.

The most traditional communities dedicate an altar and sometimes a whole day to the *ánima sola** the lone soul who has no one to regale it (see Figure 1.2). In Mixquic an ofrenda is set out for "todos los muertos de la región" (all the dead of the region) on the pre-Hispanic stone *tzompantli** behind the church (Guarneros). The builders of a beautiful public ofrenda in Oaxaca, *Estado de** Oaxaca, told me it was dedicated to the ánimas solas who have no one else to commemorate them. Xochimilco has a practice called *calaverear.* A group of *cargos/cargueros,* or elders (literally those in charge) appointed to take care of several ritual aspects of the fiesta, go from house to house requesting items from people's ofrendas to set up one for the ánima sola. In Puebla el altar del ánima sola is built outside the house, as these spirits seem to be considered ritually impure or even dangerous.[12] The descriptions of the ofrendas suggest that people of Puebla want to propitiate rather than celebrate and please the spirits; their offerings are meager indeed. Fredy Méndez, a young Totonaca man interviewed by Carmichael and Sayer in Tajín, Veracruz, explained:

> We cannot be sure that the wicked return from Hell, but, in case they do, we offer them their own *ofrenda*. Outside the house, on a narrow shelf or table, we put bread, chocolate and flowers. Those who have sinned may neither enter the house, nor approach the blessed altar; they must remain outside. This altar is for errant souls, for souls in torment, and for orphans. (Carmichael and Sayer 81)

In contrast to this cool treatment of las ánimas solas, Froylan Martínez Cuenca of Huaquechula, Puebla, says that in his family they are welcomed to the principal offering. His mother taught the children, "Why should the ánima sola remain by the roadside? How disrespectful! We should make these unfortunate souls as welcome as the souls of our loved ones. All should get the same treatment" (Carmichael and Sayer 91).

Esperanza Martínez, an elderly former teacher and lifelong inhabitant of Teloloapan, Guerrero, expressed a combination of the two attitudes that prevail in her community: "Creemos que a las almas que ya no tienen deudos se las traen nuestros familiares para que coman de las cosas puestas para los que vivieron con nosotros. A estas almas solas se les pone una vela fuera de la casa a manera de ofrenda" (Garduño Espinosa, "Ricos"). [We believe that our relations bring the souls who no longer have relatives so they may eat from the things set for those who lived with us. For these lone souls we set a candle outside the house as an offering.]

---

[12] This fear could be explained in part by the pre-Hispanic belief in a group of spirits called *cihuateteo* (god-women) or *cihuapipiltin*. They were the souls of women who died in childbirth and who, after four years of traveling with the sun (along with the souls of warriors who died in battle), turned into flying creatures with bare torsos, skulls for heads, and claws for hands and feet, enviously seeking to cause disease and death to children. To try to propitiate them, offerings were periodically set out at crossroads (see Figure 5.1).

Hanging out With the Dead

The ghosts return to the world of the dead, encouraged . . .
by masked mummers whose mission is to scare away any
stubborn souls who try to linger too long. Thus are the living
and the dead left at peace with each other for another year.
—Rosalind Rosoff Beimler 23

There is another place for offerings. Most families will have cleaned the
graves of their dead in preparation for their visit. In many communities the
graves are richly decorated with cempoaxóchitl* and other flowers; offerings of copal,* candles, calaveras,* and food may be placed on them
instead of, or in addition to, on home altars. According to the local practice, family members may take turns or may all stay by the grave the whole
night to enjoy the presence of the disembodied guests. In many places such
as Mixquic and Xochimilco, local priests celebrate mass in the graveyards
and take up a collection there for their fees. In Mexico City's Panteón
Dolores, priests celebrate mass in each quarter of the cemetery from a truck
bed on which an altar is improvised. Every mass includes a warning not to
be deceived by "false priests" into paying for masses to be said for the
dead: "Acostúmbrense a recibir gratuitamente la gracia de la Iglesia" [Get
used to receiving the grace of the Church free of charge].

Some people say they cannot tell if the dead really come; people in
Damián Texoloc, Tlaxcala, "aseguran haber visto desfilar a los muertos por
las calles rumbo a las casas de sus familiares" (Hernández, "Tlaxcalles")
[confirm that they had seen the dead parading toward their homes]. Many
ascertain that they can sense the presence of the dead, as does Froylan Martínez Cuenca from Huaquechula: "When the dead arrive, you feel their
presence. You can't talk with them; you don't call their names. . . . We feel
happy and peaceful; we go out to meet them, and feel glad that they have
come" (quoted in Carmichael and Sayer 90).

At the end of their visit—and again, the date varies from community
to community—the disembodied guests leave in the order in which they
arrived and are bidden farewell. Depending on the traditions of the place,
the graveyards may be lit by candles so the spirits can see their way. Music
may be played or songs entoned. Words of farewell may be spoken.
Church bells may be rung. New offerings of food, drink, and clothing may
be prepared.

The day after the dead leave the earth for their usual residence, related
to the Catholic folk concept of heaven, families share the food, the spirit or

scent of which the revenants have ingested. Many of my informants have said they can tell the flavor and the scent have been consumed. Irene Mauricio Reynoso of Huixcolotla, Puebla, told Carmichael and Sayer that for Días de muertos she cooks everything with extra flavor "because it is the flavour, or the aroma, that the dead extract. The dead don't physically eat the food: we believe that they come and kiss it. Later, we eat it ourselves. Some people eat extremely slowly, making everything last, because the *ofrenda* has been blessed by the dead" (Carmichael and Sayer 105). And Esperanza Martínez has said, "En las noches de los dos días vienen las almas a visitarnos y a comer el aroma de lo que les gustaba en esta vida, por eso ya no sabe igual después" (Garduño Espinosa, "Viva") [On the nights of the two days, the souls come to visit us and to eat the aroma of what they used to enjoy in this life; that's why it doesn't taste the same afterward].

Many also point out that the water level in the glasses on the altar is low because the spirits have drunk. María Antonieta Sánchez de Escamilla, a kindergarten teacher and administrator, explains, "It is the spirit, or the essence, that the dead extract. I've never noticed a change in food, but we always offer water and, do you know, the level really does go down! This can't be evaporation because there's no heat—just the flames of the candles. . . . This tells you how thirsty our visitors are" (quoted in Carmichael and Sayer 21).

There are two primary ways for the living to share the food the dead have left; one is by having dinner together. This is likely to include extended family members, ritual kin, and close friends. The other way is to prepare a basket with new or freshly washed napkins on which the various dishes are arranged. Often, the godchildren are charged with taking these baskets to their godparents with whom they may eat before returning home, the basket filled anew with some of the delicacies that were on the godparents' altar. The almost formulaic words on delivering the basket are "Mire, madrina (o abuelita, tía, padrino), le traemos lo que le dejaron los muertitos*" [Look, godmother (or grandma, aunt, godfather), we've brought you what the dead left for you].

Calaveras*

Como te ves me vi	As you look I looked,
y como me ves te verás.	and as I look you will look.
—Traditional	

Plate 1 *A boy decks a grave. Mixquic graveyard*

Plate 2 *Family reunion. Panteón General, Oaxaca, Oaxaca*

Plate 3 Home ofrenda. Oaxaca, Oaxaca

Plate 4 Detail of home ofrenda with liquor, sweets, candles

Plate 5 Detail of home ofrenda with dog, chocolate, bread

Plate 6 Detail of home ofrenda with holy images, cross, calaveritas

Plate 7 Fiesta de catrines. Bazar Sábado, México, D.F.

Plate 8 Frida y Diego "Sapo" by Linares. Anahuacalli, México, D.F. (Courtesy of Dolores Olmedo Patiño)

Plate 9 Ofrenda for B. Traven. Xochimilco

Plate 10 Ofrenda to Tamayo, altar. Taller Municipal de Artes Plásticas Rufino Tamayo, Oaxaca

Plate 11 Ofrenda for AIDS dead with calavera. Oaxaca, Oaxaca

Plate 12 Children's ofrenda. Centro Cultural Ricardo Flores Magón, Oaxaca (Courtesy of CCRFM)

Plate 13 "Tlatzotzompantli," Templo Mayor, México, D.F.

Plate 14 Mayra's mausoleum. Panteón Dolores, México, D.F.;
Mayra's mausoleum, interior.

Plate 15 Ofrenda at Coordinación de Educación Tecnológica Industrial High School exhibition. México, D.F.

Plate 16 Ofrenda by La Esmeralda School of Arts. Parque Alameda, México, D.F.

Plate 17 Parque tradicional. Shop of former Museo de Artes e Industrias Populares, México, D.F.

Plate 18 Papier mâché "Gran fandango y francachela de todas las calaveras" by Linares. Anahuacalli, México, D.F. (Courtesy of Dolores Olmedo Patiño)

Plate 19 Merienda de pilón. Bakery, México, D.F.

Plate 20 Merienda exquisita. Bakery, México, D.F.

Plate 21 Conquista del jalogüín. Bakery, México, D.F.

Plate 22 Susy's grave. Mixquic graveyard

Plate 23 Children on their grandfather's grave. Xoxocotlán, Oaxaca

Plate 24 Ofrenda for Lolita, Rosita, Xochilita. Riverview Branch Library, St. Paul
(Courtesy Karen L. Hering)

Plate 25 Ofrenda for Jerry Garcia by Juanita Garciagodoy, Mani Mokalla, Morrie Norris, Timothy Priest. Macalester College, St. Paul

Plate 26 Ofrenda for our dead, Spanish 51.01, November 1995 Macalester College, St. Paul

1.3 Tamer with pan de muerto. Bakery in Mexico City

Along with the earnest practices, carnivalesque elements are also related to Días de muertos in some areas, mostly in Mexico City. For several weeks, bakeries there produce a light, sweet yeast bread known as pan de muerto,* bread of the dead. It is made in round loaves and decorated with balls and strips of dough in the form of a skull and crossbones (recently the "bones" of slightly crustier bread have multiplied; see Figure 1.3). Panes de muerto are often placed on home altars or graves as part of the ofrenda. Loaves shaped like animals, birds, or fish (see Figure 1.4) and like people (see Figure 1.5) are baked in other parts of the country to be placed on altars. Some of the forms seem to repeat in the medium of European-style wheat bread a pre-Hispanic tradition in which such loaves were made from ueuhtli, amaranth, and honey.

If they are large enough, the calaveras that are fashioned out of sweets—sugar, chocolate, amaranth—have names on them so they can serve as gifts to specific spirits, children, or friends (see Figure 1.6). In some communities they are part of the ofrendas in people's houses or on graves, as they sometimes are in Mexico City and Oaxaca. Calaveras and humorous skeletal cartoons seem to be found mostly in the most heterogeneous cities of the country where cultures have mixed together and where humor lends a wee degree of cohesion to city dwellers who laugh at similar things and identify as a group.

Sugar calaveras could be the iconic successors of the skulls the Aztecs decorated elaborately for use as masks or offerings, of sculpted skulls—

*1.4 Fish-shaped bread on offering. Museo Nacional de Culturas Populares,
México, D.F.*

usually in earthenware—or of tzompantli,* both the racks of real skulls
and the stone representations[13] (see Figures 1.7–1.9). They could as well
derive from the Catholic practice observed by the Englishman John Lloyd
Stephens who was traveling in Yucatán early in the nineteenth century. He
saw charnel houses with hanging bones and skulls bearing the names of
individuals. He saw the lovingly cleaned and arranged bones of one Man-
uela Carrillo with an inscription in verse exhorting the passerby to "Look
at yourself in this mirror, / And in its pale reflection / Behold your end!"
He saw cleaned and polished skulls, each with its name written across the

---

[13] The placement of skulls on the tzompantli served to humiliate and inspire fear in the ene-
mies of the Aztecs. The one Hernán Cortés saw in Tenochtitlan held more than ten thousand
skulls (González, "En Mixquic").

1.5 Anthropomorphic pan de muerto on offering. Museo Nacional de Culturas Populares, México, D.F.

forehead, along with a request for an Ave María or a Pater Noster. The priest, who was leading Stephens on a tour that Stephens found disturbingly macabre, knew all of the dead and explained that it was easy to forget the dead who were interred, but disinterred and labeled, they were effective *mementi mori** (Carmichael and Sayer 47ff). Perhaps these skulls were replaced by the more cheerful sugar skulls, the earliest reference to which might have been made by Fanny Calderón de la Barca in 1841.

1.6 Sugar calaveritas with names. San Miguel de Allende, Guanajuato

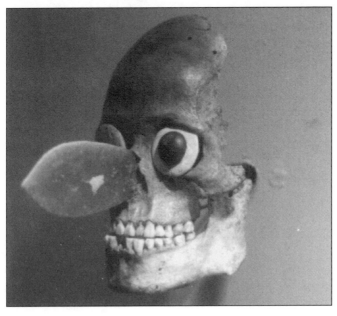

1.7 Aztec skull mask. Templo Mayor, México, D.F. (Permission given by Instituto Nacional de Antropología e Historia [INAH])

1.8 Aztec incense burner. Museum of Anthropology, México, D.F.
(Permission given by INAH)

The maker of what are surely the most elaborate sugar calaveras, Wenceslao Rivas Contreras from Toluca, Estado de México, interviewed by Carmichael and Sayer in 1989, talked about wanting to create new calaveras every year "to surprise the public" (Carmichael and Sayer 113). He confided, "At the moment I'm studying the lower jaw. It's never clearly shown by sugar-workers, but I'm hoping to create a full skull, with gaping jaws. It will look more naturalistic, more imposing" (Carmichael and Sayer 113). Later he said, "Now I can make cheerful skulls, ferocious skulls, and skulls with sad eyes. I want to give them maximum expression, I want to make them come alive" (Carmichael and Sayer 115). This impulse seems little distant from the one that moved Don Wenceslao's forebears to place diminutive tiles on human skulls, with shells and obsidian discs for the eyes, to "look more imposing" and even "alive" than a naked skull or a totally fabricated skull mask.

I read various sources and spoke with several informants about the meaning of the practice of giving and eating sugar skulls, a custom outsiders often find appalling and morbid to the point at which immigrants can be considered to have gone native when they adopt—or at least accept—the custom themselves. In Mexico City's newspaper *Uno más uno* (1 Nov. 1992), journalist Bulmaro Villarruel Velasco offered this explanation:

1.9 Templo Mayor tzompantli (detail). México, D.F. (Permission given by INAH)

1.10 A girl guards a grave. Xoxocotlán, Oaxaca

El hombre común, cuya vida no es valorada por la sociedad, carece de miedos ante la muerte, se burla de ella, se come su propia calavera y con ello se inmortaliza; es decir lo que la vida no le da, se lo arrebata a La Parca.* La tradición mestiza recupera la inmortalidad azteca y la combina con la religión cristiana.

The common man, whose life is not valued by society, has no fear before death, laughs at her, eats his own skull, and in so doing, immortalizes himself; that is to say, what life does not give him he snatches away from Tightfist (Death). The mestizo tradition recovers Aztec immortality and combines it with the Christian religion.

Villarruel's is a valid interpretation, as long as we keep in mind that it is his own. He gives no evidence of basing his explanation on the expressed opinions or interpretations of "the common man" he renders.

An anthropology student at the National Institute of Anthropology and History (INAH)* in Mexico City, Carlos Krauss, gave a fairly typical response in an interview with me on July 16, 1992, echoing part of Villarruel's thoughts.

| Regalar calaveras de azúcar es, en esto de acuerdo conmigo, confirmar la identidad mexicana. No es regalar la muerte porque no es la muerte, es un juguete o una expresión lúdica que imita la muerte. No es una calavera humana sino de azúcar. Comerla, de acuerdo conmigo, significa controlar la muerte. | Giving sugar calaveras is, according to me, confirming Mexican identity. It is not giving death because it isn't death; it's a toy or a playful expression that imitates death. It is not a human skull but a sugar one. Eating it, according to me, means controlling death. |

And yes, Krauss does give calaveras to his friends, complete with names on foreheads, and he does eat them himself, name and all. He gave his conventional response very spontaneously, showing that the official—if hidden—agenda of reconfirming national identity in celebrants of Días de muertos is served effectively, even by this simple custom. It is effective because it inspires Mexicans who eat sugar calaveras to think of ourselves as different in our attitude toward life and death from non-Mexicans who do not participate in this sweet, grotesque communion.[14] The psychoanalytical slant Krauss added as an afterthought, that to eat the calavera means to control death, is a common interpretation of the practice, twinned by the one that says mocking death is also a way to confront and conquer—or reveal—one's fear of it. For him, to eat the *calaverita** is not exactly to immortalize oneself, as it is to Villarruel, but "controlling death" by the symbolic act is perhaps like partaking, if only tangentially, in immortality.

A much more interesting interpretation was offered to me by Antonio Santana Rebollar, a young taxi driver in Mexico City, who began by saying that neither he nor his small children are *impresionados*, shocked, by eating sugar skulls with their name on them because they became used to doing it in their infancy. Then, interpreting the little objects, he said: "La calavera es como el cuerpo de uno. Es como un recordatorio al cuerpo. Porque si hay fiestas para todo, en ésta es para que el cuerpo no quede desapercibido" [The calavera is like one's body. It's like a memorial to the body. Because if there are fiestas for everything, in this one it's so the body doesn't go unrecognized].

---

[14] In Chapter 7 I meditate further on this matter.

This poetic take on *calaveritas de azúcar* is the most compelling I have read or heard. Rebollar's sense that the body should be honored both by ingesting a representation of its most important part and by dedicating a day that inspires us to remember it is entirely original. I was unable to coax him to elaborate further on his theory. It seems particularly significant that he does not mention death or the dead in his interpretation. Perhaps that is how intimately he associates death with the body; as other informants and sources will say, death resides in the body, it resides in life itself.

Don Antonio's lively consciousness of the skeleton being part of the body is shared by writer Elena Poniatowska, who celebrates Mexicans' intimacy with death, and by kindergarten director María Antonieta Sánchez de Escamilla, who carefully and diligently teaches her students to recognize the skeleton inside their body and to lose their fear of death.[15] It is also shared by a boy questioned by Alberto Beltrán—essayist, graphic artist, and founder of the newspaper *El Día*—about a sugar skull; the child said it was simply what we all carry inside us (Poniatowska). All of these interpretations, especially Rebollar's, show a sense of perspective that is an essential function of humor and a sense of humor about life and death and about the body, alive and dead.

Besides the sugar skulls, there is a tradition among some celebrants, such as people in San Miguel de Allende and Toluca, of placing *alfeñique**— molded sugar figures of animals, especially lambs—on offerings for the dead (see Figure 1.11). Capuchin friar Francisco de Ajofrín, traveling in Mexico in 1763, made the earliest report of the sweet menageries in Mexico City's markets of the season. He also mentioned "coffins, tombs and a thousand figures of the dead, clerics, monks and nuns of all denominations, bishops, [and] horsemen" (quoted in Carmichael and Sayer 46). Such figures can still be seen, mostly in central Mexico. Neapolitans were known to present their friends and relations with *ossi di zucchero* (sugar bones) a tradition that continues in Palermo and Sicily. María Teresa de Sepúlveda has confirmed that the Spanish also had such a practice. The lambs, the most common and popular sugar creatures, are a reference to Jesus as the "lamb of God" who reviews the angels, the living, and the dead in Revelations 7 (Carmichael and Sayer 47).

---

[15] For the full quotation by Sánchez de Escamilla, see Carmichael and Sayer 119 or Chapter 5, "Historical Notes on All Saints and All Souls' Days," in this book.

1.11 Borregos de alfeñique (sugar lambs). San Miguel de Allende, Guanajuato

In literate communities there are literary calaveras, too, rhymed epitaphs written for people who are very much alive, making light of some
characteristic of the individual or of his or her life or livelihood. Such calaveras are usually written about public figures; they are published, if only by
being posted in a public place, and each November 2 newspapers include
several pages of literary calaveras. This practice seems to have begun sometime in the mid-nineteenth century (Reuter 75). Earlier still, social and
political satires of newsworthy events were published as broadsheets or in
newspapers. Mexico's *prensa de un centavo* (penny press) was probably
inspired by a European tradition, especially by the Spanish *pasquines*, lam-
poons, which were satires in verse displayed in public areas (Carmichael
and Sayer 58). Since the mid-1970s, many schoolchildren have been
assigned to write calaveras. I include a few in Appendix A.

Literary calaveras have usually been accompanied, as they are to this
day, by graphic ones that might have been patterned originally on medieval
skeleton figures (Carmichael and Sayer 58). When I first saw a copy of
Joaquín Bolaños's *La portentosa vida de la muerte* (The Portentous Life of
Death) in the Colegio de México library, I thought I had come across not
only Mexico's oldest novel, published in 1792, but also our oldest calavera;
it is full of curious illustrations of what strike me as fairly lighthearted and
very animated skeletons. According to Reuter, the comical images of calaveras do, in fact, date from the eighteenth century. They represented "a
satirical and humorous Death which has very little in common with the
mementi mori of the engravings of Holbein and Dürer" (Reuter 75). He
believes the "boom" of these curious calaveras stems from José Guadalupe

1.12 Conquistadores. Bakery, México, D.F.

Posada's* engravings at the turn of the twentieth century: "More than any other artist known to us, Posada breathed life into Death" (Reuter 75). A selection of Posada's calaveras is found in Chapter 4.

In a few of the capital's more traditional neighborhoods, bakeries still sport pictorial calaveras on their windows (see Figure 1.3). Often they are quite simple, consisting of a skeleton or a skull holding or pointing to a pan de muerto. Sometimes they are elaborate cartoons that depict historical or literary figures, regional-ethnic groups, or members of certain classes or professions. As examples, I present *catrinas* and *catrines** or dandies (see Plate 7); conquistadores (see Figure 1.12); Don Juan Tenorio with Doña Inés, the nun he seduced (see Figure 1.13);[16] "Chispeante y divertida calavera de Doña Tomasa y Simón el aguador" (Witty and amusing calavera of Doña Tomasa and Simon the water carrier), by José Guadalupe Posada, and a papier mâché sculpture inspired by it (see Figures 1.14, 1.15); a

---

[16] Outside of Mexico, the nineteenth-century play *Don Juan Tenorio (DJT)* is best known for its depiction of the rascal who seduces women through pretense and deception but is saved from perdition by his true love. In Mexico, the play is best known for the subplot of the original seventeenth-century version, *El burlador de Sevilla* [*The Seducer of Seville*], in which Don Juan dispatches the father of one of his victims in a duel. Later, to mock the dead man, Don Juan invites him to dinner (this also happens in *DJT*). To his amazement, the ghost appears at the table that night, counters Don Juan's invitation, and pulls him into hell through his grave when the unrepentant murderer keeps his date.

1.13 Don Juan y Doña Inés. Bakery, México, D.F.

knocked-out boxer (see Figure 1.16); and an assortment of street vendors (see Figures 1.17–1.20). In the four years that I have been scouting for these painted calaveras, I have seen their numbers diminish dramatically—perhaps because of the expense of having the windows painted, perhaps because of growing indifference toward the genre.

In many places, artisans fashion skeletons of clay, papier mâché, wood, and various other materials. As with the pictorial calaveras, the costumes of the sculptural ones are often stereotypically coded so we can recognize who they parody. Dolores Olmedo, a close friend of deceased artists Frida Kahlo and Diego Rivera, for years has set up elaborate ofrendas to honor her two friends. In early November, the Diego Rivera Museum in Anahuacalli, which houses Rivera's pre-Hispanic collection in another building, is visited by tens of thousands who come to see that year's ofrenda. In 1990 it consisted of life-size skeletal Tehuanas* and their male partners flanking a skeleton dressed as Frida, who is patting the head of an enormous toad (Diego's nickname was Sapo [Toad]) (see Plate 8). In 1988 many of the

1.14 *"Chispeante y divertida calavera de Doña Tomasa y Simón el aguador"* *by Posada. (Permission given by Dover Press)*

1.15 *Doña Tomasa y Simón el aguador by Linares. Anahuacalli, México, D.F.* *(Courtesy of Dolores Olmedo Patiño)*

1.16 Knocked Out. Bakery, México, D.F.

*1.17 Park photographer. Shop of former Museo de Artes e Industrias Populares,
México, D.F.*

1.18 Papier mâché fruit vendor. Shop of former Museo de Artes e Industrias Populares, México, D.F.

1.19 Tortilla vendor, by Posada. (Courtesy of Universidad Nacional Autónoma de México [UNAM])

1.20 Papier mâché newspaper vendor. Shop of former Museo de Artes e Industrias Populares, México, D.F.

calaveras were from Anahuacalli's collection, including some based on engravings by Posada. The figures were life-size *cartón* (papier mâché) made in Mexico City by the famous Linares family (see Figures 1.21, 1.22).

All of the skeletal figures mentioned in this section are lighthearted, if not downright comical. The artisans or artists who conceive of and create them are usually members of las clases populares, although students and bourgeois artists sometimes make calaveras, too. Often, they are exhibited in art galleries. Some are displayed in public parks; for example, a considerable number of papier mâché sculptures made by students at La Esmeralda, an arts school, were placed at a busy corner of Alameda Park in downtown Mexico City in 1993 (see Figure 1.23).

The most important difference between calaveras authored by members of the dominant culture and those by members of the popular classes is that the former are ordinarily sculptures or elaborate and sophisticated ofrendas, whereas the latter cover the gamut of media. All may be equally complex. Compare Figure 1.22 by the Linares workshop with Figure 1.24

1.21 *"Gran fandango y francachela de todas las calaveras" (detail) by Linares. Anahuacalli, México, D.F. (Courtesy of Dolores Olmedo Patiño)*

1.22 *"Gran fandango y francachela de todas las calaveras" by Posada. (Permission given by Dover Press)*

1.23 Ofrenda by La Esmeralda School of Arts. México, D.F.

on a museum shop's display window. Although both represent an engraving by Posada (see Figure 1.22), the former is much more polished than the latter. Such sophistication frequently marks a difference between the class of the artists, as the wealthier ones will have had access to formal training. When the calaveras made by trained artists are not the result of a school assignment, the fact that members of the upper classes have chosen to create calaveras may imply a certain solidarity with and fondness for popular art and artists, as well as an interest in participating in the tradition of calaveras for their own amusement and that of the public.

Public Offerings, a Politicized Catrina*

There are also public ofrendas. Sometimes they honor a local hero, as did an enormous one for naturalized German writer B. Traven. Between 1930 and 1941 he wrote six novels set in the Chiapas mahogany forests, where he traveled many times while he lived in Tampico, Tamaulipas, and in Mexico City, where he died in 1969[17] (see Plate 9).

1.24 Painted "Gran fandango." Former Museo de Artes e Industrias Populares, México, D.F.

The artists at the Taller Municipal de Artes Plásticas Rufino Tamayo (Rufino Tamayo Municipal Studio Arts Workshop) had a very elaborate offering for Tamayo, who founded the institute; it consisted of a traditional ofrenda on a table and an enormous, high-relief sand sculpture of a skull flanked by two candles in the form of embalmed figures—one each for Tamayo and Francisco Toledo, the other internationally known artist from Oaxaca (see Plate 10, Figure 1.25). Several public ofrendas—more every year—have been dedicated to people who have died of SIDA (AIDS) (see Plate 11). Such ofrendas may have a strong political agenda, such as drawing attention to the presence of homosexuals or other marginalized groups and to their political, civil, and human rights. There are also many traditional altars built in public places, such as at the Museo Nacional de

---

[17] His novel *Macario* (1950) takes place on November 2 and reveals some interesting ideas about death. B. Traven told his widow, Rosa Elena Luján, that the plot was based on an Indian legend (Guthke 360). In Xochimilco I was told he was being honored there because he had lived there, although no evidence exists of B. Traven, a.k.a. Ret Marut a.k.a. Hal Croves a.k.a. Traven Torsvan, having lived there. I find it amusing that given his laborious creations of contradictory autobiographical information, his life story was still being fictionalized in 1991. He would have enjoyed that.

1.25 Ofrenda to Tamayo with calavera. Taller Municipal de Artes Plásticas Rufino Tamayo, Oaxaca

Culturas Populares and the Museum of Anthropology. These are authentic ofrendas such as those set in private homes. People are invited to build them outside of their true context to educate the residents of Mexico City about the traditions of the rest of the country and to rekindle a sense of national pride and solidarity with fellow citizens who live largely according to their ancestral traditions.

Those who prepare public altars express no qualms about taking a relatively intimate work into the open. In fact, when a builder of altars from Huaquechula, Puebla—where what are perhaps the most elaborate altars in the country are made—was interviewed by Carmichael and Sayer, he told them with great pride about having been invited by the government of Puebla to set up an altar in a public space: "There it was seen by many people, and photographed for the regional newspaper" (Carmichael and Sayer 97). José Camacho of Cocula, Jalisco, a collector and restorer of religious antiques, makes elaborate public ofrendas for Días de muertos, inviting visitors to place on them the photographs of their own dead. He told me he builds the offerings to teach those who visit them about local traditions. He wishes someone would learn the practice from him so the tradition might continue after he dies.

Días de muertos is an event through which celebrants can explore and reflect on the significance of life and death not only as metaphysical constructs but also as lived experience, as social conventions, and as the stage on which familial, political, economic, and social dramas are played out. Each celebration reveals an interpretation of what is meaningful in life and death. It deconstructs the meanings assigned to subordinated cultures by dominant cultures by focusing on the meanings the celebrants assign to their own existential knowledge of life, death, and society.

Let us consider, for example, one ofrenda set out by a number of sex workers on the edge of the Alameda park (half a block away from the one set out by La Esmeralda's students) in 1993 (see Figure 1.26). It includes several traditional elements: fresh flowers, cones of *piloncillo,* unrefined sugar, pan de muerto,* sugar calaveras and coffins, ears of corn, a new earthenware *jarrito* of water, and new earthenware *ollitas,* pots, of food. Four of the panes de muerto are the familiar round loaves; five are the circular loaves reminiscent of pre-Hispanic "stellar eyes"* associated with funerary and death gods. All of these elements confirm the Mexican identification of those who created and those who are honored by the ofrenda. Politically, the fact that these individuals are making an offering to their dead identifies them with their audience. Even the inclusion of Posada's* most famous calavera, "La calavera catrina" (see Figure 1.27), draws the sex workers into the larger company of celebrants of the holiday; it is an image one sees often in this season, copied or executed in many media. But the nude body below the Posada head and the sexual placement of certain elements of the offering set these commemorators apart from the crowd in a revealing manner.

It is appropriate for sex workers to represent their professional nudity, so to speak, through this drawing. In it, the dead colleagues are shown in their naked sexuality but with a death's head to show their current state. Passersby can enjoy the mischievous pleasure the memorializers must have taken when they gave their central figure fresh cempoaxóchitl* for her hat and an arm corsage, a stellar-eye bread bracelet, plus a pan de muerto and more cempoaxóchitl to cover or represent her genitals. The bowl, another genital symbol, that rests on the Catrina's left thigh contains a pink flower, which may also allude to female genitals; a small sweet roll that may allude to her livelihood—the staff of life; a lime that may indicate the bitterness of hard work; and the showiest element, a large wrapped *tamal,* phallically positioned. *Tamal* is also slang for the female private parts, so there is a gender-bending pun in this detail.

We see clearly the combined carnivalesque and earnest elements of Días de muertos in the ofrenda. Whereas this version of La Catrina reflects the

1.26 Ofrenda by sex workers. Alameda Park, México, D.F.

1.27 "La calavera catrina" by Posada (Permission given by Dover Press)

livelihood, life, and death of those honored, it is also a mirror not only for
the living sex workers' professional nudity and eventual demise but also for
the general audience's unprofessional nudity, if you will, and our guaranteed
eventual death. The ofrenda carries a political message that might go something like this.

> We sex workers are here among you, serving you sometimes in and
> near the Alameda. Our work may bring pleasure, but it also entails at
> least the risk, and sometimes the reality, of sexually transmitted dis-
> ease and the risk of violence, aside from emotional, psychological, and
> moral risks.
>
> When those who are dear to us die, we grieve for them, just as
> you grieve for your dead. We remember them on their day as you do,
> even as we hope to be remembered after we die, as you do. A majority
> of you may prefer to forget that we exist; that we are sometimes hired
> by you, your parents, spouses, siblings, children, friends; that either
> literally or philosophically speaking we are you, your parents,
> spouses, siblings, children, friends. A majority of you may consider us

to be radically different from—and inferior to—you, but we work for a living; we budget to pay our bills and support our dependents; we struggle with our ethics and our compromises; and both you and we all have a body, naked under our clothes, skeletal under our flesh. Death will not distinguish among us. Today we move from the repressed margins of your attention to its center.

This is only one illustration of the construction of meaning and pleasure that characterizes many public ofrendas. The politics of identity are often especially clear in the humorous objects that in some celebrating communities are essential to the fiesta. Both the festival and its paraphernalia reveal an intertextuality that includes rejection, reinterpretation, and appropriation of various cultural resources—ancient and modern; Mesoamerican,* Spanish, and (U.S.) North American; Indigenous, Catholic, "high," and popular. The humor evident in the various kinds of calaveras offers a critique of the codes and signs, the values and the processes of making meaning that their creators see in the dominant culture. The comical calaveras that are self-referential permit us to say about their genre what Jonathan Culler said about literature: "In so far as literature turns back on itself and examines, parodies, or treats ironically its own signifying procedures, it becomes the most complex account of signification we possess" (Culler 35f).[18]

Ritual Obligations

In Mexico . . . we are fortunate: our pre-Hispanic past and our Catholic beliefs allow us to retain our links with the dead. We know they will return to us each year, and our sense of separation is lessened. *Ofrendas** give our memories a tangible form; we express our affections in an intimate way. . . . Perhaps this is more of a consolation for us, the living.
—Sánchez de Escamilla quoted in
Carmichael and Sayer 118

Días de muertos,* as the reader can begin to see, includes a compendium of objects that appeal to the intellect, the senses, and the spirit. It is like a carnival in a marketplace where one can consume pleasures, shop for one's own gratification or for the sake of the dead, and remember, chuckle, or mourn. As in traditional carnivals, the individual is connected to her or

---

[18] I take up the matter of humor again in Chapter 7 and offer close readings of several calaveras in Chapter 8.

his community by means of all the practices she or he opts to enact. As a family prepares for the visit of its dead, men and women from three or four generations of actual and ritual kin may participate together in the purchases, preparations, and vigils. Sometimes, some of the work is divided by gender and age: Men shop; women prepare the food; children clean the graves, pull petals off flowers, run errands. Everyone's work is essential.

The participants celebrate their togetherness and wholeness and reaffirm their social bonds and obligations. John Ingham and Néstor García Canclini have suggested that all fiestas—as symbolic, ritual commemorations—sanctify, fortify, and clarify the unequal relationships among various members of the community, and, Ingham adds, particularly among *comadres* and *compadres*. *[19]

Días de muertos is a fiesta without a clear emphasis on compadrazgo because its focus is the reunion of the living and the dead; the primary relationship is one of mutual dependence. At least among las clases populares, a widespread belief inherited from Mesoamerican* anthropology—and held with a certain degree of skepticism—says that the souls of the dead attain a semidivine status[20] that makes them effective advocates on behalf of their living relatives and friends before the Christian god and saints and, in certain Indigenous communities, before Aboriginal deities.[21] Hoping to persuade the spirits to intervene in their favor, people welcome them with

---

[19] *Comadres* and *compadres*—literally, co-mothers and co-fathers—are chosen for various ritual occasions, for example, baptism and other rites of passage. When a person accepts the invitation to be a comadre or a compadre, she or he takes on obligations according to the occasion for which she or he was invited to be a "coparent." In the case of baptism, a child can have a godmother and a godfather who are not married to each other; the spouses are involved by the obligation of the accepting godparent, and so the network grows, along with the insurance it is intended to provide. Godparents provide the godchild with clothes for the baptismal ceremony and for the rest of her or his childhood. They are expected to be a moral and spiritual example and guide for the godchild and to give her or him occasional gifts. Should the child be orphaned, the godparent becomes a prime candidate to adopt the child, although a closer relative may adopt the orphan. *Compadrazgo* is the relationship, godparent-hood. Also see Ingham's chapter on ritual kinship.

[20] Of the ancient inhabitants of what the Spaniards called Nueva España, Sahagún wrote: "Y cuando alguno se moría, de él solían decir que ya era *teotl*, que quiere decir que ya era muerto, para ser espíritu, o dios; y creían los antiguos, engañándose, que los señores cuando morían se volvían en dioses" (Volume 3, Book 10, chapter 29, § 2, ¶117, p. 210) [And when one of them died, of him they would say that now he was *teotl*, which means he had died to become spirit or god; and the ancients believed, deceiving themselves, that when the lords died they became gods].

gifts and feasting. Thus, the dead rely on the living to provide them with sustenance and pleasure for their special needs, which are related to the journeys they are believed to make; the living rely on the dead to exert whatever influence they have on the circumstances of the living.

The ofrenda is not to be understood as a commercial transaction. Fredy Méndez is a prize-winning embroidery artist in Veracruz who was in his early twenties when, in an interview with Carmichael and Sayer, he explained the importance of giving freely to the dead. Let me note that the solemnity to which he alludes is not universal; in fact, he may be indirectly expressing disapproval of the carnivalesque quality Días de muertos can have in some communities.

> Each year during Todos Santos* the dead return. This is the most important festival of the year. It is not a time for making merry. It is a sad and solemn time . . . yet it gives us pleasure to receive our dead. We do the things our ancestors did: my father follows his parents' teachings, and I will continue to do the same. The dead . . . come to consume our offerings. . . . Souls do not force us to give them anything. If we give, it must be because we truly want to. (Carmichael and Sayer 77)

Sacred Time, Alterity*

Because the Days of the Dead occur in sacred time, they are like open doors that allow access to a place where the past and the present can meet and, through the consciousness of dead and living people, enjoy the meeting. Rolly Kent and Heather Valencia convey the Yaquis' understanding of this phenomenon with a nice metaphor: "There are certain days when the wall between worlds becomes so porous that the living and the dead can pass through without being subject to the laws of space or time" (Kent and Valencia 187). These are days whose sacred nature allows a kind of unmasking of time as a human construct that arbitrarily divides the flow of life and experience into measurable, quantified fragments that to the mythopoetic seem like obstacles built to divorce memory from experience, memory from memory, and experience from experience. During these days, through the power of sacred time, obstacles vanish that ordinarily effectively prevent the family, constituted of the dead as well as the living, from

---

[21] For a thorough exposition on Mexico's religious syncretism and the survival of Indigenous gods, I recommend Luis Weckmann's *The Medieval Heritage of Mexico*.

being together. In numerous Mexican groups, particularly those of Indigenous people, time and space are understood differently from the way they are understood by Westerners, and people feel themselves to be in constant interaction with the so-called dead (Kent and Valencia, chapters 7–10).

Enabled by this quality of time to enjoy reunion, people who feel fragmented—atomized by the means of production, which can require the sacrifice of wholeness at the individual and social levels—relax and return, as it were, to the seamless bosom of their whole, real family. Whereas the modern experience of fragmentation reduces subordinated people's freedom to make decisions that affect their lives and circumstances, during Días de muertos those who are home, en su tierra,* remember and recover their power, at least for the duration of the fiesta.* That is why so many historians and ethnographers who describe this contemporary event trace its historical path to remote times when civilizations innocent of Christianity and the European Enlightenment directed and controlled the historical processes of our continent. In the practices of Días de muertos* these scholars can perceive the dignity of the actors and their actions, the air of otherness that separates the celebrants from the witnesses, who appear, in comparison to the former, to remain fragmented and outside the spell of sacred time.

Some scholars, especially some of us who are Mexican, feel drawn almost magnetically to the sites of celebration. But as entranced as I may be by the pungent smoke of copal* and the multiplying flames of candles, I feel my separateness, my otherness; I know my discourse is a tribute to my experience of visiting my compatriots', my others' sacred time and sacred place and is a sure sign of my status as an outsider. But I comfort myself that my reaction is the opposite of the one Wlad Godzich described when he said, "Western thought has always thematized the other as a threat to be reduced, as a potential same-to-be, a yet-not-same" (Godzich xiii). I want to pay homage and bear witness to the irreducible otherness and radical realness of Días de muertos. Paraphrasing Emmanuel Lévinas, Godzich has written:

There is a form of truth that is totally alien to me, that I do not discover within myself, but that calls on me from beyond me, and it requires me to leave the realms of the known and of the same in order to settle in a land that is under its rule. . . . And this other is not a threat to be reduced . . . but that which constitutes me as an ethical being: in my originary encounter I discover my responsibility for the existence of this other, a responsibility that will lie at the root of all my subsequent ethical decisions. (Godzich xvi)

Being There

It isn't like simple voyeurism, I don't think—it's holier or more
reverent than that, because when I'm in that mood I don't
want to exist. I don't mean I want to kill myself, I mean that
I'm a man and a man is a watcher and a watcher disturbs the
purity of the event, so I don't want to exist, I want to be faded
away to almost nothing.
— Nicholson Baker 62

Before I close this introductory chapter, I will say a little about how it
feels to be present at Días de muertos* celebrations. In a word, I find it very
moving. The amount of love lavished on the dead—evident in the time,
effort, preparations, and expense on the part of the living commemorators—is astounding, used as I am to the much less expressive style typical of
cosmopolitan bourgeoisies. I have never visited the grave or cremation urn
of a dead relative, nor have I been invited to do so by any family member;
and I think it is significant that I do not even know if anyone pays such visits. My family, as far as I recall, never spoke of the dead within earshot of
my infant or adolescent ears, although more recently I have spoken with my
siblings and my parents about dead relatives. Jeweler and theorist of popular culture Víctor Fosado Vázquez, one of Carmichael and Sayer's informants, observed: "Among 'educated' city-dwellers, this sense of the 'sacred'
has diminished, and intimacy with death has lessened. The dead are still
remembered, but communication with them becomes more difficult; the
dead are honoured, yet increasingly they become marginalised" (Carmichael
and Sayer 134). I have witnessed this phenomenon in my own family.

Even among the living members of bourgeois families there is a pau-
city of expression of affection, aside from the requisite, conventional greet-
ings and the notable exception of love showered on young children and
infants. There are clear limits on the time, effort, and expense spent on relatives and friends. I remember noticing as a child that the poor appeared
more generous and willing to share the little they had than the wealthy,
and about 16 million of Mexico's population of 81 million in 1993 was
considered to be poor, so I can extend my generalization. That generosity
may come in part from the continuing viability of sympathetic magic. One
gives that one may receive in kind. And it is a generosity resulting from
sincere empathy and deeply instilled values that predate, but have been
fortified by, the best of Christianity.

On an intellectual level, I find the humor of Días de muertos absolutely winning. I often laugh aloud when I look at pictorial or sculptural calaveras, and I cannot stop thinking about what it means to multiply so many witty images of death and the dead. What I experience is that the normal illusion of immortality and the normal hierarchy of life as superior to and stronger than (even victorious over, in Christian terms) and more natural than death are deconstructed by the fiesta.* The illusion is exposed as culturally specific and idiosyncratic. Especially during these days dedicated to death and the dead, I know profoundly rather than merely intellectually that I am the skeleton that will be bared when my flesh is dead and rotted or burned away.

Finally, when I am in Mexico during Días de muertos, I enjoy feeling entirely Mexican in spite of my bilingualism, pale skin, and *ojos de color* (light eyes). It feels good to enjoy honestly a fiesta that tends to be scorned by most members of my native class. Since the majority of Mexicans are part of the popular classes, being with them and enjoying what they enjoy makes me feel closer to them than I usually am. It feels much the way taking communion during a phase of my youth made me feel, as though I were communing with all communicants past, present, and future in all the world. To laugh at the same jokes, to relish the same foods, to be moved by the same things gives me a sense of identification and solidarity with them. During this fiesta I hold and enjoy my limited patriotism and the breakdown of my classism. Thus I, too, reinforce my national identity by attending the celebrations of Días de muertos.

A Key Commemoration

Ofrendar es compartir con los parientes difuntos ciertos goces de la vida y algo de los frutos obtenidos en la anualidad pasada. Si el servicio de la comunidad para sus muertos se identifica básicamente en el modo de ofrendar, la ofrenda no se otorga como una dádiva sino como un ofrecimiento o sufragio coaccionado por una tradición que hace realidad la existencia de las ánimas.
— Jesús Angel Ochoa Zazueta 151

Making an offering is sharing with dead relatives certain pleasures of life and something of the fruits obtained in the previous year. If the service of the community on behalf of its dead is identified basically in the manner of offering, the offering is not given as a gift but as a sacrifice or suffrage compelled by a tradition that makes real the existence of the spirits.

Of all the fiestas* that punctuate the ritual calendar—Independence on September 15–16, Epiphany on January 6, and those to local patron saints—Días de muertos* is, according to a variety of sources, the most important one in rural communities, in communities of transplanted rural people in Mexico's urban centers, and even in some expatriate Mexican and Mexican-American communities in the United States. If, as Monica Wilson has said, "rituals reveal values at their deepest level," which, in turn, reveal "the essential constitution of human societies" (quoted in Turner 6), a similar claim could be made for festivals. A festival is more than a set of rituals, and those it encompasses tend to be less conventionalized or obligatory than true rituals are. As described earlier, certain actions are taken in regaling the dead; they vary among communities throughout Mexico. Invariably, there is a ritual feast, and there are ritual offerings. I am not interested in arguing whether the whole of Días de muertos is a ritual, but my interest in reading the fiesta was aroused by, among other things, a realization that it reveals values at a deep level, as I have expressed in previous sections. And I believe it reveals something vitally important in the constitution of certain Mexican societies.

Días de muertos finesses the notion that has preoccupied many citizens and politicians in the United States during the 1990s under the rubric of *family values*. It is a celebration that demonstrates the intensity of familial fidelity that reaches beyond the grave, but it also embraces friends and strangers if we keep in mind the offerings made to el ánima sola,* or *el muerto desconocido* (the unknown dead). With that practice it opens up the circle of concern in a much more generous way than if participants cared only for their friends and relations. This solidarity attests to the widespread Mesoamerican* commitment to what we might call an organic socialism. No member of society—not the female, not the infant, not the aged, not the infirm, not the dead—is considered dispensable. Everyone is respected, and the contribution of each one is expected and valued.[22]

Juan Gamiño Espinosa couches this function of the fiesta in terms of memory. He has written:

---

[22] For rich detail about Mesoamerican culture, I recommend Guillermo Bonfil Batalla, *México profundo*.

Desde el conjunto de creencias sobre las almas de los muertos, el Miccaílhuitl* pone en movimiento un potente recurso de lo imaginario: la memoria. Ella establece un imperativo para toda la festividad: no olvidar, a muertos ni a vivos desde el momento en que la ofrenda se pone hasta el que se reparte. (Gamiño Espinosa 73)

From the set of beliefs about the souls of the dead, Miccaílhuitl* puts into action a powerful resource of the imaginary: memory. It establishes an imperative for the whole celebration: not to forget the dead or the living from the moment in which the offering is placed until it is distributed.

Memory is the means of communal solidarity, even with its transformative creativity, that does no disservice to what is remembered but rather preserves it in renewed versions that keep it fresh and relevant.

Días de muertos looks not only back to the past but also toward the present and the future, and another reason it is important is that it fosters hope: Those who give offerings trust that their survivors will take care of them after they die, thus assuring their immortality—at least in a limited sense—and ensuring the future of traditions that provide meaning, continuity, and identity to their society. Hope serves to hearten the humble so they can continue to struggle to provide stability to their group with some optimism in the face of deep necessity, little if any access to a system of justice, virtually nonexistent opportunities for social or economic advancement, and the disdain of those who control the country's power and purse. From the perspective of the hegemonic class, hope is also politically useful, as it keeps the hopeful docile and orderly. Only when hope is frustrated and repressive means are deployed do popular uprisings occur, as in the revolt of the Zapatista Army for National Liberation (EZLN) in Chiapas on January 1, 1994.

Días de muertos is a constellation of practices that serves as a channel for what power its celebrants wield. They save for, purchase, and give great gifts and meals to both the dead and the living. They renew and strengthen social, familial, and political relationships with the living and the dead. They sacrifice money, energy, and time for the sake of someone else, and sacrifice—as its etymology reveals—makes whole and holy the gift and, I would say, the giver as well. In addition, the process of giving is empowering because whether rooted in excess or in deprivation, it grants the giver a position of high status because she or he is bestowing affection, time, creativity, and wealth—however limited any of these may be.

Participants in this fiesta find an opportunity to practice openly an element of their culture. García Canclini has usefully defined culture as an
instrument for the understanding, reproduction, and transformation of the
social system of each social class. He considers the cultures of las clases
populares an elaboration of their life's conditions and their conflictive inter-
actions with the dominant class (García Canclini 17). In Mexico's more
cosmopolitan and heterogeneous cities, said culture is ordinarily practiced
only privately with any degree of freedom; whatever bits of it leak into the
public forum during any other time of the year are apt to draw scorn or
derision, as do class-revealing speech and dress. Since the holiday is kept
primarily by the humble, the perceptions visitors have of its celebrants may
shift during this time, with negative prejudice giving way to respect, admiration, or at least a sense of nostalgia for the traditions of the deep past of
what Guillermo Bonfil Batalla calls México profundo. *[23]

Because Días de muertos is "a palimpsest for ideologies of . . . nation-
hood," to borrow a phrase from Purnima Mankekar (470), there is a limited subversion of values in which the low are exalted and the high admire
or even envy them. By provoking this admiration, memory, and desire, the
humble, in a predictably humble way, invade and undermine high culture
with its "First-World" identity. During Días de muertos, the subordinate
are the authors and agents who create and define the fiesta that draws so
much public attention. They are agents in spite of being turned into spec-
ters and objects by national and international tourists and journalists, who
come to look, photograph or videotape, and write what they can ostensibly
to appropriate what belongs radically to the Other.[24] These few days that
rupture the usual order of the social classes permit or inspire members of
the bourgeoisie to feel affected by their national alter, potentially to the
point of opening the possibility of social critique and a longer lived distur-
bance of the unjust status quo.

---

[23] Bonfil Batalla distinguishes between México profundo and México imaginario. The former
constitutes the people who share the Mesoamerican culture, one that is very different from the
Western culture shared by México imaginario. México profundo includes the Indigenous people who identify themselves as such and a less clear category of Mexicans who live aspects of
Native traditions but do not identify with any particular Indian group. México imaginario is
so named because it denies the deep, ancient, living Mesoamerican culture, preferring to
impose a Western European culture that is ill suited to the large Indigenous population and
culture. See Bonfil Batalla's superb, visionary México profundo.

[24] See "Words and Pictures" in Chapter 2 and Roland Barthes's Camera Lucida.

2

Reading Días de muertos

Semiotic Practices

When a literary scholar such as I approaches a cultural text, she or he discovers many of the same strategies of communication as those employed in a literary text. A festival, a rock video, a commercial all make selective use of anecdote, metaphor, symbolism, and other figures traditionally associated with written works. Different kinds of texts all build representations of reality in their own discourse, incorporating more than verbal language and figures, for those representations may include—as does the celebration of Días de muertos*—codes of ritual, sacrifice, economics, and so on. The work of literary semioticians is based on one principal activity: reading. By reading, literary critics regard the complexity of the discourse before them. Their work is not so much an aesthetic quest or critique as it is a kind of archaeological inquiry that leads them to the important signs and the system of signs of any given text.[1] As

---

[1] Jonathan Culler defines the reader and her or his role in the process of signification like this: "The reader becomes the name of the place where the various codes can be located: a virtual site. Semiotics* attempts to make explicit the implicit knowledge which enables signs to have meaning, so it needs the reader not as a person but as a function: the repository of the codes which account for the intelligibility of the text" (Culler 38).

Jonathan Culler has put it, "The semiotician wants to discover what are the species of signs, how they differ from one another, how they function in their native habitat, how they interact with other species" (Culler vii).

A literary critic brings her or his own set of knowledge to bear on a text. She or he understands how stories are woven, how narrativity functions to create (*fingere*) fictions, texts, and accounts. To the literary scholar a cultural text is as legible as a literary one, and what I present in this book is a reading of Mexico's Días de muertos even as Bakhtin—a giant of a literary critic—reads the medieval European carnival and as John Fiske reads the shopping mall and the beach.

How self-conscious are the celebrants of Días de muertos? Most have minimal official education and many have little to do with the systems of signification familiar to the dominant classes, so they are less likely to think and to create meaning along the lines of the Western academic observer than along the lines of their own culture. It is not hard to see, however, that the practices of this fiesta* are "a continual exploration of and reflection upon signification" (Culler 35) that concentrate on the juxtaposition of life and death, our own and that of others.

The practice of spending time with the dead reveals an interpretation of the common human experience of dreaming and thinking about the dead, of remembering them with such vividness that they seem very much alive. The creation and visual contemplation of calaveras* constitute an exploration and a critique of the creative and persuasive powers of the dominant systems of signification and distribution of power, wealth, prestige, and cultural resources. Because it fulfills these vital roles of critique, exploration, reflection, and interpretation, Días de muertos can be considered a body of literature, although the systems of signs it uses are less literary than iconic,[2] or visual or pragmatic, in the sense that they are practices performed by the human body (Culler 35f).

In a world in which the academic disciplines have found meeting points for fruitful dialogue, some still pretend to keep the disciplines separate, each talking only to itself. In his foreword to *Heterologies*, Wlad Godzich describes Michel de Certeau's "scandalous attitude" toward the fragmentation of the disciplines:

---

[2] Charles Peirce called arbitrary signs "symbols" and motivated signs "indices" and "icons." Icons have a "natural resemblance" to their signifier, albeit one "determined by semiotic convention" (quoted in Culler 24).

> [De Certeau] seeks to exacerbate the fragmentation by deliberately uncovering the ways in which the various disciplinary enterprises rely upon models and paradigms borrowed from each other, and never less so than when they proclaim their independence, so that the mutual relation of the disciplines is never one of autonomy or heteronomy, but some sort of complicated set of textual relations that needs to be unraveled. (Godzich x)

I do not pretend to attempt such an unraveling, but I will deploy models and paradigms from disciplines as varied as literary analysis, anthropology, studies of popular culture, and the history of religions. Semiotics is a discipline that is encouraging interdisciplinary efforts and communications because it leads researchers to the units of meaning of whatever text they are reading, as well as to the vast universe of intertextuality that allows signs to be comprehensible. That is, semiotics not only directs the critic's attention to discrete units of signification, but it shows that those units or *semes* (signs) produce meaning within the relationship of signs and codes. Codes are different systems of signifying, such as poetry, liturgical action, or body language. Semiotics foregrounds the phenomenon of intertextuality; every text is readable only in conjunction with the many other (inter)texts of which it is made. Umberto Eco has said, "Books always talk about other books, and each story tells a story which has already been told" (Eco 26).

In this project I seek to discover and read the signs of a folk-popular fiesta in several different communities in Mexico. Although I do not concentrate on differences in the ways various cultural groups perform elements of Días de muertos, I focus on signs for the celebration, signs within the holiday, and signs for the annual commemoration of the dead in contemporary and pre-Hispanic Mexico and make a few observations about similar matters in the United States. The principal differences are found between the celebrations of traditional communities and celebrations of people who have left their communities, in some cases lost touch with them, and altered the traditions according to their experience in their new environment. A large section of the book is devoted to the humorous, parodic signs prevalent in and near Mexico City.

A Word About the Literature

Most of the articles and books about Días de muertos* fall into two categories: ethnographies and histories. The Instituto Nacional de Antropología e

Historia (INAH) [National Institute of Anthropology and History] has sponsored many ethnographers of the fiesta* and has published their findings. Such works detail the activities and paraphernalia of the celebration in a particular community. They are valuable for giving access to the ethnographers' accounts of the customs, traditions, objects, and diet of specific celebrants.

What I have garnered from reading a good number of these (I include a selection in the Works Consulted) is, on the one hand, that a wealth of variants exists around funerary traditions, which are often included, although they are only tangentially relevant to the principal topic, and variants of celebrations of Días de muertos. For example, some Mayan communities bury their dead with clothing, food, and possessions; some communities in Oaxaca and in the Mayan area regale the dead for a full month; in Huaquechula, a town in Puebla, along with the traditional offering, a *tableau vivant* is enacted by the youngest relatives of the recently deceased in which the children are dressed as angels.

Ethnographies are valuable because they allow one to recognize elements that are virtually universal, such as dedicating different days according to the way people died—a day for those who died violently, a day for those who died as children, another for those who died as adults;[3] cleaning and adorning graves; and offering incense, candles, flowers, and food on special altars for the occasion. The majority of ethnographies I have read present data in a fairly objective manner. They do not offer readings of the fiesta, although several include Marxist analyses of its function in the community's economy. Most accounts of Días de muertos are synchronic; that is, they offer a kind of snapshot that freezes the fiesta in a moment, whether they have primarily a historical or an ethnographic emphasis. The ethnographic accounts come closer than the historical ones to being diachronic studies; that is, they offer a kind of motion picture of the fiesta that shows how it operates.

The other substantial body of literature on Días de muertos traces its origins to pre-Hispanic practices and traditions. Most Mexican versions say little or nothing about the Spanish contribution of official and popular Catholic elements. The writers lead readers to recognize and value their

---

[3] Ancient Mexicans, unlike Christians, believed one's fate after this life depended on the manner of death. Thus, for example, warriors who died in war, sacrificial victims, and women who died in childbirth all became the companions of Huitzilopochtli, the god of war and the sun. More details are given in Chapter 5.

ancient, Indigenous forebears and to identify this venerable celebration with what is most "Mexican," most worthy as a focal point for the construction of a national identity different from those of other Latin American countries, Mexico's geographical, linguistic, and historical siblings; different from that of Spain, one of Mexico's historical, linguistic, and cultural parents; and certainly different from that of the United States, Mexico's looming geographical neighbor that can be seen as a historical, linguistic, and cultural step-sibling.

What I attempt in this book is to make intelligible some of the aspects and functions of Días de muertos and its place as an integral element of the Mexican popular imaginary rather than to anthologize ethnographies or elaborate another myth of origin that may convince readers to recast or reconfirm their perspective on what the fiesta is and what it means. I duly attend to important aspects of its probable historical evolution, and I do not deny that I, too, have been seduced by the romance of my country's ancient history and idiosyncratic identity.

Many histories of Días de muertos have been written, and many are published seasonally in the Mexican press. One of the best available in English is *The Skeleton at the Feast* by Elizabeth Carmichael and Chloë Sayer, a text limited neither to history nor to ethnography but that includes foreign travelers' accounts of the fiesta and a superb section containing interviews of celebrants.

A smaller but growing number of articles published in Mexican newspapers focus on the differences between Días de muertos and Hallowe'en, most showing the superiority of the former or at least its greater appropriateness to the Mexican idiosyncrasy. These articles frequently have a defensive, even an angry tone; many reify Hallowe'en and turn it into an icon of "Yankee imperialism," whether consciously or not I cannot say. I explore this polemic further in Chapter 6, "Días de muertos Versus Hallowe'en: A Fight to the Death?"

A third category of material about this fiesta is derived from Octavio Paz's widely read, translated, and taught *The Labyrinth of Solitude,* published in 1950. One chapter is entitled "Todos santos,* día de muertos" (All Saints, Day of the Dead), which, with the rest of the book, essentializes *"el mexicano,"* "the Mexican." Paz presents his observations in the "ethnographic present," which, as Sally Price observed, is "a device that abstracts cultural expression from the flow of historical time and hence collapses individuals and whole generations into a composite figure alleged to represent his fellows past and present" (Price 57).

Paz's book is beautifully written, sometimes couched convincingly in psychoanalytic terms, and fortified by unacknowledged mining of serious sources of popular culture analysis. Considering their dates of publication in French, his hidden bibliography might include Mircea Eliade, Carl Jung, Karl Kerényi, Paul Radin, and Adolf Bandelier. Paz is never specific; he never interviews or actually introduces el mexicano. He writes winningly in the first person plural, making statements such as "Somos un pueblo ritual" (Paz 42) [We are a ritual people] and "Nuestra pobreza puede medirse por el número y suntuosidad de las fiestas populares" (Paz 43) [Our poverty can be measured by the number and sumptuousness of popular fiestas].

Paz claims—based on the lyrics of popular music, on observations of the classes below his, and on Mexican and U.S. media images—that el mexicano is indifferent to death because he is indifferent to life;[4] death is desirable, and the sooner the better; el mexicano thinks about it almost constantly (Paz 52); he finds life meaningless, and so on. Paz inserts some defensible generalizations and theories based on research and personal experience, but they are so thoroughly surrounded by unfounded platitudes and unflattering stereotypes that I warn the reader who has had little contact with members of Mexican popular classes that the portrait is not entirely reliable. Unfortunately, because of his excellence as a poet and his international reputation as a Nobel laureate, a diplomat, and an occasional instructor at Harvard University, many of his compatriots and many non-Mexicans believe in Octavio Paz's mexicano and dismiss las mexicanas and los mexicanos de carne y hueso (flesh-and-blood Mexicans), female and male, as a picturesque, exotic, largely dysfunctional, neurotic lot.

Carlos Navarrete is quoted in Carmichael and Sayer as deliberately and responsibly refusing to feed "the long list of generalisations which have been written on the theme of Death in Mexico [that fuel] the myth of Death and the Mexican being. . . . It is necessary to take in hand the task of demystifying the myth, to question it, and demonstrate the fragility as a component of a premeditated national prototype" (Carmichael and Sayer 10). That is part of my project, too.

I take up somewhat gingerly the matter of contemporary attitudes toward death in Mexico in Chapter 7. The generalizations I dare to make are based on sources—formal, informal, read, recorded, or published—that reputable scholars would find reliable. Although it is possible and interesting

---

[4] Paz only rarely considers women in this book, and I am not certain that he means "el mexicano" to be inclusive.

to generalize about national character, it is essential to keep in mind the individuals, moments, experiences, and study that bring one to the point of postulating broad statements. Human societies are constituted of individuals, and although we may share so much personal and communal history, philosophy, socialization, and experience that we have much in common within given groups, it is indefensible to hide from one's reader the evidence and the thought processes that have carried one to such conclusions. I resolve to be humble and careful. I invite alert reading.

Words and Pictures

For this book I have constructed a narrative to tell my experience with, involvement in, and readings of and about Días de muertos.* I do not pretend to have told everything that can be thought and told about the fiesta,* only my version, which is necessarily partial. Contemporary literary studies have made clear that to speak (in Spanish, *hablar,* from Latin *fabulare,* which also gives us the English noun *fable*) is to fictionalize (from Latin *fingere,* meaning to mold, form, or devise, which gives us the Spanish verb *fingir,* to pretend) because any account is built of lexical and grammatological choices. Hence, it is not the same as living what we call reality, history, or experience. So let the reader beware.

Neither my account nor the accounts I adduce are the events we narrate. They are more or less self-conscious constructions of what the speakers remember (*recordamos*) with our minds and our "hearts," built out of the language we can command. Culler would see the usefulness of a personal reading of Días de muertos (or of anything else):

> In attempting to make explicit the assumptions, conventions, and interpretive operations at work in one's own responses, one casts them in a generalizable form and exposes them to judgment, both one's own and others'. In any case, since one's notions of how to read and of what is involved in interpretation are acquired in commerce with others, there is every likelihood that an explicit formulation of one's own interpretive operations would have considerable general validity. (Culler 53)

My readings are open to more readings, especially because the objects I read are not in themselves univocal but multilingual, polysemous, as the products of popular culture are always made from resources harvested from the dominant culture, as well as from their own. The signs and elements of

Días de muertos simultaneously reveal multiple intertexts: traces of beliefs, practices, and traditions that are "high" and "low"; medieval, colonial, Renaissant, and contemporary; "raw" and "cooked"; "civilized" and "barbarian"; Christian and Indigenous; abstracted from historical records and from mythical grounds, and all of which may, at different times or points, oppose and conflict with each other. My discourse will also inevitably reveal similarly contradictory traces from the language and the texts, the cultures and the historicity from which it is made.

I incorporate many photographs in this study as illustrations but also because I do not assume that my readers have been to Mexico during Días de muertos, if at all. For them, words cannot make vivid the orange of cempoaxóchitl* (the flower of the dead), the heaps of candy skulls, the rich colors and forms of offerings, the pre-Hispanic representations of skulls, the whimsy of sculpted and pictorial calaveras.* I am not an accomplished photographer or a student of the art, but the moments captured by my lens permit my readers to see some of what I have seen. By looking at the images, you can form your own impressions, judgments, and opinions.

I present my photographs as witnesses. As Susan Sontag has said: "A photograph is not only an image . . . an interpretation of the real; it is also a trace, something directly stenciled off the real, like a footprint or a death mask. . . . A photograph is never less than the registering of an emanation . . . a material vestige of its subject" (Sontag 350).

The magical aspect of photography takes me in enough to make me believe that by showing photos taken during Días de muertos I make the celebration present to my readers to a limited extent. Writing about the gradual secularization of Western societies, Sontag recognized the power of images that was experienced when people inhabited a sacred world and that is felt again in this ostensibly secular art:

> What defines the originality of photography is that, at the very moment in the long, increasingly secular history of painting when secularism is entirely triumphant, it revives—in wholly secular terms—something like the primitive status of images. Our irrepressible feeling that the photographic process is something magical has a genuine basis. . . . A photograph is part of, an extension of [its] subject; and a potent means of acquiring it, of gaining control of it. (Sontag 351)

In *Camera Lucida* Barthes philosophizes at length about the return of the dead who have been photographed, and I do not want to make too much of this point in a book about a celebration of the yearly return of the dead because we are not talking about the same thing. His meditation begins, perhaps, with calling the object photographed a *spectrum*; it is "the target, the referent, a kind of little simulacrum . . . emitted by the object, which I should like to call the *Spectrum* of the Photograph, because this word retains, through its root, a relation to spectacle and adds to it that rather terrible thing which is there in every photograph: the return of the dead" (Barthes, *Camera Lucida*, 9). Barthes is referring to the frisson that comes when looking at a photograph of someone who has died or of someone—including oneself—who will die in the future. Photographs cause him to feel he is being turned into a specter because they turn subjects into objects, into "Total-Image, which is to say, Death in person" (Barthes, *Camera Lucida*, 14). According to this impression, the person photographed is already dead in and because of the photograph.

Superficially, this notion is close to the Mexican one that to be born is to begin to die, to be living is to be dying, but the Mexican idea has nothing to do with images, photographic or otherwise. I see it as coming out of a radical realism that cannot forget the clear and simple fact that death incontrovertibly follows life.[5] Días de muertos celebrates the intimate, continuing relationship between the living and the dead. Like the celebration of a birthday, it reconfirms annually the love, goodwill, and generosity that the beloved can count on, no matter that they are dead. Whereas for Barthes the spectrum in the photograph is always already dead, for the typical celebrant of Días de muertos, the *ánima* (the spirit) never referred to as a specter or ghost—is always continually living, as its etymology implies, regardless of whether it is seen (*spectus*), heard, or sensed. This celebrant may also consider anyone alive as already an ánima or spirit—but remember the derivation of that latinate word—in the sense that many Mexicans believe we bear our death from the moment we are born.

---

[5] Life also follows death, which, as we see in the works of modern South American writers, as well as ancient and modern Mexican writers (for a challenging read, try *Distant Relations* by Carlos Fuentes), is fertile; it supports and gives rise to life, as in agriculture. But, as in agriculture—and this varies with the anthropology of each community—there may be feelings of true loss; one will only have this life with this body and this consciousness, although in death one may enjoy continued existence. The afterlife as usually understood by Días de muertos does imply perpetuation of personality and individual consciousness. See "An Anthropology in Días de muertos" in Chapter 10.

A valuable next stage from this study would be to continue to read seriously this and other events of popular culture in Mexico, the rest of Latin America, and the world. By imbricating many aspects of dominant local cultures, popular texts can reveal much about those cultures, as well as about the subgroups and social locations of the individuals who have created them. Ultimately, I hope familiarity reduces xenophobia in all its manifestations, to the point that the popular classes stop being subordinated and become so fully respected that their multiple visions alter the perspective of the whole until Mexico becomes the multiethnic, multilingual nation that it would be if its leaders developed the courage, the commitment to justice, and the wisdom to share their power and wealth and truly to know their compatriots.

International Attention

People from the United States and other parts of the industrialized world seem to be showing a growing curiosity about what they call the Third World and its traditions and worldviews. For hundreds of years, European and U.S. travelers have visited Mexico, and their writings sometimes betray something akin to a depleted sense of reality, which they supplement with what they consider the exoticism, picturesqueness, charm, and, above all, vitality of our landscapes and our people.

In 1993, for example, Quality Paperback Books (QPB) offered subscribers a box entitled "Mexico: The Day of the Dead." It included a small anthology of travelers' impressions of the fiesta edited by Chloë Sayer, a poster showing a detail from Diego Rivera's mural depicting the fiesta,*[6] and a tin calavera.* In spring 1994 I received an invitation to "have the time of [my] life on the Day of the Dead" in Oaxaca with a history professor from Texas A&M University. Colleagues have sent me mail-order catalogs that offer kits and activities books for and classroom celebrations of Días de muertos.* On seeing a *New Yorker* cartoon by William Hamilton that showed a fashionable cocktail party with the caption "Darling, spotting Todd Mason dressed as a woman—was that at the Palio in Siena or the Day of the Dead in Oaxaca?" (November 13, 1993), I recognized that the holiday had become a vacation destination for the

---

[6] The publication does not offer the title, which is "Day of the Dead: Street Festival." It was painted in 1923–1924 and is a detail of the south wall fresco *Court of the Fiestas* in the Secretaría de Educación Pública, Mexico City. My thanks to Rina Epelstein, curator of the Frederick Weisman Museum, Minneapolis, for this information.

sophisticated tourist, as well as for the celebrant, the anthropologist, and the student of popular culture.

I predict that canny merchants and tour guides will capitalize more and more on the concerns, curiosities, and desires to see how other cultures—especially Mexico—live with death. Mexican essayist Alberto Beltrán considered the fact that of all Mexico's traditions, foreigners are most interested in Días de muertos. He concluded that this is the case because the way a community remembers the dead is also the way it contemplates the unknown, which gives rise to myths and religions that, in turn, formalize such contemplations.

A number of my students at Macalester College in Saint Paul, most from the United States, have also expressed enthusiasm and pleasure at the opportunity to discuss without embarrassment Mexican and South American texts in which death is a central concern; in which children discover, ponder, and live with death; in which the dead are in close communication with the living.[7] These young people, Days of the Dead travelers, and the purchasers of QPB's box seem to recognize that life is incomplete without death; that death and thoughts about death cannot be postponed and ignored forever; that the people of traditional societies, and of Mexico in particular, can help them satisfy their hunger for living more intimately with death even though the foreign seekers have been socialized in a culture that pretends people can be young and beautiful (that is, alive) forever with the right diet, doctor, exercise program, cosmetics, and clothing (that is, with enough money). Susan Sontag has written: "A society which makes it normative to aspire never to experience privation, failure, misery, pain, dread disease, and in which death itself is regarded not as natural and inevitable but as a cruel, unmerited disaster creates a tremendous curiosity about these events—a curiosity that is partly satisfied through picture-taking" (Sontag 359).[8] It is a curiosity that is maturing into a serious interest in some members of the privileged classes, about whom it seems Sontag wrote the previous quotation, and it may be satisfied in part with picture looking and in part with dwelling—however briefly—with the practices of other societies, whether by reading, traveling, or interviewing.

---

[7] They were most impressed by Mexican Elena Garro's *La semana de colores,* a collection of short stories.

[8] I see my picture taking less as the result of what Sontag might describe as morbid curiosity than as an additional form of inscription.

Even within the United States, or whatever countries Sontag had in mind, many experience profound privation, failure, misery, and disease. To them, death is as close a companion as it is to the majority of people in the developing world. Newspaper articles occasionally cite statistics indicating that young African American boys do not expect to reach adulthood, surrounded as they are by violence. Perhaps the AIDS epidemic, which has infiltrated all classes of society, is part of what is fueling the interest in ways of considering death.

To what extent are practices and philosophies about death eroticized in industrialized societies? The violence in popular entertainment raises this question. In the consciousness of those for whom (violent) death is stimulating, a great distance may remain between their awareness and their death.

As a Mexican, although the celebrant of Días de muertos is not a member of my social class, neither is she or he entirely exotic. I was influenced profoundly by the popular religion of my nana,* or nursemaid, who spent hours socializing me throughout my infancy, childhood, and early adolescence. Eventually, I learned and, to some extent, internalized the prejudices of my class that overlay the sweetness and vitality of my lived experience, but Rosita Ortiz Torres could never become a mere other to be simplistically rejected. What I learned from her and from a Christian upbringing shaped my worldview, as well as my eventual power to become conscious of the cruelty and stupidity of such prejudice. Now, as an adult, I return to consider the matters a popular fiesta makes available.

Romancing the Bone

Si te llevo en mí prendida	If I carry you attached to me
y te acaricio y escondo;	and I caress and hide you;
si te alimento en el fondo	if I feed you in the depths
de mi más secreta herida;	of my most secret wound;
si mi muerte te da vida	if my death gives you life
y goce mi frenesí,	and my joy gives you ecstasy,
¿qué será, Muerte, de ti	what, Death, will become of you
cuando al salir yo del mundo,	when, upon my leaving the world,
deshecho el nudo profundo,	the deep knot undone,
tengas que salir de mí?	you have to emerge from me?
—Xavier Villaurrutia, 9,	
"Décima muerte"	

As this section title suggests, I have taken the position of a suitor in this project, and I feel justified in courting as a woman rather than as a man, given the flexibility contemporary society has begun to accept in gender relations and identities and given the nature of intellectual pursuit, which feels androgynous to me. My research and writing has consisted of romancing *La Huesuda, La Flaca,** *La Calaca,** (Bony, Skinny, Skull)—a few of the myriad Mexican nicknames for Death. Paradoxically, they are ironic terms of endearment that are so rich semiotically that whereas they refer superficially to the skeleton—an almost universal representation of death— to be better understood they need to be followed, pursued, romanced, if you will. These terms are not used exclusively during Días de muertos,* but this is the season when *La Muerte** is most remembered, represented, and consumed. This is the time when death-related intertexts are most accessible to the cultural semiotician, as if they, too, were attending a great reunion, perhaps a ball, waiting for the reader who will invite them to dance and explore their meaning deep into the night.

If I pose as a romancer of La Calaca, it is in part because I was raised to celebrate Hallowe'en rather than Días de muertos; thus, the event was not culturally mine, and I felt a need to earn gently and persistently the right to associate with everything related to it. It is also because a semiotic analysis can be a bit like a romance. It is joyful in its creatively spun net of associations. It is intense and focused. It is humble because of its inevitable partiality, sometimes dejected in the face of unyielding signs. I approach an object of study with enthusiasm and zeal, as its etymology dictates—eager to know it, to attend to its complexity and nuances; eager to make public my growing knowledge of something very worthy of being studied and known.

Self-Portrait With Calavera*

Vida y muerte no son mundos
contrarios
Somos un solo tallo con dos flores
gemelas.

        —Juan Rulfo

Life and death are not contrary
worlds
We are a single stem with two twin
flowers.

"Dos catrinas"* (Figure 2.1) is a snapshot I asked my father to take at the entrance of Mexico City's Museo Nacional de Culturas Populares, which had a double display for Días de muertos* in 1990. At the entrance and all through the patio were larger-than-life-size papier mâché calaveras (skeleton sculptures). In the enormous circular exhibition space were fifty-one ofrendas,* built in situ by people from eleven states of the republic[9] according to their traditions.

A *catrina* is a female dandy. No such a word exists in English, but it is not unusual in Spanish. All calaveras catrinas are directly or indirectly inspired by the one created by José Guadalupe Posada* in the first decade of the twentieth century (see Figure 1.27). According to the grandson of Posada's colleague, the famous printer and journalist Antonio Vanegas Arroyo, Posada's "Calavera catrina" was intended to make fun of women from the lower classes who were imitating women from the upper classes— "maids who dress up in their mistress' cast off finery" (quoted in Carmichael and Sayer 126). To my eye, neither the engraving nor the drawings and sculptures that came after it make this intention patent.[10] Most calaveras catrinas exhibit signs of turn-of-the-century wealth, and they are frequently accompanied by a calavera *catrín*, the male counterpart (see Plate 7, Figure 2.2).

When I saw this towering sculpture, I felt drawn to it, and I wanted to preserve my delight by having a photograph of myself holding her hand.[11] Working on Días de muertos for several years, gazing long at and thinking hard about its signs and images—especially the comical calaveras, which I find enormously engaging—have altered my perspective on life, death, and the body to the point that I feel clearly the dry skeleton under my clothes and flesh and I know so intimately that it feels like part of my identity. I am my skeleton. So I was drawn to La Catrina as like is drawn to like with no analytical thought, with only a sense of fun because of the photo opportunity.

This study has been more than an intellectual exercise. Although, as I have said, I am not of the classes or the ethnic groups that celebrate Días de muertos as part of their tradition, I am from the same country, and I feel

---

[9] The states represented were Chiapas, Guerrero, Michoacán, Morelos, Oaxaca, Puebla, Querétaro, Estado de* México, Yucatán, Tlaxcala, San Luis Potosí, and the city within Mexico City, Xochimilco. During the opening ceremony, there were neo-Aztec dance groups, tzeltal prayers, and music from Chochos, Nahuas, and Mixe.

[10] One of the most frequently admired qualities of the work of Posada, whose origins were humble, is his democratic gaze, which does not betray a classist prejudice.

[11] I doubt if I have been the only one so tempted; in fact, Chloë Sayer published a photograph taken between 1929 and 1931 by Grigori Alexandrov of Sergei Eisenstein with his arm hooked through that of a calavera catrina (Sayer 40).

2.1 Dos catrinas. Museo Nacional de Culturas Populares, México, D.F. Photo by Jorge Garciagodoy.

2.2 Papier mâché catrina by Linares. Anahuacalli, México, D.F. (Courtesy of Dolores Olmedo Patiño)

addressed by some of its icons and images, as well as by much of its philosophy, in a very direct way. I feel I have been ingesting death, my death, and Días de muertos all my life through the sweets and all the other elements of the event. By setting a yearly ofrenda for my dead, I have joined the numbers of Mexican intellectuals and artists at home and abroad, the children and grandchildren of emigrants, and the internationals who are drawn to celebrate Días de muertos. Through this photograph and its accompanying reading, I offer my credentials and a sort of calling card that helps to portray me and my relationship with my project.

"Dos catrinas" is not a calavera because its medium is too much of a collage compared to the real calaveras and because it was created neither by a member of las clases populares nor for that class. But it may be as close as a bilingual, bicultural (Minnesotan Mexican), bourgeois intellectual can come to making a calavera. It comes out of my social location and represents it. It is a product of my syncretic "culture."

Vis-à-vis Días de muertos, I am a literary critic and a critic of popular culture, not an anthropologist nor a sociologist; and I am a Mexican tourist, one of many Mexicans who visit the communities that celebrate th˙   ˙val as their own. We urban professionals who make these visits do s⌀   enjoy the journey to our national otherness, to our small-town oɪ   - patriots who live according to older norms than do those of us who ⌐   or the most part according to homogenizing global standards with our faxes, laptops, and televisions and our appetite for Hollywood movies and international books and cuisines. To some extent, such excursions complete us as nationally identified beings. From Freud onward, students of meaning have shown that we do not discover the world and ourselves through identity alone but also—and primarily—through alterity,* through the other, even through many others. At least momentarily and partially, the visits heal fragmentation by class, education, and ethnicity. We travel to traditional communities to enjoy the sights, smells, tastes, and sounds, as well as to enjoy— more or less self-consciously—our National Heritage, in upper case, as official government sources encourage us to do.

"Dos catrinas" can be read as I read real calaveras—teasing out their signs, pursuing their possible messages to their readers, watching for their most informative intertexts. To do so, I will switch from first to third person for the rest of this section. As Barthes has said, "The Photograph is the advent of myself as other: a cunning dissociation of consciousness from identity" (Barthes, *Camera Lucida,* 12).

2.3 Earthenware word processor. Oaxaca, Oaxaca.

The first element to remark about is the medium of this faux calavera. Calaveras are sculpted in papier mâché, candy, clay, wood, et cetera; drawn and painted on glass or paper (see Figures 1.1, 1.24, 2.2, 2.3); or printed like those of Posada (see Figures 1.14, 1.27). Except for broadsides and newspaper calaveras, the media chosen are low technology and tend to be managed by individuals or in small workshops.[12] This one is a photograph of a person with a calavera. Whereas tourists, journalists, and serious photographers have photographed Días de muertos, a photograph is not a calavera.

Calaveras are decidedly for public consumption. Some are produced in great quantities, such as the sugar and chocolate skulls that take over many traditional markets during this season. Most are unique and are displayed in public spaces. Frequently, they are part of public ofrendas that can have

---

[12] For interviews with sugar workers, see Carmichael and Sayer, Part 2.

a humorous tone, compared with private ofrendas, which are usually entirely earnest. The primary audience for "Dos catrinas" is not the buyers of sugar calaveras who frequent the markets and squares of Mexico in October and November. Rather, it is literally a memento, a way to remember a place, a moment, a sculpture, the photographer, and so on. In this sense, the most direct intertexts of "Dos catrinas" are the tourist photos of the subject reclining next to a Chac Mool, the subject pointing at an iguana on La Sagrada Familia, the subject waving from the Stone Arch Bridge.

Let me move into the frame to see the field of signification in which the subject and the catrina stand. In the photograph, behind the living woman and the catrina are a display of cempoaxóchitl,* some votive candles, and part of the museum buildings and grounds. The first two elements are signs of Días de muertos. The museum buildings and grounds are signs of official stature and intellectual discipline and seriousness. Beyond the museum we see a bit of sky. At the level of the calavera's upper teeth and to her right are the museum's doorbell and the sidewalk beyond the brick wall. I will return to an analysis of these semes.

The fingers of the foregrounded figures are interlaced. The calavera wears white clothing highlighted in pink, typical of the first decade or two of the twentieth century. The fleshed human wears casual, middle-class urban garb and carries a cloth shoulder bag. The calavera's mouth is open, perhaps greeting the visitors who were beginning to stream into the museum complex. Her expression is complacent. The woman, smaller than the calavera, is smiling. Both figures could be, to judge from their posture and dress, in the prime of life.

The photographer has joined life and death, the first and last decades of the twentieth century, a sculpted female calavera and a living woman not yet entirely, but certainly containing, a calavera. The photograph, significantly, was taken at both an architectural and an astronomical threshold. It is nearly dusk, and the sky, already colorless, shows neither day nor night. There is, on the secondary, connotative order of signification anomaly, not only because of the cited thresholds but also in the principal figures—one skeletal, one fleshed. A possible intertext is the pre-Hispanic masks of faces, which are also half fleshed and half skeletal (see Figure 7.2).

On first look, because of the intimate gesture of interlaced fingers and the side-by-side position, no hierarchical distinction appears to be drawn between the sculpture and the woman. On second look, the calavera's clothing connotes sexual attractiveness and elegance. The living woman's clothing connotes leisure, her bag, work; it is a briefcase or book bag, cloth rather than expensive leather. Clothing, as Marshall Sahlins observed in "La Pensée Bourgeoise," is not chosen simply to cover, warm, and protect the body but also to show an identification with some social formation. In "Dos catrinas," the calavera's garb and demeanor signify her identification with a wealthy class, as those of the live woman signify her identification with an intellectual class and with a generation, the U.S. baby boomers. The calavera enjoys a higher status in the capitalist hierarchy than does the woman. Both figures represent urban milieus. The calavera's larger size connotes superiority.

The woman is on the left, the "sinister" side of the calavera. This suggests death or ill fate. The calavera holds the woman's right (dominant) hand as if the latter were surrendering to the former, and the calavera is closer to the sidewalk with its connotation of the activity of the city and, therefore, of life. Symbolically, then, she is more alive, in greater control of life than the living woman, and at the same time she stands between the woman and the street as a guardian who has the power to allow or disallow passage. The woman has passed into the territory of the calavera. She seems to have agreed to follow Mictecacíhuatl, the Lady of the Realm of the Dead, into Mictlan* (the Realm of the Dead)—smiling, complete with bag and baggage, scrip and scrippage—as an obedient child might follow her mother, go where she goes, when she wants, as long as she wants; as a devotee might follow a teacher; as Naomi followed Ruth: "Wherever you go I will go, wherever you stay I will stay. Your people shall be my people, and your god, my god. Wherever you die I shall die and there I will be buried" (Ruth I:16–17a).

In a parallel manner, while researching this book I traveled into the territories of ethnic and socioeconomic groups that my own class and the United States—my country of residence—dominate according to their interests. As in "Dos catrinas," during recent Días de muertos I have placed myself in the territory of that carnival and, if not in the realm of the dead, at least firmly in the realm of the fiesta.* I do not pretend that my perspective is that of the typical celebrant, but my perspective has been altered profoundly by my experience of Días de muertos because I have stood in its theater rather than remaining on the audience's side of the proscenium. I have moved and I do move back and forth. I am writing with the *simpatía* (the sympathy), empathy, and goodwill I hope are represented by the humor and the fun of this photo and my reading of it.

❰3❱

Días de muertos and National Identity

ías de muertos* is a celebration that distills several symbolically important matters relating to Mexico's national and cultural identity. It is a prime example of the syncretism that characterizes Mexican popular religion, having evolved primarily from a pre-Hispanic constellation of practices and having drawn on popular cultural traditions from Spanish Catholicism.

Días de muertos is earnestly celebrated, mostly in rural communities and by the first generations of urban immigrants—typically by las clases populares. The communities that celebrate Días de muertos, however, are visited by other Mexicans who do not hold it as part of their own familial and social tradition but who may incorporate details of it into a discourse or a practice of national identity. A taxi driver told me he and his family had visited friends in Mixquic for the previous year's Días de muertos because the celebration "es muy bonita, muy tradicional; es muy mexicana" [it's very beautiful, very traditional; it's very Mexican]. Others have told me that although they do not set offerings for their dead, they enjoy eating the seasonal pan de muerto* and giving and eating candy skulls because they simply like the sweets or because "es la tradición" [it's the tradition].

Since the mid-1920s, the government has supported and promoted Días de muertos, especially at the neighborhood level—not only the fiesta* per se but knowledge and appreciation of it by those who do not celebrate it themselves. On November 2, 1992, the national newspaper, *Novedades,* ran an article about the various activities surrounding Días de muertos in one neighborhood. It clearly stated, "Los festejos tienen como finalidad fortalecer las tradiciones y costumbres de nuestra mexicanidad" [The festivities have as their end the fortification of the traditions and customs of our Mexicanness].

The broadsides illustrated by José Guadalupe Posada* (1852–1913) intrigued Jean Charlot, the French artist who went to Mexico as a young man and worked with Diego Rivera for an interesting reason: He felt his quest and project, shared by other Mexico City muralists, were satisfied and inspired by Posada's vision. Those artists wanted to do what they believed Posada had done in his illustrations: to marry Indigenous and mestizo* Mexico and to harmonize their country's nineteenth and twentieth centuries through their art. In other words, they intended to create a coherent—if occasionally ironic—portrait of Mexico.

Eric Hobsbawm's discussion of invented tradition, although limited to Europe, is useful for considering official Mexican interest in promoting Días de muertos. To begin with the appropriate definitions, Hobsbawm wrote:

> "Invented tradition" is taken to mean a set of practices . . . of a ritual or symbolic nature, which seek to inculcate certain values and norms of behaviour by repetition. . . . They are responses to novel situations which take the form of reference to old situations, or which establish their own past by quasi-obligatory repetition. . . . The object and characteristic of "traditions," including invented ones, is invariance. . . . "Custom" in traditional societies . . . does not preclude innovation and change up to a point. . . . What it does is to give any desired change (or resistance to innovation) the sanction of precedent, social continuity and natural law as expressed in history. (Hobsbawm 1f)

Días de muertos fits the kind of invented tradition Hobsbawm finds most interesting, that which is adopted and adapted, which is, one might say, reclaimed from *old traditions*—a term I prefer to *custom,* which seems to lack weight. An illustration of the kind of discourse that participates in this dynamic is found in the November 3, 1992, issue of *Uno más uno,* in the article "Expresó Clariond Reyes su defensa por las tradiciones de nuestros antepasados" [Clariond Reyes expressed his defense for the traditions of our ancestors]. The newspaper reported that Benjamín Clariond Reyes, the mayor of Monterrey, Nuevo León, encouraged holding contests for altars of Días de muertos, expressing his concern that Mexican traditions be upheld and not be replaced by *"americanismos"* (Americanisms). At the awards ceremony (first prize, one and a half million pesos*), he was quoted as saying:

Los jóvenes de Monterrey pueden estar seguros que seguiremos impulsando el nuevo Monterrey . . . pero también nos seguiremos preocupando por fomentar y difundir nuestras tradiciones. Con este concurso de altares de muertos, sin duda alguna, quien más sale ganando es nuestra cultura. . . . Nuestra ciudad, por sus características industriales y comerciales sin duda está a la vanguardia de las inovaciones y de los cambios. Sin embargo, por eso mismo es doblemente importante que busquemos difundir nuestra cultura, que es el orgullo del pasado y en el que fincamos nuestro futuro. (*Uno más uno,* November 3, 1992)

The young people of Monterrey can be sure that we will continue to impel the new Monterrey . . . but we will also continue to be concerned with fomenting and divulging our traditions. With this contest of altars for the dead, without a doubt it is our culture that wins in the end. . . . Our city, because of its industrial and commercial characteristics, is doubtlessly on the vanguard of innovation and change. For that very reason, however, it is doubly important that we seek to divulge our culture, which is the pride of the past and on which we base our future.

Here, the modernizing, internationalizing future is founded discursively on the oldest local traditions. The mayor's speech legitimizes the new while reaffirming the old; it explicitly promises the youth of the city that the city leaders will continue to modernize and to preserve traditions, and it implicitly implores whoever keeps the old traditions to continue them. Whereas Reyes, again implicitly, reaches out to the United States and Canada—identifying Monterrey with the commercial and industrial vanguard—he also reaches out to the deeply rooted Mexican tradition, thereby reconfirming Monterrey's Mexican identity.

An article in the daily *Novedades* on October 30 that same year listed a combination of activities—one commemorative, the rest practical: A "monumental pre-Hispanic" carpet was made of tinted sand, cempoaxóchitl,* votive candles, "et cetera," designed by seven artists from Oaxaca under the direction of theater scene designer Antonio López Mancera. Note the use of the adjective *pre-Hispanic*; this carpet falls into the category I call neo-pre-Hispanic, as it is really an imaginative contemporary work inspired by familiarity with pre-Hispanic art that yet cannot ignore the artists' familiarity with contemporary art and all the ways in which they participate in modern life. The practical activities in various neighborhoods included the establishment of portable toilets, parking areas, free transportation to Mixquic, where Días de muertos is the principal fiesta of the year, and arrangements for medical attention and water. The article spoke of the importance and long standing of this holiday in Mixquic:

[El delegado José Ramón Martell López] explicó que esta ceremonia del culto a los muertos que se viene realizando en Mixquic desde la época prehispánica, es un ritual en el que se enlazan las culturas que han dado sustento a nuestra identidad.

Afirmó que Tláhuac es un santuario de símbolos, leyendas y de arraigo a la tierra y a las costumbres ancestrales donde hombres y mujeres se esfuerzan por conservar su tradición y sus formas de organización haciendo del pasado un presente digno de la cultura actual. (Cited in González, "En Mixquic")

[Delegate José Ramón Martell López] explained that this ceremony of the cult to the dead, which has been realized in Mixquic since pre-Hispanic times, is a ritual in which the cultures that have given sustenance to our identity are interwoven.

He affirmed that Tláhuac [the borough in which Mixquic is located] is a sanctuary of symbols, legends, and attachment to the earth and the ancestral customs where men and women strive to conserve their tradition and their forms of organization, making of the past a present worthy of contemporary culture.

Just as this brief article juxtaposes descriptions of high art and of the humblest sanitary necessities, the high-sounding official discourse of Martell López describes an earnest practice to which the humblest citizens are, for their own reasons, profoundly committed. I would venture that they are less concerned with the interweaving of cultures for the sake of national identity than with remembering and honoring the dead with hopes that the dead will care for them.

Days of the Dead is a living tradition that has no need for revival, no interest in invention (Hobsbawm 8), nor, perhaps, anything to gain or lose by being tailored to fit what a ruling group may call the national interest. It has its own life and its own integrity as it is kept by people in much of Mexico. The typical celebrant in Mixquic or Cuetzalan neither knows nor cares what journalists, mayors, or scholars say about the fiesta. Celebrants do not know or care about the nostalgia and the worry of those who fear changes in the fiesta's observation. They are not concerned about the perceived threat of "Americanization" that some fear. They set out offerings; they visit and adorn the graves of loved ones; they offer *tamales** *de frijol* to guests. They sleep peacefully at night, knowing they are behaving correctly toward the dead—in their eyes and in the eyes of the living.

But some of Mexico's intelligentsia—and I include educators at all levels, politicians, artists, and the intellectuals who concern themselves with these matters—project their anxiety nationally. How many of them know and respect, rather than patronize, an individual who faithfully commemorates the dead? What can they do except fret, preach, generalize, and make herculean efforts to promote this celebration, which they fear will change or disappear and thereby stop aiding the construction of national identity and patriotism as the officials conceive of them?

A worried, conservative attitude is apparent among many Mexican writers. Hugo Nutini begins his *Todos Santos** in Rural Tlaxcala* as follows:

> This is a book about culture loss and decay. . . . It is a work of salvage ethnography. In the relatively short period of twenty-five years, the configuration of the institution, especially its physical manifestation and ritual and ceremonial discharge, has changed almost beyond recognition. From a well-integrated, smoothly functioning, and exquisitely expressed ensemble, the cult of the dead has become a disorganized, marginally discharged institution within the also changing socioreligious system. (Nutini ix)

Change is not loss and decay but the opposite. Petrification signals the loss and decay that would lead to apathy and the abandonment of a cult, a ritual, a tradition, a cultural practice. Nutini's admittedly "conservative view of society" (Nutini ix) smacks of what Renato Rosaldo has called imperialist nostalgia—the tendency of the intellectual laborer to mourn the changing or passing of her or his object of study, which his or her gaze and presence are helping to change. The inventors of tradition seem to have such a passionate interest in the preservation of custom that this interest keeps them from appreciating its dynamic vitality.

The world of the celebrants changes, and the celebrants change to accommodate constantly varying circumstances and to exploit ever new resources as they become available, as we see in the incorporation of some of Hallowe'en's icons. Rosalind Rosoff Beimler's relaxed attitude toward this holiday seems much more in tune with the event and its participants than that of anxious conservatives. She wrote, "Symbols here become mixed, but the message is always the same—mock death, partake of it, join it, because there is no escaping it" (25).

The officials and the conservative preservers of tradition are interested not in the survival of Días de muertos as an event that integrates the societies in which it is observed but rather in the survival of a political, economic, and social order that favors their class and conforms to their ideas of what is desirable. The establishment of nations produced citizens where previously there had been atomistically independent groups, many of whom knew or cared little about each other's existence. But those in power thought (or think) they all had to be made to feel and behave as part of "Mexico." As Hobsbawm wrote,

> The state, seen from above in the perspective of its formal rulers or dominant groups, raised unprecedented problems of how to maintain or even establish the obedience, loyalty and cooperation of its subjects or members, or its own legitimacy in their eyes. The very fact that its direct and increasingly intrusive and regular relations with the subjects or citizens as individuals (or at most, heads of families) became increasingly central to its operations tended to weaken the older devices by means of which social subordination had largely been maintained. (Hobsbawm 265)

One of the state's strategies in Mexico has been to exploit a folk cultural event that is virtually universal throughout the country by giving it its stamp of approval; by incorporating the captive audience of grade-school children, some of whom manage to involve their families; by inviting visits by noncelebrants; and by permitting or inviting the introduction of Hallowe'en. By making Días de muertos an officially encouraged holiday, the government has tried to perpetuate and assure its universality. If all Mexicans—at least those who could be spared from their work—were free to commune with the living and the dead at the same time, unencumbered by routine duties, there would be an opportunity for solidarity or even for a quasi-mystical communion with each other, as there is for Christians during the Eucharist.[1] Everyone would be able to partake of warm, pronational feelings that would attest to the effectiveness of this strategy.

Identification with fellow citizens—dead or alive, continuity with an ostensibly common past, and appreciation for the government-sanctioned holiday all serve the national interest. I cannot count the number of informants who answered my questions about the meaning of Días de muertos for them, their reasons for performing a particular aspect of it, and their reason(s) to celebrate it at all by saying "es muy mexicano" [it's very Mexican] or "porque somos mexicanos" [because we're Mexican]. Many of us feel more patriotic during and because of this celebration, in part because we think our way of relating to death and the dead—and, by implication, to life—is unique in the world, setting us apart from (and at least a little above) everyone else. We are *más machos* (braver) and we have *más corazón* (more heart) than other cultures.[2] As writer George Rabasa observed, "It's also a way of saying [we celebrate the dead] because we are who we are—Mexicans. Because we are Mexicans we cannot possibly behave in any other way but to carry out the rituals of being Mexican. This is not so much [a reflection of] patriotism but a reflection of the Mexican in a higher, more global, less individualized identity" (personal communication). Rabasa points to the essentializing of the Mexican by himself or herself, which indicates the success of the official agenda of appropriating a grassroots tradition.

Both Víctor Fosado Vázquez, son of a lifelong collector and promoter of Mexican folk art who is an authority on popular art and an informant of Carmichael and Sayer, and Ana Ortiz perceive a discrepancy between the invented tradition promoted by "the Government" and observed "for the wrong reasons" and the old traditions observed "for the right reasons." Both have speculated about official motives for supporting Días de muertos, and both have questioned the effectiveness of what they seem to consider a charade rather than a true commemoration of the dead. They cast doubt on the authenticity of the urban, (post)modern resident who has lost his or her traditions:

---

[1] During the presidency of Salinas de Gortari, November 1 was a national holiday on which the state-of-the-union address was given, coinciding conveniently with the first of the Days of the Dead.

[2] An interesting side effect of this belief may be that we find ourselves exotic, other, by considering what the rest of the world does and thinks about death and the dead to be "normal." We may feel, literally, etymologically "alienated" by our essentialized difference.

Why, you may ask, should the Government worry about our traditions? . . . The goal is social and political stability. The DIF[3] was formed to foster family values and family well-being. The Government encourages loyalty to one's family, one's region and one's traditions. It would be optimistic to imagine that everyone now upholding tradition is doing so out of deep conviction. There is a strong element of snobbery and affectation, and many people are merely following the official line. . . . With or without feeling, for the right or the wrong reasons, our traditions are being promoted and perpetuated. (Fosado Vásquez, quoted in Carmichael and Sayer 134f)

Otra clase social de otro nivel ya . . . ha ido perdiendo [las costumbres de Días de muertos] para absorber costumbres de otros lugares. Yo veo en muchas casas ya no se ponen ofrendas o se ponen con un deseo de conservar una tradición, pero no con una creencia profunda, pero con el deseo de conservar formas aunque los contenidos se han eliminado. (Ortiz's interview in Alfonso Olvero's "Celebrating the Day of the Dead")	Another social class from another level has been in the process of losing . . . [the customs of Días de muertos] to absorb customs from other places. I see that in many houses offerings are no longer set out, or if they are it is with a desire to preserve tradition but not with a profound belief, rather with the desire to preserve forms although the contents have been eliminated.

Neither Ortiz nor Fosado Vázquez allows for the possibility that some, if not all, of the people who adopt practices borrowed or mimicked from other social classes and ethnic groups—possibly boosted by the patriotism fostered by official support for Días de muertos—find the performance of the practices so rich that their beliefs and feelings are transformed by them. Thus, a composer like Jorge Reyes might find himself believing that the spirits of his dead visit the monumental altar he and his audience erect in his concert space on November 2, even though celebrating the holiday may be relatively new to him. Similarly, some of the mostly middle-class members of his audience may feel the power of ritual and tradition altering their own view of the relationship between the living and the dead.

---

[3] Desarrollo Integral de la Familia [Whole Development of the Family], a government agency.

*3.1 Ofrendas workshop. Centro Cultural Ricardo Flores Magón (CCRFM), Oaxaca
(Courtesy of CCRFM)*

I would like to return briefly to the role played by public schools in the preservation of Días de muertos and in the invention of tradition. Hobsbawm considered primary education, "imbued with revolutionary and republican principles and content, and conducted by the secular equivalent of the priesthood," to have functioned as an effective substitute for the church and its moral and ideological leadership in the French Republic from the 1860s onward (Hobsbawm 271). Education plays a similar role in Mexico and has for approximately the same period of time. When a school teaches children to observe a holiday, the family's practices are fortified if they also observe it and are criticized and perhaps brought somewhat into line if they do not. All public schools are obligated to teach elementary students about the fiesta by having them build an altar, set an offering, decorate it with their own art, and, in many cases, write literary calaveras* or create plastic ones. In Oaxaca the Taller de Artes Plásticas Rufino Tamayo, an arts studio, held workshops to teach and sponsor children ages four to twelve to make elaborate altars with their own calaveras (see Figure 3.1, Plate 12).

An article by Patrick Johansson in the daily *El Nacional* ("Sincretismo evangelizador y muerte precolombina," November 2, 1993) announced a documentary on Days of the Dead in Parque Hundido, a city park, concluding with the weighty advice: "Recuerde que es nuestra obligación enseñar a los niños el origen y el porqué de nuestras tradiciones" [Remember that it is our obligation to teach children the origin and the reason of our traditions]. Of course it is children who can preserve or discontinue traditions, based in part on what their parents or caregivers have taught them to value.

If the promotion of Días de muertos is effective, it is so, as Hobsbawm observed, because it enjoys a "genuine popular resonance" (Hobsbawm 264) and because official manipulation of the fiesta manages to "exploit practices which clearly meet a felt—not necessarily a clearly understood—need among particular bodies of people" (Hobsbawm 307). Días de muertos as encouraged by official leaders merges folkloric, popular, and occasionally high cultural elements and identification with the nation-state (Hobsbawm 6f).

Who are the people to whom Fosado Vázquez refers as perpetuating "our traditions" to "follow the official line" or out of "affectation or snobbery" rather than sincerely? Some are the same teachers to whom María Antonieta Sánchez de Escamilla refers, commanded to do so by the Secretaría de Educación Pública (Ministry of Public Education). Some are individuals who, out of a sense of nostalgia for the ways of their ancestors, a sense of solidarity with las clases populares, or a sense of aesthetic or spiritual or ritual appreciation for the fiesta follow some of its traditions, although they were not taught them by their parents. Some are members of the middle-class elite whom it is necessary to include in any nationalist project (Hobsbawm, "Mass-Produced Traditions"). Since most members of that group cannot be as easily obligated to do what a government ministry orders and few are likely to be profoundly affected by what their school-age offspring are taught, other strategies have to be deployed for their involvement.

One of the more curious and paradoxical of those strategies is to open the way for the introduction and adaptation of Hallowe'en. I limit myself to saying that doing so gives the fiesta a cosmopolitan air and an international cachet that appeals to a certain segment of the middle class, to those who aspire to that class, and to a great number of those who innocently adopt and adapt icons and practices that please them.

Perhaps the most effective strategy for involving the middle class is to invite them to visit sites where Días de muertos is celebrated. The promotion of such tourism not only moves money from the country's national and state capitals to its peripheral communities; it also involves the tourists' thoughts and actions in several ways. They must plan, discuss, and transport themselves. They think about or discuss the appropriate dress and behavior when visiting communities with which they are unfamiliar. They alter their diet somewhat by eating at the site they have chosen. They may be tempted into buying some of the sweets of the fiesta. The visitors may sacrifice their usual bedtimes; many communities have *velación* (a vigil), *danzas* (dances), processions, and other practices that take place deep into the night.

In 1992 I became aware of organized tours that arranged visits for a price. I joined two in the state of Oaxaca. One, on November 1, went to two graveyards in Xoxocotlán.[4] We were each given a bouquet of flowers, two *veladoras* (votive candles), and torches that consisted of a candle set into a split bamboo shaft and protected by orange cellophane paper. Before the tour departed, we were given a short lecture (once in Spanish, once in English) about the importance of Días de muertos. We were reminded that we would be guests at a spiritually important event and were counseled to behave appropriately. And we were instructed to place our flowers and candles on graves that were unadorned and untended; we would gain spiritual merit this way and be rewarded in the hereafter. A majority of the people on the tour were from the United States; a few were from Canada, Europe, and Mexico. The bilingual guides were Mexican.

Tourists are spectators of traditions that, even if they might have been kept by their grandparents, are not theirs. Whatever they do, whatever the extent of their participation or of the merging and mingling of "audience" and "actors," because they are present at a commemoration of the dead, their bodies and minds draw them into the circle of a celebration that to many feels intimate and a bit magical. In this way, many are brought into the "we" of national identity and affirmation. What is the effect for the international visitors? Some have expressed great enthusiasm about the fiesta and humbleness and gratitude for the opportunity to witness it. Several have said they found it very moving. They are as earnest as Mexican tourists, with the advantage that they travel with an attitude of openness some nationals have lost through lifelong familiarity.

The theatrical aspects of Días de muertos have proven to be a lasting element in public symbolic discourse. They have attracted the concern of a group that fears the disappearance of the celebration. They have attracted the attention, attendance, and spending of an enormous number of national and international tourists. They have infiltrated international intellectual,

---

[4] Pronounce the *x* as a *j* in Spanish, that is, as a vigorously aspirated *h* in English.

commercial, and journalistic circles, granting the fiesta additional legitimacy. They continue successfully to serve two masters: the earnest celebrants who would perpetuate their practices in honor of the dead even if only their community and their dead were watching and the forgers of an official and distinctive "Mexican" culture.

◄4►
Two Manifestations of Días de muertos

D ías de muertos* celebrations vary from community to community. Although the great majority maintain a core of practices, the history of each celebrating group determines the variations, which may be as simple as the different flowers, fruits, and vegetables that are in season in a particular region or as complex and arcane as how syncretism has woven together Christian and Indigenous strands of beliefs and traditions in a specific social system. I am not concerned in this book about such singularities, as interesting as they can be.[1]

One basic difference, however, falls within the bounds of this work: that between the folkloric and popular forms of the fiesta.* I often think of the two aspects as the earnest and the carnivalesque, which does not preclude the earnestness and gravity in the latter. In *Understanding Popular Culture,* John Fiske draws the distinction neatly:

---

[1] Several ethnographies are included in the Works Consulted. Many more can be consulted in Mexican libraries, and a number are available in collections in the United States.

Folk culture, unlike popular culture, is the product of a comparatively stable, traditional social order, in which social differences are not conflictual, and that is therefore characterized by social consensus rather than social conflict. . . . Folk cultures are much more homogeneous and do not have to encompass the variety of social allegiances formed by members of elaborated societies. (Fiske, *Understanding Popular Culture*, 170)

Mexico, officially a Spanish-speaking nation-state, is made up of many heterogeneous subcommunities. Twenty-three distinct ethnic groups are found in its one Federal District (D.F.) and thirty-one provinces, in which more than fifty languages are spoken. It is a relatively large country, encompassing 1,972,546 square kilometers; around 10 percent of its population is considered purely Indigenous, 75 percent is mestizo,* and 15 percent is "European," according to the 1992 *Cambridge Encyclopedia of Latin America and the Caribbean*. In many towns and villages, one can witness genuine folk culture. People live fairly harmoniously according to commonly held values and traditions, and tolerating well each other's rather minimal differences. I speculate that in most areas where this is true, we would find examples of what Bonfil Batalla calls México profundo,* societies strongly identified—whether consciously or only existentially—with the ancient Mesoamerican* philosophy that has survived, resisted, or conformed to Christian and Western conversion.

Popular culture shows the opposite traits. It is hosted by a social order unevenly divided between identification with vestiges of ancient local traditions and identification with foreign, "modern" ways and values—the proponents of which are often at odds culturally and philosophically but also through the dynamics of domination, exploitation, and (neo)colonization. Popular culture is usually found in large cities, whose numbers alone preclude homogeneity and guarantee a variety of social allegiances. Mexico City and other cosmopolitan cities exhibit this pattern, and I include in this group large towns that host so many commuters and vacationers from the D.F.* that their culture exhibits features of the capital's, including a number of elements of popular culture.

Although these distinctions can be described efficiently, the outsider who visits a rural community is apt to find elements of dress, language, music, diet, and so on that can be observed in a state capital. Similarly, even in the national capital pockets reminiscent of village life can be found. Human action, reaction, and interaction being as complex as they are, any contact between people and cultures can inspire imitation, adaptation, or adoption of details that one or two generations ago might have drawn scorn or sanction. Even so, for historical and geographical reasons, Mexico does, in fact, host societies that exhibit the values and practices of folk culture.

In the two kinds of cultures I can generalize about certain characteristics of Días de muertos. Most simply, where folk culture dominates, Días de muertos consists virtually entirely of the earnest and oldest elements of the fiesta:* preparation of elaborate ofrendas* containing key elements, visits with the dead, and sharing of the ofrendas. Where popular culture dominates, some people keep one or more of the earnest aspects of the commemoration, and others do not. In the second circle, a number ignore the fiesta altogether, especially if their parents or grandparents did not celebrate it; some prefer a Mexicanized version of U.S. Hallowe'en; some enjoy one or more kinds of the myriad calaveras*—literary and sculptural, edible and enjoyable as art, folk art, popular art, and humorous artifacts.

In this chapter I will describe what I observed of the folk cultural version of Días de muertos in Cuetzalan, Puebla, in 1991 and some of what I have observed of the idiosyncratic celebrations in Mexico City, especially in 1990 and 1993 but also during my life there. I will end by considering the impact José Guadalupe Posada* has had on the iconography of the popular fiesta.

In the Folk Culture of Cuetzalan

Nacer es solamente comenzar a morir.   To be born is only to begin to die.
        —José Gorostiza
    (Quoted in Villaseñor)

For one familiar with Mexico City's version of the fiesta,* Días de muertos* is very different in Cuetzalan, Puebla, in the Sierra Madre Oriental, where the culture seems much less contested—to the point of conforming to John Fiske's definition of folk culture. In this mountain town, Catholicism has been so transformed by Indigenous beliefs and traditions, and the local practices so firmly established, that there seems to be little else to transform, subvert, or resist. Relations among Indians, Indian mestizos,* and the white mestizo bourgeoisie seem casual and easy. While I was there, I conversed with several residents, including a family of middle-class mestizos, a Jewish man, and a formerly Catholic woman; the last two worked in the city's Tourism Bureau. All of them recognized differences between their own and the *Indígenas'* culture. Their recognition seemed gracious, amiable, and utterly nondismissive. They talked about the language and some of the traditions of the Indígenas in a quietly accepting way. They did not act or speak in a patronizing or exoticizing manner, and they made no effort to separate themselves from the Indígenas with any discursive violence. Neither did they speak with the gingerly care of "political correctness."

Cuetzalan is a municipality of around 45,000 inhabitants (Centro de Estudios Históricos de la Sierra Norte de Puebla [CEHSNP] 8), 55 percent of whom are Indigenous and 45 percent mestizos, usually Indigenous and Spanish. Only about 15,000 live within the city limits of Cuetzalan, and the rest live in seven *Juntas Auxiliares* (villages and surrounding rural areas). The Indígenas belong to two ethnic groups: the Totonaca and the Náhuatl*, with the latter the predominant one whose language virtually everyone speaks. Most residents are bilingual and also speak Spanish.

Compared with some neighboring towns, two of which had been established by 481 c.e., Cuetzalan is not an old city (CEHSNP 12). In 1531 the Franciscan convent Our Lady of the Assumption was established in Tlatlauquitepec, now part of the municipality of Cuetzalan. When Cuetzalan was first mentioned in a historical document, it was still part of the Franciscan mission, which had been taken over by secular clergy by 1570. In brief, so little documentation exists about Cuetzalan that the CEHSNP believes the Spanish conquerors and colonists had little interest in it. It was—and still is—fairly isolated, it lacks plains for agriculture and husbandry, and it has no mines. Local society maintained many traditions unchallenged by external agents until the mid-nineteenth century (CEHSNP 15ff).

Eleven Cuetzaltecos participated in the famous May 5, 1862, battle against the French, and Cuetzalan began to expand with the new *Leyes de Reforma* (laws of reform), which did not recognize communal property held by the Indígenas. Outsiders were given those lands, and they displaced the local people by violent means. By the 1890s, Cuetzalan had a new cemetery adjoining the church, a growing coffee industry, a telephone line, schools for boys and for girls, gas lighting, and three orchestras. The road joining Cuetzalan with the closest large town was roughed out in 1920 and smoothed out in 1962, and on October 4, 1986, Cuetzalan was granted the status of a city (CEHSNP 19ff).

The CEHSNP maintains that Días de muertos, to which it refers as All Saints and All Hallows, is the most important fiesta for all the Indigenous groups in the municipality (CEHSNP 24). The Indígenas call it *Animaílhuitl,*

4.1 Doña Ocotlán at her mother's grave. Cuetzalan, Puebla

which, in a Náhuatl*-Spanish neologism, means fiesta of the ánimas, or spirits. The only public signs of the celebration are found in the cemetery where graves are cleaned, weeded, and decked with offerings of flowers.

According to Doña Ocotlán Reyes, who became my most helpful, generous informant in Cuetzalan, the most important days are October 31, when the ánimas of those who died as children are regaled, and November 1, when the ánimas of those who died as adults pay their visit. November 2 is the day for the ánimas solas,* the spirits of individuals who died far from home or who no longer have relatives to care for them.

She was going to the *camposanto* (the graveyard), not for the sake of el ánima sola but to greet again the spirits of her grandson, who had died of an intestinal disorder when he was ten months old, and her mother. Doña Ocotlán had cleaned their graves and put bouquets of cempoaxóchitl* on them on the appropriate days (see Figure 4.1). On November 2, after rearranging the flowers, she went into the church where a mass was just ending. Having received the blessing, she came back out, invited my family to her son's house, and returned to her mother's grave, where she bowed her head briefly and crossed herself.

The graveyard was full of people, many doing what Doña Ocotlán had done, many just then cleaning and decking the graves according to their means. Some were ostensibly settled in for a long visit with the revenants, standing still, facing the graves. The ground was very wet and muddy. It had rained for several days and was so foggy that I could not usually see why the church was called Iglesia de los Jarritos,[2] and I was never able to discern the characteristic reddish color of the earthenware jugs.

The weather had kept many people at home the nights of October 31 and November 1, which made new visits necessary on the following days to relight votive candles on the graves. When I asked Doña Ocotlán about the fluidity or flexibility of time, she explained that it does not matter if the graves are not visited exactly on the traditionally prescribed date, as long as they are visited near that time. A poor woman who had been, in her word, *regalada,* "given" to a wealthier woman as a servant when she was seven years old because her parents were too poor to raise her themselves, Doña Ocotlán sympathized with people whose obligations prevented them from observing the holy days "on time." This contradicted the notion I had held of sacred time, derived largely from Mircea Eliade (*The Sacred and the Profane*), which had led me to believe that only certain, very specific times are considered sacred by mythopoetic people and that those times cannot be postponed or moved back for the convenience of the celebrant.

The transposing of Día de los angelitos,* (Day of the Little Angels), and Día de muertos, (Day of the [Adult] Dead), from October 31 and November 1, respectively, to el Día del ánima sola on November 2 surprised me for that reason, but Doña Ocotlán showed me that the notion of sacred time is more elastic than I had believed. The upper echelons of society have more power to bend rules in our working schedules and have less need to adhere to schedules we ourselves establish and enforce less tolerantly for those we employ. The spirits that visit relatives who are not free on the traditional dates must be patient enough to visit when their hosts are free. We remember that the Catholic missionaries and colonizers shrank the chronologically scattered and abundant observances for the dead to a mere two days to coincide with their feasts of All Saints and All Souls'; celebrants and celebrated adjusted to the imposed changes. Although the conquered Mesoamericans* concentrated their commemorations of the dead to culminate on the Catholic holidays, the folk-popular celebration still poaches on the last days of October and beyond November 2 in many communities.

---

[2] It is named Church of the Clay Pots because clay pitchers are strung on cables along its spires.

In contrast to the carnivalesque celebration in México, D.F., the customs surrounding Días de muertos in Cuetzalan invite an attitude of normalcy and convention. The people with whom I spoke there communicated a sense of duty about the fiesta—not unpleasant or resentful but with no sense of resistance to the hegemonic culture; no sense of revelry, carousal, and fun; and no publicly expressed intense feeling of any kind. We were often proudly offered tamales* de frijol (bean tamales), which reminded me of the way many people in the United States talk about Thanksgiving: The special food and its preparation seem as important as those who gather for the meal, and rarely does the informant talk about what she or he is thankful for.

Thinking about how holiday food departs from the daily diet reminded me of what Inga Clendinnen has written about the elaborate communal preparations for pre-Hispanic Náhuatl feasts and "the 'neighborhood' dimension of city life" (Clendinnen 59), beginning with the fact that the sharing of food in Mexica* society extended beyond the family to neighbors, as does the distribution of the ofrenda* at the end of Días de muertos:

We have occasional glimpses of the gaiety of the preparation for some festivals, with whole neighborhoods staying up all night, stirring the stewpots and simmering with anticipation, before a general joyful celebration, while at the festival of Izcalli[3] women were out in the streets at first light with their baskets of fresh-cooked tamales scurrying to be the first to distribute them to neighbours and kin. (Clendinnen 59)

This may be true because food affords us the "logic of the concrete" that Claude Lévi-Strauss wrote about. It is the material, apprehensible dimension of experience on which the more abstract, spiritual dimensions are mapped. Ultimately, tamales signify not merely the corn cakes but also the elaborate preparation they entail in the company of friends or relations, the love with which the cook remembers those who will consume them, the anticipation and, later, enjoyment of the food and of the reunion of living and dead, and so forth. Días de muertos in Cuetzalan is an integral part of the year, of the season of harvest. It does not stick out grotesquely as it does in Mexico City with its excessive fun, its outrageous calaveras,* and its energetic presence.

---

[3] The Izcalli festival celebrating growth and rebirth took place in the month that lasted from January 19 to February 7. Some of the customs equated the growth of babies and children with that of corn (Clendinnen 297).

In the Popular Culture of Mexico City

> I don't know why people in Mexico City like death to be
> shown so cheerfully. . . . Here [San Salvador Huixcolotla,
> Puebla] people want living things: angels, birds, the chalice,
> crosses—maybe even coffins, but never skeletons.
> —Vivanco (Quoted in Carmichael and Sayer 103)

Resistance is very visible in and around the overpopulated, over-crowded, overcentralized capital of Mexico. In this ethnically diverse city people dress, speak, gesture, relate, and move in areas and ways that preserve and make clear their ethnic and class origins. A frequently quoted aphorism propounds, "Dime con quién andas y te diré quién eres" [Tell me who you spend time with, and I'll tell you who you are]. How one spends leisure time is one of the indicators of identity, and this includes what national and international holidays one observes and how. Whereas groups of people identify with one another through positive means such as what they own, think, believe, and do in common, they also define their identity by distinguishing themselves from other groups.

For example, people sometimes use the words *indio* and *india* to insult someone they consider inferior. Mestizos* or mestizo-identified Indígenas distance themselves from the Indígenas who preserve and continue to embody their ways. Members of the dominant classes may not make fine distinctions among people in the popular classes, who usually share similar hair and skin coloring although their dress and physical posture vary; such distancing may be particularly important as mestizos seek to join socioeconomic classes higher than the class of most Indígenas and higher than their own. Like the members of the lower middle class whom Bourdieu described as wanting to separate themselves from "Nature" to draw closer to "Civilization," in Mexico members of parallel formations consider Indigenous people undesirably "natural" or "primitive" and prefer to draw closer to the industrial, modern, or "civilized"—which implies foreign residents and foreign-identified nationals, including those with non-Mexican parents.

Even well-to-do members of the bourgeoisie may refer to fellow metropolitans whose dress or style they judge to be common as indios or as *nacos,* a word of uncertain etymology that means variously lower class, uncool, lacking in taste, barbarous, uneducated. Thus, we see in Mexico City and other large cities elaborated societies in social conflict, which is rarely life threatening but plays out through the kinds of systemic violence perpetrated by economic liberalism's concentration of wealth in the hands of a very few.

The Mexica* or Aztecs were guided by their tutelary god Huitzilopochtli to the site where they built the grand city of México-Tenochtitlan, beginning in 1325 C.E. In 1427 the Machiavellian counselor Tlacaélel masterminded the beginning of the Aztec empire under three kings. He actualized his vision of a warrior mysticism by rewriting history, reforming the religious pantheon, redistributing lands and titles, reorganizing the army and the *pochtecas* (merchants), and consolidating the Triple Alliance with Texcoco and Tlacopan, now called Tacuba (León-Portilla, *Los Antiguos Mexicanos* 40ff).

When Hernán Cortés and his troops of Spaniards and Native allies finally arrived in Tenochtitlan on November 8, 1519, they were amazed at the city's size and beauty, its streets and canals, its high buildings, and its imposing temples. The seat of the empire fell to the foreign invaders on August 13, 1521, and Cortés went about turning it into a Spanish city. He sent for "*Los Doce*," the twelve Franciscan friars who arrived in 1524 to begin what is known as the spiritual conquest of Mexico. As the conquerors mixed with the Amerindians, they devised a rigid hierarchy based on ethnicity and relative wealth and power. The National University, founded in 1551, was the third university in America.

After almost three centuries of Spanish domination, the Mexican-born *criollos* * spearheaded the war of independence from Spain from 1810 to 1821. Mexico City continued to be the capital of an empire that became a republic in 1824. Currently occupying more than 950 square miles and inhabited by around 20 million people, the city has outgrown itself, and although it still has beautiful areas and is continually richer in cultural activity, it has become somewhat chaotic politically, economically, ecologically, and socially.

In this, one of the world's megacities, Días de muertos* has been celebrated by popular classes year after year, and as I said earlier, in the most cosmopolitan parts of the country, its "earnest" aspects are only a fraction of the celebration. Typically, within two generations of immigration to the city, rural people lose the tradition. Días de muertos has become mainly an event featuring ordinary and extraordinary popular pleasures in which the serious and the comical, images of life and death, work and fun are juxtaposed in practices of the body and the mind.

Numerous *mises en scène* of related themes, both in Mexico City and other places, are inclined toward a carnivalesque atmosphere during Días de muertos. For centuries Mixquic, an independent town officially within the *delegación* or borough of Mexico City, has been famous for its "death cult." (An informant told journalists Simón Cuevas and Romualdo Galindo that Mixquintli, the goddess of life and death, presides over the town "donde 'los muertos están vivos siempre y los vivos no dejan de recordar-los'" [where 'the dead are always living and the living always remember them'] (Cuevas and Galindo). A visitors' center housed in the library makes available a mimeographed schedule with events and performances that last three days. A platform is erected, and hundreds of folding chairs are set in rows under a tarpaulin in the center of town. There are poetry recitations, history lessons, and what I call neo-pre-Hispanic rituals and dances based on current ideas of ancient and contemporary conceptions of death, the afterlife, and the dead. There are also readings and performances of stories and plays. The stories, sometimes by nationally recognized writers such as Juan Rulfo, do not necessarily have Días de muertos as their setting or theme; they may simply focus on the death of a character or on a visit by a spirit. There are contests for the best calavera* costume or skit, as well as for the best ofrendas* in both the home and the graveyard.

Many skits are presented; they are usually crude and little more than the dramatization of a joke about tricking or being tricked by Death.[4] There may be dramatizations of a version of the story I told in "La ofrenda" in Chapter 1. Sometimes they are performed by calavera puppets and often by actors dressed as skeletons. The plays may include adaptations of Zorrilla's *Don Juan Tenorio,* which is performed annually in many theaters in Mexico during this season, and although the moralistic original continues to draw an audience, ribald and humorous versions compete with it (see Figures 1.13, 4.2). The mood in this improvised theater may be serious during the audition of a "high culture" literary piece or the performance of a ritualistic dance or pantomime, but for the most part the mood is jocose.

---

[4] Whereas Death has been personified as a trickster in other cultures, it is interesting that in Mexico it is given a role similar to that of the pre-Christian god Tezcatlipoca, whose name means the Mirror's Smoke or Smoking Mirror. He is defined by absolute arbitrariness, omnipotence, and omnipresence. He is the master of human destiny, which sometimes brings felicitous experiences and often brings misfortune. When a skit shows Death/Tezcatlipoca being tricked, it is an instance of wish fulfillment, a fact recognized by the sempiternally realistic Mexican.

4.2 *"La Calavera del Tenorio" by Posada. (Permission given by Moyer Bell)*

*4.3 "Rebumbio de calaveras" (Skeleton Hubbub) by Posada.
(From Berdecio and Applebaum)*

Beyond the humble auditorium, a market takes over most of Mixquic with stall after stall of calaveras made of bread, chocolate, or sugar—as in other parts of the country—but most distinctively of amaranth, a crop that has been grown in this area for around seven hundred years. A few entrepreneurs sell T-shirts printed with Posada's* designs (see Figures 1.14, 1.27, 4.2, 4.3) or with a commemorative motif. Many sell skeletal toys, jewelry, clothing, crafts, and souvenirs. One can eat a meal at one of the myriad improvised *comedores* (refectories) or stalls that line the streets. For the culminating days of the celebration, great crowds consume the food and enliven the scene; people come from Mexico City proper, from other villages and states, and from South and Central America, the United States, Canada, and Europe.

What is more visible to the public at this time than either the earnest commemoration of the dead in cemeteries and private homes in the D.F.* or the plays, skits, and performances one must usually either travel or enter a theater to see is the humorous, grotesque display of sculpted or painted calaveras in the *Centro Histórico* (the historical downtown) and working-class neighborhoods. Most are images of working people going about their everyday activities (see Figures 4.4–4.6). The calaveras are seen in shop windows as merchandise and in display cases as ofrendas. They are displayed in many

4.4 Earthenware hair stylist. Oaxaca, Oaxaca.

museums, kiosks, schoolyards, and open spaces. On the first two days of November, they are seen in parks and plazas, including the Plaza de Armas in front of the National Palace, where they hope to draw attention from the public and politicians, perhaps including the president (see Figure 4.7).

The calaveras found in the country's largest metropolis during this time combine the sadness of unpleasant, miserably remunerated work with the delight of irritating the wealthy by reminding them of the situation of the subordinated and of the former's role in that subordination. The exhibits combine life and death by depicting activities of people's livelihoods per-formed by skeletons. They make fun of stereotypes—including relations

*4.5 Papier mâché band with marimba by Linares. Anahuacalli, México, D.F.
(Courtesy of Dolores Olmedo Patiño)*

*4.6 The dead bury the dead. Window of former Museo de Artes e Industrias
Populares, México, D.F.*

4.7 Ofrenda in optical shop. Mexico, D.F.

4.8 Ofrenda to homosexuals who died in silence.
Parque Alameda, México, D.F.

between men and women, professionals and clients, family members, and others—by presenting them in material form in paintings and sculptures. Calaveras are clear examples of popular culture, the culture of the subordinated, which, if read with attention, show how such groups express resentment, resistance, or evasion of a system or a group that holds dominion over them.[5]

This kind of parody has a political nature insofar as it comments on relations of power. Other marginalized groups draw attention to their cause through large public ofrendas that usually include pictorial or sculptural and sometimes literary calaveras. This set might include ecologists whose ofrendas honor destroyed forests, homosexuals whose ofrendas honor companions who have died of AIDS or who have died still closeted (see Figure 4.8), social activists whose ofrendas honor victims of the 1985 earthquake and remind the government that, years later, it has not yet honored its promise of affordable housing, and so forth.

All of these groups, from the working poor to the socially peripheral, are earnestly honoring their dead through their ofrendas. But by taking over public space from which the dominant classes usually exclude them, they are commanding attention not only to their legitimate concerns but to their very existence. They are, in a Bakhtinian sense, turning social order upside down; in bell hooks's sense, they are bringing the margins to the center. By naming themselves in the agora, they make themselves recognized by those who prefer to forget their inconvenient actuality and their unpopular cries from the social wilderness. Through their ofrendas they hope to open the consciousness of members of the bourgeoisie, obliging them to make room for the other in their awareness with the hope that such consciousness will stir the privileged to the point of effective action on behalf of those normally forgotten. This is a serious analysis of what appears humorous to those predisposed only to chuckle at calaveras, which are or appear to be lighthearted much of the time. Calaveras are multilingual—comical and tragic, ingenuous and purposeful—as is much of the discourse of the subordinated. I hope to further the work of *concientización* (consciousness raising) imbricated in the showy, parodic, politically charged ofrendas to which I refer.

---

[5] See Fiske, *Understanding Popular Culture*, 169.

Posada: X Rays of Fin de Siècle Mexico

Hubo un día en que la muerte buscó a un niño por todas las ciudades, La vieron asomar el rostro enjuto en las esquinas de las calles.	One day death was looking for a child through every city. Her skinny face was seen peering around the street corners.
Dio con él en una plaza mimosa, rodeada de árboles. Entregole un cofre de madera lleno de arena. En la arena se veían dos pisadas de niño. "Ya puedes morir", le dijo, "te he traído tu huella". —Jerónimo Arellano	She finally found him in a graceful plaza, surrounded by trees. She handed him a wooden chest full of sand. On the sand could be seen a child's two footmarks. "Now you can die," she said to him. "I've brought you your prints."

The serious fun that those raised in Mexico City find in Días de muertos* has a respected source in the art of José Guadalupe Posada.* His internationally known and, in Mexico, frequently reproduced engravings of calaveras* probably inspired the proliferation of the seasonal calaveras we see today (Reuter 76). He, in turn, seems to have been inspired by French engravers, as well as by the Spanish custom of published calaveras.

Posada was born to humble, illiterate parents in Aguascalientes in central Mexico on February 2, 1852 (see Figure 4.9). A professional draftsman and engraver from adolescence, he illustrated all manner of publications from religious tracts and yellow journalism to political commentaries (see Figures 4.10–12). He spent some time working in León, Guanajuato, and emigrated to Mexico City in 1888, where he set up shop and soon became affiliated with Antonio Vanegas Arroyo. They worked together from then on, and it was during their collaboration that Posada created his best-known works. Although he enjoyed recognition during his lifetime, he died penniless in 1913, and his bones were tossed into a common grave with

4.9 Posada (right) with La Catrina, Frida Kahlo, Diego Rivera by Diego Rivera. Detail from his mural "Sueño de una tarde de domingo en la Alameda" (Dream of a Sunday Afternoon in the Alameda). (Permission given by Dover Press)

4.10 *"Calavera revolucionaria" by Posada. (Permission given by Dover Press)*

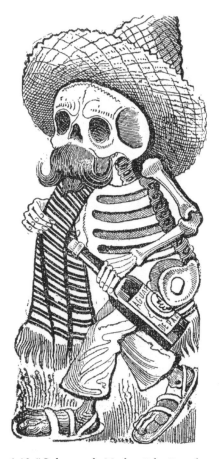

4.11 *"Calavera de un revolucionario*
zapatista" by Posada.
(Permission given by Dover Press)

4.12 *"Calavera de Madero" by Posada.*
(Permission given by Dover Press)

those of other poor people—an uncannily appropriate end for the supreme calaverista (see Figures 4.13, 4.14).

What was the importance of this humble man, and why does he have a place in this chapter? It is unusual, virtually unique, that one artist should stand out in a field occupied by artists who neither sign their work nor in any other way seek individual recognition. Working as he did during the francophile dictatorship of General Porfirio Díaz, Posada's colloquial, accessible art presented and represented the lives, concerns, interests, and tastes of the country's common people (see Figures 4.15–4.16). He also

4.13 "Gran calavera eléctrica" by Posada. (Permission given by Dover Press)

4.14 "Calaveras Mourning the Dead" by Posada. (Permission given by Moyer Bell)

4.15 "Skeletons' Banquet" by Posada. (Permission given by Moyer Bell)

multiplied images of skulls and bones as no one had since Aztec artisans produced high and low bas-reliefs of tzompantli* and partially skeletal human figures in stone and earthenware. Innocently, he initiated what is sometimes known as the Mexican renaissance, a movement that exalted and idealized folk art and, to a growing extent, pre-Hispanic art as an alternative to the Eurocentric "high" art of the time. This "Mexicanism" soon crossed the Atlantic and fueled the modernist avant-garde's enthusiasm for new imagery from beyond its cultural and class ken (Wollen 16f).[6]

Posada's genius was his capacity to amalgamate Spanish and Mexican cultural influences simply and powerfully, ironically and earnestly, comically

---

[6] Wollen applies Thomas Gretton's descriptive phrase *blithe gruesomeness* to Posada's illustrations, and he considers them in the context of Mexican and European art: "For Rivera Posada's skeletons and skulls provided a link with the politically repressed world of the Aztecs, and were a symptomatic return of values and motifs repressed for centuries by post-Conquest rulers as 'Indian,' but for Breton they represented a link with the death instinct, with the repressed impulses of sadism, with the unconscious. Allied to nonsense and to laughter, they threatened the bourgeois order of constraining reason and hypocritical virtue" (Wollen 18f).

4.16 "Calavera de los patinadores" (. . . of the Streetcleaners) by Posada.
(Permission given by Dover Press)

and tragically such that the result was a clear, unsentimental portrait of his
people and his time (see Figures 4.17–4.22). As Mexico was emerging from
the ten-year revolution of 1910, with leaders in all fields seeking to propose
an identity that would help Mexicans to imagine themselves as a nation,
Posada's work was useful for its innate syncretism, but in a tremendously
important way it also inspired the following generations of artists who
would continue his work, now deliberately, to fuse the cultures that had
come to compose the country (see Figures 4.23, 4.24). Jacques Lafaye, in his
chapter "From Daily Life to Eternity" in *Posada's Mexico*, put an interesting spin on Posada's calaveras: "What Posada offers us with his calavera is
thus a sort of X ray of a collective soul. But this must be understood in a
psychological and satirical sense" (Lafaye 137f). It seems important to me
that in Posada's "X rays" of Mexico we have clinically realistic engravings
that show his class origins, whereas in the romantic portraits of Mexico's
humble people by Diego Rivera and David Alfaro Siqueiros we have idealized paintings that reveal their class.

Posada behaved like a radiologist in another sense. Just as X-rays are
taken to examine the bones, his calaveras and other engravings were often
drawn ostensibly to examine society, which accounts for his role as cultural

EL GRAN PANTEON AMOROSO.

Leed, pues, este Panteón de los Amores
Todos los que habitáis aquí en la tierra,

Y hallaréis muchos gustos y dolores
Que el gran secreto de la tumba encierra.

Aquí van con sus amores
Gozando dos calaveras:
La que en vida fué Dolores,
Y él de apellido Contreras.

Aquí yace un buen torero,
Que murió de la aflicción
De ser mal banderillero,
Silbado en cada función;
Ha muerto de un revolcón
Que recibió en la trasera,
Y era tanta su tontera
Que en el sepulcro ya estaba
Y á los muertos los toreaba
Convertido en calavera.

General que fué de suerte
Y mil acciones ganó
Y sólo una la perdió
La que tuvo con la muerte;
Nadie hay que al mirarle acierte
Si fué un sabio ó de tontera,
Hoy es una calavera
Con gorro en verdad montado,
Y aunque esté condecorado
Hoy ya no es lo que antes era.

Aquí tienen á dos muertos,
Tal cual para cada quien,
Casados por desaciertos,
Paseando y vistiendo bien.

—¿Usted no sabe de amores?
—A según cuando conviene.
—¿Quiere ir conmigo á Dolores?
—Charrito, sí aquí me tiene.

—Adiós; no ande de celoso,
—Me cree con los ojos tuertos.
—Si alguno me hiciera el oso
Se contaba entre los muertos.

—No quiero más amistad.
—Mi amor no me ha sido quimera.
—Dejadme en la soledad
Y en paz, torpe calavera.

Y aquel charrito celoso
Pudo al fin tragar el queso,
Y con su muerte afanoso
Marchóse á llorar el hueso.

—Métale á la penca, vale.
—Atórele á los ardores.
—Ojas; pero no me jale.
—Pos vamos para Dolores.

No he visto mujer más fina
Pa cantar una canción
Ni en toditito el Japón
Ni en toditita la China,
Con tal aire y tal sal salero,
Que no hay en el mundo entero
Quien cante bien sus amores,
Como ésta que vi en Dolores
Junto á un sepulcro ratero.

No me eche una rata muerta
Vestida de colorado,
El muerto chino taimado
Que me ha espiado ya la puerta,
Mi calavera no es tuerta,
Y sí canto sin quimera
Es hoy por la vez postrera,
Pues pronto la muerte flaca
Ya mero mis restos saca
Y á Dios de mi calavera.

—Con tal de llorar el hueso
Con usted, preciosa güera,
Me va á dar pa copa y queso
Por muerto y por calavera.

4.17–19 *"Gran panteón amoroso"* (Great Pantheon of Lovers) by Posada.
(Permission given by Moyer Bell)

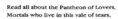

Read all about the Pantheon of Lovers,　　And in the silence of the tomb
Mortals who live in this vale of tears,　　You'll find all manner of joys and fears.

Here lies a brave toreador
Who died of distress,
Booed by the public
For always making a mess;
A butt in the backside
Took him to the land of the blessed.
And when he got there
He was such a blockhead
That thinking they were bulls
He started to fight the dead.

This brilliant general
Won a thousand battles,
The only one he lost
Was with death's rattle.
Now you can't tell
Whether he's a genius or a nit,
Today on a skull
His general's hat does sit,
And despite all his medals
he's changed quite a bit.

Here are two skeletons
Parading without shame:
In this life she was Dolores
And Contreras was his name

This fancy couple here
Are birds of a feather;
They did not marry for love
But see how they stride out together.

'Are you game for love?'
'That depends on the price and the day.'
'Can I take you to Dolores' place?'
'OK cowboy, right away!'

'Come now, don't be so jealous.'
'You think I've got no eyes in my head.'
'If anyone plays Romeo to me
He can count himself dead.'

'I want no more of your love!'
'I've been faithful and true!'
'Revolting skeleton, leave me alone,
I want to be rid of you.'

And the jealous cowboy
Finally rose to the bait,
And went off to the grave
To mourn his mate.

'Drown your sorrows.'
'Have another one on me.'
'OK, but what's the hurry?'
'We're off Dolores to see.'

A fairer lass
I never did see
In the whole of Japan
Or the China Sea,
She sang with such grace
Tra-la-la tra-la-lee;
No one sang a song
Of love so sweet
As the girl at Dolores' place
Who by a grave I did meet.

Don't throw a dead rat
Into my vault,
That crafty old skeleton
Has got his eyes on the door-bolt;
My skull is not blind,
And if loud I do sing
Today is the last time,
For soon Death's sting
Will dispose of my remains
And my skeleton will be nothing.

'If I can do penance
With you, my fair dame,
Then for the grave
I am ready and game.'

4.20–22 *"Gran panteón amoroso" (Great Pantheon of Lovers) by Posada.*
(Permission given by Moyer Bell)

4.23 *Calavera depicting contemporary newspapers as skeleton cyclists by Posada.* *(Permission given by Dover Press)*

4.24 *"Calavera de Don Quijote" by Posada. (Permission given by Dover Press)*

critic. Based on this aspect of Posada's work, Lafaye believes some of Posada's calaveras are allegorical, and he writes about the illustrator's "moral intention," which he finds as evident in his prints as in Spain's mystery plays. For Lafaye, the calaveras illustrate the vanity of life (Lafaye 138).[7]

However any viewer of Posada's peculiar calaveras sees them, they are even more popular now than they were during his life. Their reception is so easy that they are a fairly intimate part of contemporary Mexicans' cultural background. I would venture that they influence Mexicans' lack of nervousness and fear and sense of humor about death, and they are one of the elements of Días de muertos many enjoy most. They held a different appeal one hundred years ago, when Posada's contemporaries had seen fewer of them than have mine. People bought them perhaps with what Peter Wollen, adducing Stallybrass and White's insight, sees as the nervous attraction carnivals hold for "respectable" society, which would like to circumscribe the chaotic ambiance of the fairground as they do their own less than virtuous desire for entropy and anarchy. Wollen recognizes a similar situation for the respectable lover of "high" art who is faced with Posada's works and whose response is less spontaneous and embracing than that of people who are more open to alternative aesthetics and values.

> [Posada's prints] both threaten the conventions of the art world, transgress its implicit rules and standards, and at the same time reinforce by both revealing and yet holding at a distance, by reinvigorating without overwhelming. In many ways, the art world acts as a mediator between the world of carnival and fairground and the respectable world of high culture. . . . In Mexico, the influence of Posada made possible the mix of populism and modernism which the artists of the renaissance wanted. It gave them street credibility, so to speak, while they pursued their monumental ambitions. (Wollen 21)

Wollen speculates that Posada might simply have been engraving in two dimensions the three-dimensional skeletal sweets that, then as now, were sold, given, and consumed during Días de muertos. In our time his

---

[7] In medieval Europe, dance-of-death depictions fulfilled a similar role. Death was shown dancing with members of society, who were stereotyped by their dress or accoutrements and often accused of hypocrisy or immorality. The harshest portrayals were of community leaders such as priests and judges.

calaveras, in turn, have been given three dimensions by at least one family of papier mâché artists: the famous Linares family in Mexico City (see Figures 1.15, 1.21, 2.2). Whether printed or sculpted, imitated, quoted, or reproduced, Posada's insightful and humorous calaveras have helped to shape Mexico City's idiosyncratic approach to death and the Days of the Dead. They are now an indispensable component of the popular culture fiesta for which Mexico is known.

5

Pre-Híspaníc and Peninsular Traces in Días de muertos

Stories of Origin

Knowledge of all human activities in the past is possible only
through a knowledge of their traces . . . the marks, perceptible
to the senses, which some phenomenon, in itself inaccessible,
has left behind. Just to apprehend such marks as traces of
something, as evidence, is already to have gone beyond the
stage of merely making statements about the marks themselves; to count something as evidence is to make a
statement about something else, namely, about that for
which it is taken as evidence.
—Connerton 13

S tories of origin are somewhat untrustworthy because they usually
have a political or ideological agenda that dictates what details
will be included and excluded and how they will be presented rhe-
torically. In the case of Mexico's Días de muertos,* it is widely believed
that most of the practices are little changed from pre-Hispanic times and
that only a few were introduced by Spanish Catholicism. Certain icons and
customs used in the fiesta* today would be unrecognizable to pre-Hispanic

celebrants, such as images of Jesus, Christian saints, and Hallowe'en figures. Objects such as bottled drinks, manufactured garments, and plastic toys would also be foreign to them. Some articles and symbols would, however, be the same, including the cross, some forms of which were used by ancient Mesoamericans* as a discrete cosmology and an instrument of orientation for both the dead and the living.

The story of the origin of Días de muertos is lost, but traces of the multicentenary celebration have perdured into the late twentieth century. Although aspects of the contemporary observances are new, such as the ofrendas* with a political charge—including those that commemorate Emiliano Zapata; children who died of hunger; homosexuals who died "in silence"; or sex workers who died of AIDS—in important respects the celebration is very close to what it was before Spanish Catholics insisted that the dead be remembered exclusively on the first two days of November and before a majority of celebrants converted to Catholicism and adopted its iconography, language, and ritual. For that matter, people in what is now Mexico made offerings to their dead much like those made in most of the world, including sixteenth-century Spain. I will present a mosaic of pre-Hispanic and peninsular marks that are perceptible in celebrations of Días de muertos in the last decade of the twentieth century, inviting the reader to join me in following Jonathan Culler's advice that "one does better to look for symbolic rather than causal relationships" (Culler 19).

Pre-Hispanic Commemorations of the Dead

To begin chronologically in America, a brief history of burial offerings follows. During the early preclassic period, roughly between 1500 and 500 B.C.E., bodies were buried with a dusting of red color. They were wrapped in petates* and buried in the home or near the neighborhood of the deceased with offerings of utensils used in life, clay figurines, and vessels with food. In the middle preclassic period, from 500 to 200 B.C.E., the offering was more abundant; it included jewelry, pyrite mirrors, and a sacrificed dog. In the late preclassic era, circa 150 B.C.E. until the beginning of the Common Era, rudimentary graves were constructed, or the dead were buried on platforms, among shell and polychrome ceramic objects. They were still offered personal utensils and a dog (Aviña). Some scholars suppose that from the earliest period, people believed the dead would need the components of the offering on a four-year journey to Mictlan*, the place of the dead. Rosalind Rosoff Beimler mentions the pre-Hispanic practice of making offerings to the dead at death, eighty days later, and on the anniversary of the death for the next four years, at which time the soul was supposed to have reached Mictlan (Rosoff Beimler 19). Provisions needed to be supplemented on each of these occasions.

From 1300 to 800 B.C.E., collective oblations consisting of ceramics were found at interment sites, where individuals were placed in fetal position and wrapped in a petate, according to Piña Chan. He describes burials of one man with several women and of women with sacrificed children and others, all with beautiful pottery vessels, personal ornaments, food and drink, small toys, and, in some cases, sacrificed dogs (quoted in Ochoa Zazueta 32f).

Several texts compiled and written early in Mexico's colonial period describe beliefs and practices whose vestiges can be seen in current traditions of Días de muertos.* Bernardino de Sahagún, a Spanish Franciscan friar, was a missionary to Mexico in the sixteenth century. Comparing himself to a physician who needs to know everything possible about a patient to treat her or him, Sahagún amassed and preserved an encyclopedia of Indigenous culture as it existed on the eve of its destruction and "salvation" through Christian conversion. He considered the Indians' "idolatry" a mortal disease of the soul. Sahagún compiled a twelve-volume work entitled *Historia general de las cosas de la Nueva España* [*General History of the Things of New Spain*] (as Spaniards called what is denominated as Mexico). The work is really two parallel texts: His informants' Náhuatl* accounts of their culture and his Spanish translation of and commentary on those accounts. Sahagún asked the old people of Anáhuac, the Valley of Mexico, to dictate their knowledge of traditions, stories, beliefs, and so on; and he asked young men who had been taught the Latin alphabet to write down what the elders said. The Náhuatl text was finished in 1547, the Spanish one thirty years later (Sahagún Book 1, Introduction, 10–18).

In this extensive, if not always accurate, work, we read about traditions that existed for many generations before Sahagún learned of them and that exist today—virtually uninterrupted, although certainly altered, by Spain's military and ideological conquest and by U.S. ideological and economic influence. Numerous entries shed light on the celebration of Días de muertos.

For ten days during the month of Quecholli, between October 24 and November 20 according to the Gregorian calendar, the Nahuas celebrated a fiesta* to the war god Mixcóatl (Cloud Snake) and to those who had died at war (Sahagún Book 2, chapter 14, 126f). The fiesta included offerings of special sweet tamales*; *amatl* (bark paper); the shield, blanket, and *maxtle* (loincloth) of the deceased; and small bundles containing four miniature arrows and four miniature torches—all of which were placed on the tombs of the dead—and "muchas ceremonias por los difuntos en esta misma fiesta" [many ceremonies for the deceased during this same fiesta] (Sahagún Book 2, chapter 14, 126f). The celebrants sat by the graveside all day and all night. At night they lit the torches and arrows. On the last day of the month, all of the gifts except the tamales were ignited. Women burned their weaving implements and jewelry at the burial site: "Decían que todas estas alhajas que quemaban se las habían de dar en el otro mundo donde iban después de la muerte" [They said that all these implements they burned were to be given to them in the other world where they went after death] (Sahagún Book 2, chapter 33, §28, 205).

In the month of Tóxcatl (April 23 to May 12 of the Gregorian calendar), the following offerings were made to the dead: "muchas gallinas y maíz y mantas y vestidos y comida y otras cosas, y en particular cada uno en su casa gran fiesta; y a las imágenes que tenían de sus padres y papas y otros difuntos sahumaban con incienso" [many hens and corn and blankets and dresses and food and other things, and in particular each one at home [held] a grand fiesta; and the images they had of their parents and priests and other deceased were offered incense] (Sepúlveda 4).

Ancient Mexicans commemorated the dead in the ninth and tenth months of their calendar during the postclassic era. The ninth month, Tlaxcochimaco, began on August 5 of our calendar, and its first day marked the beginning of Miccailhuitontli, the fiesta of the little dead, those who had died as children.[1] It lasted the twenty days of the month, and vegetables were offered. Xocohuetzi, the tenth month, which extended from our August 25 until September 14, was for Miccaílhuitl, the commemoration of the adult dead.[2] There was weeping, and food was presented (Durán Book 1, chapters 12 and 13). Diego Durán says the main activity was to erect a xócotl (tree trunk) on top of which was placed an image of a bird made of amaranth dough and at the foot of which were placed offerings of food and pulque. Then there was a procession around the xócotl.

The thirteenth month, called Tepeílhuitl, which coincides with the Gregorian October, was the fiesta of finados, the dead. During that month the gods of rain and the high mountains where clouds are formed were celebrated, and those who had died from being struck by lightning or who had drowned were also remembered (Sahagún Book 2, chapter 13, 124f).

---

[1] María Teresa Sepúlveda claims this month extended from July 12 to July 31 (Sepúlveda 4).
[2] Sepúlveda gives the dates August 1–20 and calls the fiesta Ueymiccailhuitl. An alternate spelling is Huey Miccaílhuitl.

The *mocihuaquetzque,* women who had died in their first childbirth, were honored during the month of Títitl, which lasted from December 19 to January 27: "Comían este día un pan acedo, que ellos llamaban xocotamalli, que quiere decir pan acedo o agrio. . . . Bebían también unas puchas acedas de maíz morado. De esta comida y bebida ofrecían en los templos y cada uno en su oratorio" [This day they ate a sour bread that they call *xocotamalli,* which means sour or acid bread. . . . They also drank some sour gourds of purple corn. This food and drink they offered in their temples and each one in their oratory] (Durán Book 1, chapter 22, 289). Midwives mourned the deaths of these "brave women," but according to Sahagún their families rejoiced because, along with the women who had died in war, this group would dwell joyfully with the sun. They were petitioned by living relatives to intercede to "our Lord" on behalf of the supplicants (Durán Book 6, chapter 29, §16, 182). Offerings similar to some made for the dead today were made during Xochílhuitl (Fiesta of Flowers) honoring Xochipilli, the god of flowers and poetry. Xochílhuitl was a movable feast, its dates determined by astrono-mer-astrologers. I have read of Días de muertos being called *Fiesta de las flores.* Aurea Acosta, writing in the newspaper *Excélsior,* affirmed that this is so because flowers, then as now, signify "el carácter perecedero de la vida, pero también de su renacimiento" [the perishable nature of life but also its rebirth]. According to Sahagún, in Xochílhuitl

la otra gente ofrecía diversas cosas: unos ofrecían maíz tostado, otros maíz tostado revuelto con miel y con harina de semilla de bledos; otros hecho de pan una manera de rayo, como cuando cae del cielo, que llaman *xonecuilli;* otros ofrecían pan hecho a manera de mariposa . . . otros ofrecían unas tortas hechas a manera de rodela . . . otros hacían saetas, otros espadas . . . otros ofrecían muñecas, hechas de la misma masa. (Sahagún Book 1, chapter 14, §10, 60)

the other people offered several things: Some offered toasted corn, others toasted corn mixed with honey and with flour from amaranth[3] seeds; others made from bread a kind of ray such as when it falls from the sky, which they call *xonecuilli;* others offered bread made in the manner of a butterfly . . . others offered some cakes made in the manner of a shield . . . others made arrows, others swords . . . others offered dolls made from the same dough.

---

[3] There is an edible plant called blite, which is what my *Larousse Gran Diccionario Moderno Español-Inglés English-Spanish* gives as a translation for *bledo.* I believe, however, that Sebastián Verti correctly identifies it as a Spanish word for Mexican amaranth (also called *huautli, tzoalli,* and *alegría)* in *Tradiciones mexicanas* 310.

Sahagún wrote about certain festivals that were held in honor of mountain deities believed to afflict people with, or relieve them of, illnesses related to the cold. I will quote him on two practices that might have marked Días de muertos. Anthropomorphic figures of the gods were fashioned by priests out of *tzoalli*, a paste made of amaranth seeds and honey from honey ants (Verti 311): "Los que las [figuras] hacían poníanles dientes de pepitas de calabaza, y las ponían en lugar de ojos unos frijoles negros . . . ayocotli" [Those who made the figures gave them teeth of squash pips, and they put in them, in place of eyes, some black beans] (Sahagún Book 1, chapter 21, §9, 72f). These figures sound similar in nature and medium to the calaveras* made of several sweets, particularly to those popular in Mixquic, which are made of amaranth and honey and have teeth made of squash pips or peanuts, although their eyes are usually raisins rather than black beans. Sahagún goes on:

También ponían estos mismos papeles goteados con *ulli*, y colgados de unos cordeles delante de las mismas imágenes, de manera que los papeles estaban asidos los unos de los otros, y meneábalos el aire porque estaban los cordeles en que estaban los papeles colgados atados a las puntas de unos varales, o báculos, que estaban hincados en el suelo y de la una punta del uno a la del otro estaba atado el cordel o *mecatl*. (Sahagún Book 1, chapter 21, §9, 72f)

They also put these same papers, dripped with rubber and hung from cords, before the same images; the papers were tied together, and the air moved them because the cords on which the papers were hanging were tied to the ends of some rods or scepters that were fastened in the ground, and between the tips of the rods the cord was tied.

Vestiges of this custom can be seen in the traditional ofrendas of Oaxaca and other places where not the bark paper amatl but rather brightly colored, artfully cut tissue paper is offered to the dead. The Oaxacan altar is always framed by an arch, usually made of sugarcane rods tied together at the top (see Plates 3, 11).

Sahagún continues, "Ofrecían asimismo a estas imágenes vino, u octli o pulcre, que es el vino de la tierra" [They also offered these images . . . the wine of the land] (Sahagún Book 1, chapter 21, §13, 73). In the center of Plate 4 is a bottle of liquor, an example of a contemporary "wine" still offered to the dead. *Octli* or *pulcre* (pulque) is a drink of fermented maguey juice that is still favored by many members of las clases populares and is included in many ofrendas.[4]

The following quotation from *Historia de las cosas de la Nueva España* is rich in terms of what might have survived of pre-Hispanic traditions memorializing the dead.

Aquellos por cuyo voto se hacían convidaban a los sátrapas para el quinto día, después de hechas las imágenes (en que) se había de hacer la fiesta . . . (pasaban) aquella noche velando, cantando y bailando a honra de aquellas imágenes, y de los dioses que representaban. . . .

A todos daban comida cuatro veces en aquella noche, y todas cuatro veces tocaban instrumentos musicales, los que ellos usaban. . . .

Después de acabada la fiesta, otro día luego de mañana el que había hecho la fiesta juntaba a sus parientes y a sus amigos, y a los de su barrio, con todos los de su casa, y acababan de comer y beber todo lo que había sobrado de la fiesta; a esto llamaban *apeoalo*, que quiere decir añadidura a lo que estaba comido y bebido; ninguna cosa quedaba de comer, ni de beber para otro día [parentheses in original]. (Sahagún Book 1, chapter 21, §§15–16, 24, 73f)

Those for whose vow they were made invited the satraps for the fifth day, after the images were made around which the fiesta was to be held . . . they passed the night awake, singing and dancing in honor of those images and of the gods they represented. . . .

To everyone they gave food four times that night, and all four times they played musical instruments, the ones they used.

After the fiesta was over, the next day in the morning he who had given the fiesta gathered his relatives and his friends and his neighbors, with everyone from his household, and they finished eating and drinking all that was left over from the fiesta; this they called addition to what was eaten and drunk; not one thing remained to eat or drink for the following day.

The reader will recognize similarities between these observances and Días de muertos. After preparing the ofrenda, which might include pan de

---

[4] Inebriation was punishable by death in Aztec society, except among the elderly and on ritual occasions, at which time it was not only encouraged but obligatory, at least according to Diego Durán. Children were only rarely permitted to partake (Clendinnen; Soustelle).

muerto* and sugar calaveras—both of which are something like the images mentioned by Sahagún—in many communities members of the household of the dead keep a vigil, either in the graveyard or at home. Although there is no formally established serving of tamales* or other foods, those keeping vigil eat periodically, and the householder is expected to provide the food three or four times during the event. I find it interesting that if a household has welcomed the spirits of the dead on October 28,[5] the vigil and the feast for the dead can be held on the fifth night now as then. In the third paragraph of the quotation we recognize the communal feast in which the living eat the food the dead have left after consuming their part of it.

For another example, we read that to appease the goddesses known as *cihuapipiltin* (celestial women) or *cihuateteo** (divine women)—those who died in their first childbirth—parents bestowed on them toasted corn, tamales, and loaves of bread in various shapes such as butterflies and lightning during the five days One Deer, One Rain, One Monkey, One House, and One Eagle, when at crossroads the cihuapipiltin were believed to curse children with illnesses (Sahagún Book 1, chapter 10, §1, 49) (see Figure 5.1). These presents are identical to parts of the offerings that are set out for the dead today in the last days of October and the first days of November. Although few communities shape their bread as lightning or butterflies, I have photographed altars that include loaves shaped as fish, humans, skull and crossbones, and stellar-eye* circles (see Figures 1.3, 1.4, 1.5, and Plate 9 [the circular loaves hanging over the cut tissue paper], respectively). Sculptures of cihuateteo can be seen in the National Museum of Anthropology's Teotihuacan room in Mexico City. They are described by Sahagún:

La imagen de estas diosas tienen [sic] la cara blanquecina, como si estuviese teñida con color muy blanco . . . lo mismo los brazos y piernas; tenían unas orejeras de oro, los cabellos tocados como las señoras con sus cornezuelos; el huipil era pintado de unas olas de negro, las naguas tenían labradas de diversos colores, tenían sus cotaras blancas. (Sahagún Book 1, chapter 10, §5, 50)

The image of these goddesses has a whitish face, as if it were tinted by a very white color . . . also the arms and legs; they had gold earplugs, their head dressed like ladies' in crescent shapes; their shift was painted with black waves, the skirts were worked with different colors, their sandals, white.

---

[5] That is the day on which those who died a violent or unexpected death are welcomed home.

5.1 Cihuateteo. Museum of Anthropology, Mexico City (Permission given by INAH)

Contemporary sculptural calaveras look very similar, with the notable differences that they are skeletal and that they tend to have a humorous air. The white skin of the cihuapipiltin represented the pallor of death. It is interesting that they were dressed elegantly, "como las señoras" (like ladies), as are the comical skeletal catrinas* that abound now during Días de muertos, after Posada* (see Figures 1.27, 2.2). Again, I am not implying that the catrinas are directly derived from the cihuapipiltin, but they may be symbolically related to them.

When Sahagún describes the goddess of water, Chalchiutlicue (She of the Precious Stone, meaning turquoise), he says she was venerated along with two others: Chicomecóatl (Seven Snake), the goddess of food, and Uixtocíhuatl (Salt Woman), the goddess of salt (Sahagún Book 1, chapter 11, §8, 51). In traditional ofrendas there should always be a glass of pure water to slake the thirst of the visiting spirit, a little plate of salt, and items of food. It is impossible to say for certain that water, salt, and food are offered because of the connection with the three goddesses because people the world over consume them. Still, one can speculate that the veneration with which these items are placed on the altar is related to the sense of sacredness that has always surrounded the fact and the act of sustenance for mythopoetic groups—a sense that is reflected in the trio of goddesses, worship of whom may have marked the elements of the contemporary ofrenda.

Many traditional ofrendas include new items of clothing, new work implements, or new miniature clay images of tools laid out on a new petate,* along with candles, food, and incense on a bed of coal in a new incense burner (see Figure 5.2, Plate 1). In his description of the Náhuatl* rite of confession, which necessitated a benefaction, Sahagún mentions three of these items, if we can consider that firewood has been replaced by the coals in the incense burner and by candles: "Llegado el día que le había mandado que volviese, el penitente compraba un petate nuevo e incienso blanco, que llaman copalli; y leña para el fuego en que se había de quemar el copalli" [When the day arrived that he had been told to return, the penitent bought a new petate and white incense, which they call copalli; and wood for the fire on which the copalli was to be burned] (Sahagún Book 1, chapter 12, §7, 52). These objects were not used exclusively in commemorations of the dead; they were required as oblations that marked the sacred space and time of ritual occasions.

5.2 Ofrenda to children who died of hunger. Puebla, Puebla

Pre-Hispanic Traces in Contemporary Beliefs

Traces of pre-Hispanic beliefs subsist along with traces of practices. As is evident from the many commemorations to the dead mentioned previously, Mesoamericans* had different categories of the dead, each requiring its own recognition. The way of death determined the person's afterlife—not, as in Christian belief, the way of life. Thus, warriors who had died in battle accompanied the sun from dawn until noon, at which time the women who had died in childbirth or war accompanied the sun from midday until sunset when it, under the name Tzontémoc (He Who Falls Head First), descended into Mictlan (Sahagún Book 6, chapter 29, 179ff). The sun's warrior companions had the form of *papalotl* (butterflies) or of hummingbirds, both of which were associated with resurrection. Children went to the vicinity of the tree Chichicuáhuitl, whose branches dripped milk for their sustenance. They were the only ones who were believed to reincarnate (Sepúlveda 22). If one died of old age or of various illnesses, one went to Mictlan* ("the beyond" or Place of the Dead), a shadowy region not unlike the Hebrew Sheol and the Greek Hades, presided over by Mictecacíhuatl and Mictlantecuhtli, lady and lord of Mictlan.[6] Mictlan was reached after a four-year journey during which the River Chiconauapan (Seven Tests) had to be crossed with the help of a dog, which explains why itzcuintli* were found sacrificed in burials. Those who had died of any diseases associated with water, by drowning, or by lightning went to Tlalocan, the happy place of Tláloc, the rain god. Also welcomed to Tlalocan were those who had died of incurable diseases such as leprosy, because they had suffered more than others in this life. Tláloc received such protégés directly, sparing them a journey to and through Mictlan. A mural in Teotihuacan shows residents of Tlalocan playing marbles and other games, swimming, reciting poetry, and chasing butterflies. Tlalocan was the image converts had in mind when Christian missionaries talked to them about heaven, just as those missionaries deliberately equated Mictlan with hell.

The various categories of the dead recognized by ancient Mesoamericans are still respected to some degree in contemporary Días de muertos,* accounting for the plural Días spilling out of the officially allotted All Saints Day. In an interview published in Mexico City's newspaper *Uno más uno*, Tlaxcala resident Juan Tecpa Uribe offered a neat explanation:

Los días de fiesta de muertos están dividos porque algunos muertos necesitan de más tiempo para estar con su familia: el 28 de octubre llegan los de muerte violenta, que como no pudieron despedirse de su familia en vida, llegan antes que los demás espíritus para reconciliarse con el mundo que dejaron; el 29 vienen los que murieron ahogados y de los cuales se piensa fueron elegidos por el dios de la lluvia para estar con él en su reino;[7]

The holidays of the dead are divided because some dead need more time to be with their family; on October 28 arrive those of violent death who, having been unable to bid farewell to their family before dying, come before the rest of the spirits to be reconciled to the world they left; on the twenty-ninth come those who drowned and who we believe were chosen by the god of rain to be with him in his kingdom;

---

[6] According to Ariès, in its early days "Christianity also adopted the ancient idea of survival in a gray and gloomy lower region" (Ariès 95).

[7] Notice the unself-conscious mention of the god of rain and the sense of privilege associated with this category of the dead.

el 30 llegan los espíritus de los niños y el 31 "los grandes." El primero de noviembre es cuando todos los muertos reunidos conviven y comen todos los alimentos puestos en la ofrenda, de los cuales se cree pierden sus propiedades nutritivas luego de estas fechas. (Quoted in Hernández, "Tlaxcalles")

on the thirtieth come the spirits of the children, and on the thirty-first "the grown-ups." The first of November is when all the dead are together and eat all the food placed on the offering, from which it is believed the nutritional properties are lost after these dates.

Working in Totonacan villages in Veracruz and Puebla, anthropologist Crescencio García Ramos reports that in that community *Ninín*, Días de muertos, begins even earlier: "[El Día de San Lucas] is really the beginning of celebrations for the dead. San Lucas is the patron saint of those who die a violent death: those who are murdered or drowned, and those who die from strange diseases, are guided by evil or by the female deity of water and of rivers; they are identified as *los malos aires* (harmful winds) which bring sickness" (quoted in Carmichael and Sayer 148, note 14).

A visit to a Totonaca cemetery on the night of November 2 reveals other marks of the pre-Christian cosmology, as well as of the syncretic nature of the fiesta.* On the graves are placed a cross, the picture of a saint, and an arch with twelve stars woven of palm leaf for women and thirteen stars for men; the stars signify the planes of existence above the earth (Carmichael and Sayer 65). Only those who set the offering know whether the Christian icons are intended to bless or to mask the presence of the Pagan elements. In conclusion, the celebration of numerous days of the dead, along with the preservation of pre-Hispanic symbols, signify the survival of Native traditions and beliefs in the face of the constraints that concurrent Christian traditions and beliefs necessarily imply. In some cases, I think of these elements as examples of transgressive syncretism, because through them the celebrants are actively and perhaps consciously constructing a ritual system that contains what they find meaningful in their pre-Hispanic spirituality and religion alongside what they find meaningful in the European ones. I will return to this subject at the end of this chapter.

Many details of Mesoamerican culture subsist in the Mexican diet, language, and physiognomy. Many recognize the pre-Hispanic builders of Mexico as our true forebears, even if our bloodlines happen to be purely European. Those ancestors are idealized, as most ancestors tend to be,

5.3 Paper Tlaltecuhtli. Tecómitl

although often, tragically, at the expense of contemporary Indígenas, who continue to be marginalized and exploited by the dominant minority; a significant number of Mexicans distance themselves as much as they can from the Amerindians, ancient and modern. Still, our vigorous relationship with precolonial culture is illustrated by the following account.

Traveling to Míxquic from central Mexico City, one must pass through the plaza of the town of Tecómitl in the borough of Tláhuac,[8] which in 1990 offered an interesting testimony to Mexicans' love of the past. Over the arch leading into the churchyard of a sixteenth-century church, an enormous image of Tlaltecuhtli fashioned of thin wood had been placed (see Figure 5.3). Tlaltecuhtli was a funerary god of the Nahuas, the lord of the earth and the night. He was depicted as and often called the earth monster, feet in the air, head down, his tongue a sacrificial knife, his hair decked with the stellar eyes* associated with the gods of death (see Figure 5.4). Alejandro Jara Ampudia, an instructor in Coordinación de Educación Tecnológica Industrial, Mexico City's vocational high school, having done fieldwork in Tecómitl, informed me that Tlaltecuhtli was part of the town's logo. The other part is a clay pot Tlaltecuhtli holds between his hands; it stands for the valley in which the town lies. According to Jara Ampudia, the whole logo represents souls who are descending into the town where they will live. The choice of this figure as an emblem for their home makes clear the sympathies of the townsfolk.

As if it were not enough to have a representation of Tlaltecuhtli as their symbol, on this occasion, by obliging churchgoers to file beneath Tlaltecuhtli's skeletal embrace, the people of Tecómitl had pronounced Tlaltecuhtli's semiotic triumph over the religion of the conquerors to which most of them subscribe. Nor was the image a mere duplication of the earth monsters one might see at archaeological sites and museums. This one had been reinterpreted by the artist(s) as a contemporary calavera, depicting him as a skeleton. I have never known of any other skeletal Tlaltecuhtli. To reinterpret and recreate the body of a god is more than a tribute; it is a reincorporation of the deity into the life of the town. It suggests his continuing relevance in the imagination of the creators of the enormous image and in that of the townspeople who permitted the work to be placed in honorable sacred space.

In the town square was another contemporary representation of an ancient Mexican practice. There were two tzompantli* (see Figure 5.5), one with cutout silhouettes of skulls in profile, the other showing exactly how they used to be threaded on the original tzompantli by piercing the

---

[8] Greater Mexico City, the Federal District (D.F.), includes many towns and rural areas. One travels through one or two of each before reaching Tecómitl.

5.4 Tlaltecuhtli. Templo Mayor, México, D.F. (Permission given by INAH)

detached heads through the temples and slipping them onto poles, like beads on an abacus (see Figure 5.6).

During the long prime ministership of Tlacaélel (1486–1521), the then-ancient rites of human sacrifice were intensified.[9] Tlacaélel promoted the poetic notion that the red of sunrise and sunset was evidence that the sun loses blood daily battling the forces of night and therefore must be given generous transfusions of human sacrificial blood. The victim's heart was ripped out by the most skillful priests in seven seconds such that it could be

5.5 Paper tzompantli. Tecómitl

lifted up while still beating. Most victims were then beheaded, becoming part of a tzompantli until birds of carrion and time left only bare skulls.

Three years after seeing the construction paper tzompantli in Tecómitl, an ofrenda* set outside the entrance of the Templo Mayor Museum in Mexico City made patent my sense that the stacks of calaveritas de azúcar* are the iconic offspring of the grisly tzompantli of old. My impression was further confirmed by the ofrenda entitled *Tlatzotzompantli*,[10] which features five rows of eight sugar skulls each, threaded through the temples (see Plate 13; its text is presented in Appendix A).

---

[9] Most victims of human sacrifice were obtained through *guerras floridas,* florid wars, held against neighboring villages of people from whom the Aztecs gathered tribute. Thus, the victims were similar enough to the Aztecs to be considered good and proper sacrifices. The guerras floridas might have also served in the training of warriors for whom the first captive, which they were not allowed to claim until a certain age and stage of training, marked a rite of passage.

[10] *Tlatzo* means the chaff of sugarcane or corn, with rubbish as a secondary meaning. Those who set the ofrenda might have meant "sugarcane-chaff wall of skulls," or they might have been suggesting the fragility of the sugar skulls by equating them with chaff that blows away in a breeze. A spiritualist, antimaterialist interpretation, supported by the offering's text, is that the skull and, by extension, the human body are chaff or rubbish.

5.6 Tzompantli. Templo Mayor, México, D.F. (Permission given by INAH)

Raised with a memory of the society before the conquest, Mexicans are influenced by that memory in our present attitudes toward and theories of the body—how it lives and how long (read, briefly), how it dies and how long it is dead. This explains why the residents of Mexico City, the ancient capital of the Mexica* or Aztec empire, are able to find humor in a fiesta many foreigners (as well as some of the haute bourgeoisie) find sinister and macabre. For what is humor but a sense of perspective? And what appeals to a sense of humor more than that which is familiar?

Numerous ancient calaveras look much like the candy ones we have today and may be their semiotic and iconic parents. They are low and high reliefs, etchings in ceramic vessels, or paintings on incense burners, pots, and codices (see Figures 1.8, 1.9). Some are decorated in fanciful ways; most are realistic, as are the sugar, amaranth, chocolate, or sweet potato calaveras that are usually decorated with bright frosting, sequins, and foil. Cultural artifacts are never created out of nothing. It is so impossible in central Mexico to avoid familiarity with pre-Hispanic depictions and sculptures of skulls that they have marked contemporary ones.

Spanish Presence, Culture Shock

The traces of Spanish Catholic conventions that can be discerned in Días de muertos* are less easy to identify than the pre-Hispanic ones because by the time of this writing, in parts of Mexico Días de muertos has been transformed by around five hundred years of Spanish cultural influence, as well as by waves of immigration from other parts of the world—including Europe, Asia, and the United States. Spain itself, having been in close contact with numerous civilizations and cultures as both colony and empire, is an amalgam of several of those cultures. These groups have altered Aboriginal holidays in subtle and obvious ways so that it is virtually impossible to ascertain the origin of any given detail of the celebrations for the dead.

In any case, the tradition of feeding the dead is virtually universal, with exceptions developing in this twentieth century of mass migration and immigration in which many people have lost touch with their families and communities of origin, both the living and the dead. Since the industrial revolution, the individual has been proletarianized to the point that in some cases work is more necessary and absorbing than the nurture and enjoyment of familial and communal relations, including those with the dead. Further distance between modern men and women and their predecessors is a result of their becoming more concerned with economic and political ideology than with religious and spiritual practices and traditions. The effect in many cases is the malaise of alienation.

The oldest existential problem in hispanophone America is that as a conquered continent it was founded on the denial of Aboriginal traditions by the ruling classes. The conquest produced a sense of cultural transitoriness because the elites continued, and to some extent continue today, to identify with their European ancestors' countries and interests rather than with their American fatherland. They gave the Spanish, Christian culture, with all it entails, greater importance than the Indigenous cultures and religions, languages, and political systems. That frame of reference has been preserved in some measure by families of European extraction who have married only other Euro-Americans. The criollos* (American offspring of Spaniards) and those whose education, wealth, social status, and, in a few cases, Indian nobility allowed them to join the elite added to the conflicting interests of the Spanish crown, the conquerors, and the colonizers of the country to which they were born.

Along with such cases, the transition through miscegenation produced a new racial and social type who did not recognize himself or herself in either the Spanish or the Indigenous culture. Because their parents were from different ethnic groups and by being, in some instances, the product of sexual or political violence, some mestizos* lived, metaphorically, as orphans. Their imbalance was and is exacerbated if they denied their Indian roots and tried to fit into the white upper class through their dress, speech, and gestures; the latter, because of their racism and classism, rejected them.

During the Enlightenment, the European world attempted to create the "New World" in its own image, establishing the same liberal political and economic policies that were revolutionizing the Old World. Therein we have another denial of the American reality. America could not be Europe. Indians—and there were many independent and unrelated communities—mestizos, and creoles could not be Europeans. The last two groups have had the options of isolating themselves from their European forebears or living the illusion of being Europeans across the Atlantic.

Another element contributes to a potentially disturbed philosophical ground. To this day in Mexico one can perceive the overlapping of disparate historical periods: the precolonial, the colonial, the modern, and, yes, even the postmodern. Agricultural technologies in underdeveloped regions have scarcely changed since the Spaniards arrived. Virtually feudal relationships subsist in pockets of the country, and in other areas professionals and students communicate with international colleagues and friends by electronic means. In Chiapas, "Subcomandante Marcos" garnered international support for the Indian uprising he led in January 1994 by sending faxes and electronic mail to the mass media and sympathizers.

Even the concept of time added to the alienating metaphysics of America, especially during the first generations of contact with Europe. For Christians, time is linear, experience is always new and unrecognizable, and the world has a finite life. For Amerindians, time was cyclical, permitting recognition of the processes and phenomena of history and ecology, and the world was seen essentially as having a potentially infinite, although fragile, life.

Insofar as Christian missionaries were able to alienate certain groups of Amerindians from their intimate contact with nature and the earth, they produced groups whose ground of being was shaken. Insofar as the Christian Spaniards renamed the Americans, telling them they were not who they believed and said they were, they in effect illegitimized the Americans and emptied them of their identity, leaving them with nothing but the new Christian name. That was not who they had been, who they knew themselves and one another to be. In all these ways, the conquest was decentering.

Having lost the axis mundi,* the sense of life, time, and the world, how could philosophical health and legitimacy be recuperated? By living on the margins as a number of Indigenous communities have done; by eventually renewing the use of certain images, icons, and practices as segments of both Indians and the bourgeoisie have done since Mexico's independence from Spain; by accepting foreign identities—whether European or U.S.-based— as other segments of the bourgeoisie have done, some sense of self-defined identity has been restored. The members of México profundo* alone managed more or less to avoid these crises by remaining relatively aloof from Spanish influence. They saved their identity by amalgamating foreign and local cultures into a sensible metaphysics and modus vivendi.

Días de muertos as practiced in Mexico City gives evidence of some strands of orphanhood, of eccentricity, of a quest for and construction of identity. As it is lived in the provinces, Días de muertos gives evidence of compromises between the new and the original, the Christian and the Mesoamerican,* and of the harmony available on the margins of modernity, out of sight of the sometimes violent hegemonic gaze that would alter what it regards.

In the next section I will give a history of the Catholic Feasts of All Saints and All Souls', and I will relay the most relevant and interesting data I have gathered about peninsular beliefs and customs that have marked contemporary celebrations of Días de muertos.

Historical Notes on All Saints and All Souls' Days

The origins of the Catholic feasts of All Saints and All Souls' are somewhat obscure. Rosalind Rosoff Beimler claims Catholic funerary rites were an adaptation of Egypt's ceremonies for Osiris, god of life, death, and grain, who was murdered on the seventeenth day of the autumnal month of Athyr, which corresponds to November of the Gregorian calendar. Around that time, the Egyptians believed the spirits of the dead visited their family homes. Their relatives set lamps to guide the spirits to where they had prepared food for them. These practices were carried to Europe by the Romans, whose god of life and renewal, Bacchus, was influenced by Osiris. Philippe Ariès gives some interesting details about the Roman commemoration of the dead.

> Ovid relates that on the Day of the Feralia, the Day of the Dead, the Romans sacrificed to Tacita, the mute goddess, a fish with its mouth sewn shut, an allusion to the silence that reigned among the . . . spirits of the departed. This was also the day on which offerings were taken to the graves, for at certain times and in certain places, the dead emerged from their sleep like the unclear images of a dream and sometimes troubled the living. (Ariès 23)

If any human practice can be considered natural, the one of giving presents to the dead seems to be one.

Christians in their turn accepted and modified the customs of the Romans (Ariès 20) according to their philosophy. As far as I can ascertain, the rites of mourning and funerals were practiced at the time on a popular level, without official sanction or guidance.

According to Remigio Tovar, Pope Gregory III officially instituted the Feast of All Saints on November 1, 835, to cajole said saints to protect Christian Europe against the devastating incursions of Normans and Sarracens. Emperor Ludovicus Pious mandated that the celebration be observed throughout Gaul and Germany (Tovar 2). José Carlos Aviña, however, has said that the feast was established on November 1, 793, by the same Pope Gregory III, who erected a Roman chapel to "all unknown saints." He gives no reason for these events. Yet another version has been presented by two sources who claim the holiday was initiated in the seventh century by Pope Boniface IV to supersede and supplant a Pagan commemoration of the dead and that Gregory III transposed it from May to November sometime between 827 and 844 (Reyes 22; Carmichael and Sayer 14). The day was to be a recognition of Christianity's saints and martyrs—past, present, future, known, and unknown.

The last theory I will offer about the origin of All Saints Day comes from Ariès, who identifies the monastery of Cluny, France, as one in which masses for the dead were said incessantly during the ninth century and at which a holy day dedicated to the salvation of the dead began. Various communities did this for laypeople because they were not guaranteed the prayers of fellow monks or church members. Each community chose its own date:

> Including January 26, December 17 (Saint Ignatius), the Monday of Pentecost, and especially the Feast of the Maccabees.[11] . . . The date of November 2, chosen by Odilon of Cluny in 1048, was the preferred one and was eventually adopted by the entire Roman church, but not before the thirteenth century, an indication of the monastic origin of the sentiment and of the long indifference of the common people to this individualistic attitude toward the dead. (Ariès 159)

This story of origin is also described in the *New Catholic Encyclopedia*.

Catholicism still teaches that All Souls' Day (*Fieles Difuntos*), celebrated on November 2, has the purpose of interceding on behalf of the souls of the dead who are believed to be in purgatory undergoing the process of "purging" their sins. Living relatives or friends can still pray or offer masses for their dead in hopes that such actions will accelerate the purification. According to Carmichael and Sayer, it took four centuries for All Souls' Day to be widely accepted because it seemed to propitiate and honor the dead, as did certain Pagan rituals that Christian officials were trying to eradicate (Carmichael and Sayer 15). The most persistent Pagan practice seems to have been, predictably, that of feasting with the dead and other holy figures in the graveyards of the Mediterranean. All attempts to suppress this custom

---

[11] To quote Ariès again: "The Maccabees [whose name may have inspired *macchabe*, a word for *corpse*, and thence the word *macabre* (116)] had long been honored as patron saints of the dead because they were believed, rightly or wrongly, to be the originators of the prayers of intercession for the dead. Their feast day was probably replaced by the commemoration of November 2, All Souls' Day" (Ariès 116).

were in vain, and according to Rey and to Sayer and Carmichael, the Spaniards who invaded our continent perpetuated the practice.

Without indicating the period to which she refers, Elsa Malvido, coordinator of the Seminario de Demografía Histórica, INAH [Seminary of Historical Demography, National Institute of Anthropology and History], maintains that the feast of All Saints was celebrated by exhibiting the relics of each church's important saints. The faithful visiting the sanctuaries that day were granted indulgences for each visit. Plenary indulgences were an important business for the Catholic Church.

On November 2, members of a congregation took offerings or gifts to their priest for the sacraments they had received, and this practice was misinterpreted as an offering to the dead. Malvido points out that in America, for many years the Indians were persecuted for taking offerings to the graves of their dead, whereas in the same period Spaniards were buried with wine and bread, and banquets were offered to the Spanish dead in their homes. She calls this part of the Catholic Church's "game" of permitting itself what it denies others. The colonizers and conquerors were following an early Christian tradition, which Ariès explains when he describes "the commemorative meal that the first Christians took on the graves of the martyrs and the offerings they left there. . . . This act of devotion, which was inspired by pagan practices, was prohibited by Saint Ambrose and replaced by eucharistic services. It has been retained in the Eastern Christian church, and traces of it remain in our folklore" (Ariès 26). As we know, the commemorative meal has been perpetuated in Mexico's Días de muertos.*

Death in Medieval Spain and Europe

Foreign journalists and visitors sometimes refer to Días de muertos* as a dance of death. The epithet is fitting in the sense that the calaveras* that disport themselves on bakery windows, in the pages of newspapers, on the tables of merchants, and on altars to the dead appear to be dancing—if not literally, then metaphorically. The term *dance of death* or *danse macabre* alludes to a thirteenth-century French poem entitled "The Encounter of the Three Living and the Three Dead" in which three young knights encounter three corpses during a hunting trip and realize the corpses are themselves (Kastenbaum 67).

According to Robert Kastenbaum, at least by the time of Hans Holbein the younger (1497–1543) who painted a "Dance of Death," the skeletal figure of death had come to be used not only to inspire fear but also to criticize society and its morals. It was also featured in drama and was characterized by taking pleasure in "shock and destruction."

> There was often an element of parody . . . a mutual reminder that humans are mortal and will have to reckon with God's judgment. . . . Farce and even obscene humor were seldom absent for long. . . . The dance of death was also sensitive to social rank and class. The Death figure often passed judgment on peasants, merchants, clergy, and royalty, each of whom were thought to have specialized in particular forms of sloth and vice. (Kastenbaum 67)

Late medieval paintings of danses macabres sometimes portrayed the living as stiff and, well, lifeless, standing hesitantly before partially decomposed, graceful, animated corpses or skeletons who were inviting the living to dance. The death figures betray a sense of humor and fun, as do contemporary Mexican calaveras. Since the clothing of the living figures made clear their social status, Philippe Ariès believes such depictions were intended to emphasize that all are equal in death and that no one knows when death may strike (Ariès 116).

"Le paravent de la fête Dieu," a very large, painted screen that the Musée du Vieil Aix in Aix-en-Provence takes pride in exhibiting, shows a moment in the life of the town during the Middle Ages. At the end of a religious procession is a black-clad, skull-masked figure chasing children, scythe in hand. The notes that pertain to that detail read: "*La mort,* toute de noir vêtue, traîne sa faux sur le pavé et pousse des cris sinistres. Devant elle, les enfants s'enfuient épouvantés. Tous ces jeux sont terminés par la mort pour faire souvenir l'homme de la derniére fin" [*Death,* all dressed in black, dragged her scythe along the street and emitted sinister cries. Before her, children fled in fear. All these games ended with death to make people remember their final end].

T.S.R. Boase has written about the popularity of the dance of death story in all of Europe; it appeared in many paintings in churches, manuscripts, and graveyards. He describes pageants in Paris in 1422 and at Bruges in 1449 in which actors wore skeleton costumes and engaged characters who represented the various social strata and functions (Boase 104). The story was known and told in several mediums in Spain, and it entered at least two Mexican churches in the sixteenth century: the cloister of Huatlatlauhca and the confessional in Malinalco, Estado de* México (Gerlero).

It seems very likely that the spirit of social criticism and of comedy that infused European depictions and dramatizations of the dance of death were taken up and fitted to their new milieu in Mexico and were perhaps first published in 1792 by Fray Joaquín Bolaños in his tragicomic protonovel *La portentosa vida de la muerte*. This work pretends to be a religious tract in which, Death is ultimately conquered by the resurrection of Christ, but most of it reads like a typical picaresque novel told in the third person. As in that genre, the moral of the story serves more or less as an excuse for the amusing peripeteia of Death's adventures, some of which are erotic, some political. The book is generously illustrated with comical drawings. Death itself is the only skeleton.

In *The Medieval Heritage of Mexico*, Luis Weckmann reveals the origin of literary calaveras, the invention of which is sometimes erroneously attributed—along with that of pictorial ones—to José Guadalupe Posada.* Weckmann informs us that these comical pseudo-epitaphs were read on November 2 as early as the eleventh century. Then as now they were called *calaveras*. I see no reason to doubt this genealogy.

Both Mexicans and Spaniards offer their dead yellow flowers, the fittingly named *sempervivum* in Cataluña and cempoaxóchitl* in Mexico (Weckmann 201). In this instance we have a symbolic, coincidental relationship. The human eye is drawn to yellow more than to any other color, and we usually perceive the sun as yellow. Because the sun appears to rise and set, metaphorically being born and dying, and because it influences the cycles of agricultural fertility, the sun is an almost universal symbol of life. By extension, a yellow flower can be seen as an iconic twin of the sun, with all its cultural associations. Then again, in both Judeo-Christian and Mesoamerican* cultures, flowers signify the fragility and brevity of human life. As an offering to the dead, who are expected by both Christians and Mesoamericans to be reborn into an afterlife, flowers serve as symbolic companions that are momentarily as beautiful and fresh as were the deceased in their youth but that will wilt very soon. A yellow flower, even when called flor de muertos, is a sign of the ephemeral life of the body but also of the eternal life of the sun and the soul.

Weckmann makes one more observation about a medieval Spanish practice that has to do with Christmas but that I will extend to one associated with contemporary Mexico's Días de muertos. He cites Sinanoglou (without identifying the article or book) to trace the custom of Christmas supper to the (presumably late medieval) custom "of eating little figures of the Baby Jesus made of bread or sugar, to the homilies of Saint Gregory the

Great, who expressed the correlation between the eucharistic bread and the body of the newborn Christ" (Weckmann 204). Weckmann may be engaging in the kind of questionable Catholic scholarship that finds the origins of practices and symbols in theology that is a thousand years old, and he might not have realized that what he attributes to Gregory is far from unique to him, being much more common among the female mystics of the late Middle Ages (Caroline Bynum, personal communication).

There were mystics who associated the baby Jesus with the host, and if they ate sugar or pastry figures of the Christ child at Christmas, they might have experienced mystical union with Jesus similar to that experienced during the sacrament of the Eucharist in the context of the Mass.[12] In a section of her book entitled "Further Imaging of the Eucharist," Miri Rubin wrote about communicants who saw a child when the host was consecrated:

> This image which was designed to evoke compassion came to inhabit a very central place in eucharistic symbolism: the child, viewed, chewed, adored, sacrificed, appears again and again in various eucharistic registers and contexts. The image brought together two strains in eucharistic symbolism, one which stresses the presence of a real human, suffering body, a historic Christ born to a Virgin, and the other, which stresses redemption through sacrifice; and what dearer than the sacrifice of innocence, of the dearest, son by father? (Rubin 135f)

Certain panes de muerto,* such as those in Oaxaca, are in stylized human shape with armlets and leglets. The protrusion of the little flour head resembles a funeral shroud that allows only the head to be seen (see Figure 5.7). The pan de muerto typical in and around Mexico City is topped by a stylized skull and crossbones; many figures of skulls and skeletons are made of various sweets to be ingested by living and dead during Días de muertos. As "breaking bread" at any time in a deliberate or ceremonial way can be reminiscent of the Christian sacrament, the eating of anthropomorphic sweets can, by extension, invoke sacramentality as well, even if it is usually considered playful by contemporary Mexicans and given little importance. Both the medieval and modern customs have cannibalistic undertones, which I interpret as indicative of the love the eater feels

---

[12] I thank Dr. Caroline Walker Bynum for her clarifications on this point and for recommending the work of Miri Rubin.

5.7 Pan de muerto with flour head. Oaxaca, Oaxaca

toward the eaten—in which case the ingestion makes the eaten an intimate and inseparable part of the eater and alters her or him by her or his immanence with all of the attributes that made the beloved lovable.

In *Holy Feast and Holy Fast,* Bynum elaborates on the medieval practice that is parallel to the contemporary one: "Because Jesus had fed the faithful not merely as servant and waiter, preparer and multiplier of loaves and fishes, but as the very bread and wine itself, *to eat* was a powerful verb. It meant to consume, to assimilate, to become God. To eat God in the eucharist was a kind of audacious deification, a becoming of the flesh that, in its agony, fed and saved the world" (Bynum 3).

Focusing on it in another way, a cannibalistic practice indicates different desires. The eater wants magically to appropriate characteristics of the morsel, as when an Aztec runner ate a bit of the calf muscle of a sacrificed warrior who was a good runner. During Days of the Dead, by consuming a sweet skull the eater is inoculated against fear of death because she or he has taken in the peace of death or the dead. Another desire can be to dominate or destroy what is eaten, in which case the ingestion leaves the eater alone in the field. If one consumes a skull, one pronounces one's semiotic triumph over death—that is, through that action one pronounces one's immortality. None of these interpretations—and there may be more—is inappropriate for the eating of pan de muerto and calaveritas de azúcar,* whether one consciously analyzes the meaning of the act or not. As to the fact that both sweets are considered fun to eat, philosophers from Aristotle to Freud and beyond have long known the hidden seriousness of play and humor.[13]

Like the corpses in medieval European dances of death, the calaveras of Días de muertos are often heuristic figures that attempt to confront their public with the inevitability of their demise; with the intractability and injustice of their social, economic, and political systems; and with the foolishness of their vanity and self-deception. Calaveras can be distinguished from their European counterparts because they are not sententious, self-righteous little homilies addressed to others; instead, they are self-portraits. The *rotulista** (neighborhood artist), the *alfeñiquero* (sugar sculptor), and the village potter represent themselves and their beloved husbands, wives, children and parents, neighbors and acquaintances, as well as their dead, as

---

[13] In conjunction with this consideration of symbolically cannibalistic practices, remember the cannibalism of the Mexica.* Several of their rituals required the ingestion of a morsel of the flesh of a sacrificial victim. See Clendinnen for further discussion.

skeletons. It is as if they had undressed, taken off their flesh, and dressed again in their own clothes to represent themselves as they perform their work, their courtship, their play—in a word, as they function within their economic system and social hierarchy.

There is a self-reflexivity in the calaveras that I do not perceive in many of their Old World relatives. Whereas the serious medieval Death speaks in the second person, the light-hearted Flaca* or Pelona* speaks in the first. Whereas the former seems to feel it has transcended earthly life, the latter knows herself—even when fleshed and breathing—as always already skeletal. Each presents a fairly different view of human life, human significance, and the afterlife. The European Death implies that the immortal, universal spirit is real and the contingent individual is an illusion. La Calaca* implies the indissoluble union of life and death, body and spirit, and realistically knows it is the memory and the love of those who are still living that confer immortality.

Mathilde Reyes, in her article on beliefs about and tributes to the dead, describes some of the changes Catholics wrought in the Indigenous conceptualizations of death. Confession was instituted so Catholics would be prepared to die well at any time. The church taught that death was to be feared because of the suffering that awaited sinners in purgatory and hell, whereas only the righteous few could expect happiness and rest in heaven. Prayers were said for the souls in purgatory. Death figures were shown with a threatening expression in face and posture, carrying a scythe with which to cut down human life. It was not until the eighteenth century that the clergy softened their characterization of death, giving death a kind visage and encouraging their flock to face death with faith and without fear. From that time comes a prayer called "A la Santa Muerte" (To Holy Death) (Reyes 22f). Catholics were taught to befriend death.

Death in Sixteenth-Century Spain

The conquerors, colonizers, and missionaries who went to the New World in the sixteenth century carried in their cultural baggage several customs that were compatible with Indigenous death-related beliefs and traditions. Christians in both the sixteenth and seventeenth centuries, according to Ariès, had a dim view of the world, which they considered to be "permeated with the tincture of death; it ha[d] become suspect from one end to the other" (Ariès 333). Although the Indians whom the Spaniards conquered in Mexico had a deep love of the world, the god Tezcatlipoca inspired them to value life as if they were always on the brink of death. They did not trust the world to sustain them kindly and generously.

Agapito Rey lists several compatible practices, beginning with the annual visit to the cemetery that, according to him, started when Spain was a colony of imperial Rome. There were commemorative occasions at harvest. Burials were performed with great pomp and circumstance, particularly in Madrid, where when a child died there was great celebration—dances, fireworks, music—and no sadness, since the soul was believed to be innocent and to go directly to heaven.[14] When an adult died, those who attended the wake were served refreshments and bread, alms were distributed to the poor, bread was given to the local priest, and professional *plañideras* (weepers), wept (Rey 115f). The hiring of professional mourners is not widespread, as most bereaved have enough grief of their own.

Rey refers to two poetic universal offerings. The older of the two was the lighting of candles on graves, intended to help the spirits find their way in the dark. The other was the placing of water to quench the thirst of visiting spirits, both when the person was on her or his deathbed and on the night of All Souls'. Both traditions are practiced today by most celebrants of Días de muertos.*

Transgressive Syncretism

To the frustration of the purists among the early Christian missionaries (Sahagún "Exclamaciones del autor," Volume I, 95), syncretism was an early and pervasive strategy of efficient evangelization in the so-called New World, having been used since the Roman Empire in the spiritual conquest of Germans and Celts, who invaded from the north (Weckmann 184). Fray Pedro de Córdoba recognized that the Catholic doctrine had to be altered and added to in order to be taught adequately in New Spain (quoted in Weckmann 185).[15] Proselytizers were wily enough to capitalize on similarities between Native and Christian deities, beliefs, and rituals by pointing out to their targets that they already almost believed in the outsiders' "true" god and saints, that in the case of the Mesoamericans* they already almost participated in the "true" rites of passage, that they already almost

---

[14] King David also wept for his son only until he died, and upon his son's death he danced and celebrated.

[15] I recommend the thorough *Paralelismos rituales de las religiones azteca y católica* by Georgina Estrada Sagaón.

understood the "true" nature of the universe. New converts often assumed that to call their own gods by Christian names was merely part of learning the foreigners' language.[16] To accept innovations in rites of passage was part of being civil and respectful hosts. To respect whatever they could understand linguistically of the strangers' religious discourse was part of being courteous and correct.

Christians often usurped sacred times and places by destroying existing temples, altars, images, and ceremonies and installing their own, sometimes forcing the local people to use the same stones in the new buildings. The strategy was effective because it took advantage of local traditions that held certain sites and periods or days to be so special, in what believers likely considered an essential or natural way, that the distinctiveness had to be recognized ritually. Missionaries appeared to recognize the holiness of a time or a location, so the changes they wrought in renaming the deities or the times felt less violent, incredible, and arbitrary to the Native audience than if the former had attempted to establish sacred times and places that did not coincide with local ones.

The best-known instance of sanctified space thus transformed in Mexico is the case of Tonantzin (Our Mother), who was honored at a temple on the hill of Tepeyac. Although many Catholics the world over and a majority of Mexican Catholics believe in the miracle, sound scholarship shows that Father Miguel Sánchez concocted the story of a miraculous maryophany in the same place, by means of which the Virgin (Mary) of Guadalupe was established in place of Tonantzin.[17] Perhaps the best-known instance of sacred time being appropriated is Christmas, December 25, which was the holiest day for the Mithraists, practicants of a mystery religion that was so popular and widespread in the Roman Empire at the dawn of Christianity that it was one of the latter's strongest competitors.

Virtually all religions as we know them today are, willy-nilly, the products of syncretism. No missionary could ever find a potential convert who had no philosophical or religious foundation of her or his own. No convert could be so thoroughly converted or diverted that her or his past could be

---

[16] In colloquial speech, in fact, *cristiano* has come to mean not only one who professes Christianity but also both "person" and the language "Spanish," the last two suggesting that only Christians are real people and only Spanish is comprehensible to the civilized, as opposed to "barbarian" tongues.

[17] I recommend the superbly researched and amusingly presented study by Eduardo del Río García (Rius), *El mito guadalupano.*

erased to the extent that the convert would entirely forget—although she or he might refuse—her or his spiritual and philosophical worldview, practices, and observations of sacred spaces, sacred images, and sacred times. It seems inevitable that the old and the new religions, coexisting in one body and one mind—that of each convert—would mingle and mix.

In his *Mary, Michael, and Lucifer: Folk Catholicism in Central Mexico,* John M. Ingham details the practice of missionary syncretism. The proselytizers changed the lyrics of Aboriginal songs and altered their dances to make them support the European religion. Sometimes they merely permitted and other times they promoted and canonized Indigenous practices, which led to alterations in both the sanctioned Catholic liturgy and its pantheon. Ingham points out that this pantheon reveals the history of assimilation of local deities, including astronomical bodies, figures of agricultural fertility, healers, war gods, nature spirits, and the like (Ingham 8f). For example, because of his association with water, John the Baptist became one with Tláloc, the god of rain. To this day, the two are associated. Even as in ancient times it was believed that those who died by water went to Tlalocan, the place of Tláloc, some communities still say the drowned are "los peones del dios del agua San Juan Bautista" [the peons of the god of water Saint John the Baptist] (Matos Moctezuma 140).[18] What is poignantly telling in this case is that the colonial hierarchy is reproduced in the hereafter. Rather than project an afterlife of play and delight for this group of dead as in pre-Hispanic times, today it is expected that they will continue to be subjugated to a foreign god.

The roster of Catholic saints also shows traces of Christian value judgments on the Indigenous hierarchy—for example, assimilating the gods of the poor and turning those of the wealthy into satanic figures, as happened in Mexico—since as members of ascetic orders the earliest missionaries were critical of greed, excess, and power and were sympathetic to the underclass (Ingham 8f). The friars endeared themselves to the local peasants by being their advocates in the face of mistreatment and injustice by the secular conquerors and colonizers. The tables turned when secular clergy took over the friars' work and sided with the colonizing elites (Ingham 9).

The spiritual conquest of Mexico in the sixteenth century was facilitated by many similarities between the two pantheons, such that, in Ingham's

---

[18] Also see the quotation by Juan Tecpa Uribe in "Pre-Hispanic Commemorations of the Dead" in this chapter.

words, "the resulting syncretism was unusually coherent" (Ingham 9), as he, Estrada Sagaón, and others have observed. The Amerindians produced their own working version of Catholicism out of elements of their original religion, the doctrines the missionaries preached, and formalized representations of the new social order. This, as Ingham has written, "gave them not only a blueprint for survival but a critique of domination also" (Ingham 9).

So, whereas several religious Spaniards wrote about the "Indians'" docility and receptiveness toward Christianity,[19] in some cases the ostensible neophytes introduced the saints and Jesus into their own pantheons as they had with the deities of conquered and assimilated populations. In other cases they called their own gods by the names of the European gods, and sometimes they collapsed Christian and Indigenous deities into new ones.

Marta Turok reminds us that many Mexican dances managed to create an alternative language for codifying spiritual concerns and petitions that was unintelligible to the severe conquerors and missionaries (Turok 40), even as the Catholics were tailoring old dances to their own ritual. Whereas this new use of dance was designed to preserve the Native religion and protect it from Christianity, it would have seemed innocent enough to fail to alert the Spaniards to the Amerindians' veiled resistance or alter their belief in the Indians' docility. Elizabeth Carmichael and Chloë Sayer suggested that the imposition of Spanish religion and culture actually fortified the cults of Indigenous gods (Carmichael and Sayer 61), presumably by inspiring rejection of the foreign and reinvigorating adherence to the local. Still, as has been suggested, resistance and transgressive syncretism are only part of the story. Ingham nicely summarizes the Amerindian appreciation of Christianity:

> [T]he Indians responded with enthusiasm and reworked Catholic teachings according to their own needs and understandings. Folk Catholicism in rural Mexico today is not part of a state apparatus, nor is it merely a tool of provincial elites. Although it formulates and sanctifies positive sociality, it provides an idiom for critical commentary on negative social relations. It thus reflects the interests of the poor as well as those of the wealthy. Ultimately, it is as much a peasant construction as the product of theological ratiocination by elite clergy. (Ingham 2)

---

[19] For example, Bartolomé de las Casas, Bernardino de Sahagún, Motolinia, and, in general, the Franciscan missionaries.

At the same time, the Spanish crown's desire for bureaucratic order and social discipline put religious transformation to work for its own benefit. Transforming Native spiritual and cultic independence to dependence on Christian religious leadership helped to homogenize the expanding Spanish colony, as well as to make the members of society more visible, especially through the Catholic sacrament of confession.[20]

To summarize, whereas for the missionaries syncretism was a strategy of conversion, for the targeted converts it has sometimes been a strategy for cultural survival. As Anita Brenner, Estrada Sagaón, Ingham, and Weckmann have amply demonstrated, Amerindians have disguised certain cultic practices and deities as Christian ones and have continued to worship as and whom (or what) they wish. This is what I call transgressive syncretism.

The commemoration of the dead, especially in the relatively homogeneous Indigenous communities of Mexico, continues today, altered but not profoundly changed by Christianity. Rolly Kent and Heather Valencia, in their account of Yaqui culture, consider the Indigenous aspect of ritual to be the essential one, even if it is a Christian celebration: "Catholicism has helped cement the culture into a coherent structure that has nurtured the people in changing times" (Kent and Valencia 122). Traditional offerings are made and shared, protected from official sanctions by means of Christian symbols and personages—whether in the private sacred space of home or in the public one of a graveyard. The two brief days corresponding to the feasts of All Souls' and All Saints are observed, but Días de muertos* may last from October 18 through November 30, most typically from October 28 to November 2. And whereas Christians pray for the souls of their dead, whom they believe are in purgatory or in heaven (I have yet to meet anyone who thinks their dead are in hell), on the day set aside for them on the calendar, members of México profundo* remember their dead on the days determined by the way they died, as did their pre-Christian ancestors.

I cannot aver that the most traditional celebrants of Días de muertos are consciously or deliberately poaching on the religious practices of their colonizers to preserve their deepest and oldest ways and beliefs; nor can I affirm that they do so unconsciously or naively. In either case, the results are the same. Just as many biologists attribute to human beings an instinct to survive, so humans seem to have profound desires and powerful motivations to

---

[20] See Michel Foucault, *The History of Sexuality*, Volume I, especially "The Repressive Hypothesis" on the origins of complete confession and penance.

preserve their cultures. In Mexico, even in comparatively homogeneous communities, there is a clear awareness of the enormous differences in economic, educational, political, and judicial privilege between the ruling and the ruled; from that awareness follow numerous tactics of self-preservation, self-protection, and seeking and constructing meaning and pleasure. Days of the Dead is a festival that functions as a vehicle for many of those tactics. During and throughout the fiesta,* the celebrants define and reaffirm publicly their society and culture with all that those words entail regarding social, economic, and political relations, spirituality, metaphysics, anthropology, philosophy, and the rest.

Días de muertos is interesting in part because it is a popular answer to the dominant Christian mythology of All Souls' and All Saints Days, as well as to the dominant mythology about the stereotypical, provincial[21] Mexico and the nationalism it constructs. Whereas pre-Hispanic Mexican cultures seem for the most part to have given in to Spanish Catholicism, some pockets have resisted colonization, and this celebration is one of them.

The two Catholic holy days are dedicated to those who died "in Christ" and are presumed to have been "living in Christ" ever since. The church observes these days with solemnity and prayers. All Saints and All Souls' emphasize two things: the importance of being a Christian so one is guaranteed a happy afterlife and the vision of an afterlife in which the Christian's earthly sufferings will be redressed and she or he will live happily ever after.

Although I agree with John Ingham that religion is adapted by its adherents for their own constructions of meaning, I believe it is also one of the cornerstones of ideology on which the edifice of social order and control is built. Catholicism in Mexico was an important tool of the conquest and colonization by Spain, as Protestantism is now for the ideological transformation and modernization after the model of the United States. The missionaries attempted to convert the Indigenous population, convincing them to submit to Christ and the king of Spain, whom the Catholics represented almost as a double deity who would protect them as loyal subjects. Mexicans became by and large disciplined, cooperative subjects who

---

[21] I use this word as in Mexico, to refer to the relatively traditional provinces or states of Mexico in contradistinction to the modernizing, cosmopolitan cities. Provincial culture is not totally but is largely México profundo,* whereas metropolitan culture is not totally but largely México imaginario.

accepted the violence and injustice of the conquest and its hierarchy of classes because they were promised eternal happiness after death. "Blessed are the poor in spirit, for theirs is the kingdom of heaven. Blessed are those who mourn, for they shall be comforted. Blessed are the meek, for they shall inherit the earth" (Matthew 5:3–5). But evidence of resistance is visible to one who knows how, when, and where to look; and some contemporary examples of Días de muertos being used for limited political visibility are presented in Chapters 4, 8, and 9, even as evidence of syncretism is visible in the ever-changing aspects of Días de muertos, as we will see in Chapter 6.

6

Días de muertos Versus Hallowe'en: A Fight to the Death?

Hay que dar pelea para
que nuestras tradiciones
no se pierdan.
Este Día de muertos di
no al Halloween, y di
sí al grito de una limosna
para mi calavera.*

We must put up a fight so
that our traditions
are not lost.
This Day of the Dead, say
no to Hallowe'en and say
yes to the shout for alms
for my calavera.

No al Halloween. POBLACION
TEPOZTECA CONSERVA TU
TRADICION EN ESTE DIA DE
MUERTOS. NO DEJES QUE LLEGUEN
DE OTRA PARTE Y QUE TRAIGAN
COSAS AJENAS A TUS COSTUMBRES.
SE ORIGINAL.[1]

No to Hallowe'en. Residents of
Tepoztlán, preserve your tradition
on this Day of the Dead. Don't
allow anyone to come from
another place and bring things that
are alien to your customs.
Be original.

—Poster

---

[1] See Figure 6.1.

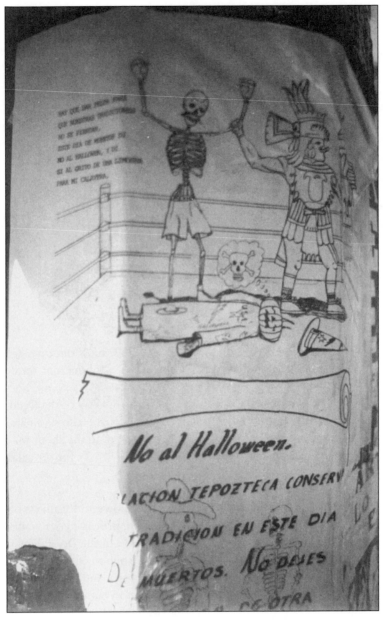

6.1 "No al Halloween." Tepoztlán. Morelos

¡Qué noche—dijo la muerte—
miedos y sustos sin fin
entre tanta bruja y duende
de aquel barrio de postín!
Y es que en vez de ir a la ofrenda
se perdió en un Jalogüín.

—Jorge Anaya

"What a night," said Death,
"scares and frights without end
among so many witches and goblins
from that poseur neighborhood!
Instead of going to the offering
it got lost in a Hallowe'en."

Where did twelve-year-old Aline Ramiro get the idea or inspiration to disguise herself and her siblings and friends after the style of U.S. Hallowe'en celebrants and go out through the streets of Cuetzalan, Puebla, asking for their calavera* in 1991? Aline did not or would not tell me. To my variously phrased questions she kept repeating *"Se me ocurrió"* [It occurred to me]. She was clearly seen as the leader of that motion by both her younger brothers and her grandmother who first told me proudly that Aline had organized the costumed activity. Aline had dressed as a witch, one of the brothers as a mummy, and the other as a *vaquero* (a cowboy).

In the nearest city, Teziutlán, I had seen some costumed children, the boys wearing industrially produced masks and capes. Most carried elaborate jack-o'-lanterns that, in addition to a carved face, often had a cross, a lightning sign, or *grecas* (geometrical designs that represent stylized lightning, the horizon, and such). These youngsters walked the streets accosting passersby with the traditional request, "¿No me da mi calavera?" [Won't you give me my calavera?]. One was then expected to put coins into the carved pumpkin. The youngest children were accompanied by adults.

During my lifetime I have seen Hallowe'en make its presence felt more and more in Mexico. In Oaxaca, Oaxaca, in 1992, mylar balloons (whose designs included a witch on a broom and a pumpkin) were imported from the United States. In Toluca, Estado de* México, in 1993, similar mylar balloons carried proudly by local children included pictures of a cartoonish ghost, a green witch, and another ghost breaking the chains of purgatory[2] (see Figure 6.2).

---

[2] In the Catholic world, Fieles Difuntos (All Souls' Day) is dedicated in part to praying for the dead in purgatory. In Mexico, a song may be sung to them with the words: "Salgan, salgan, salgan, ánimas en pena; que el Santo Rosario rompa sus cadenas" [Emerge, suffering souls; may the Holy Rosary break your chains]. The balloon I describe refers to this belief or prayer.

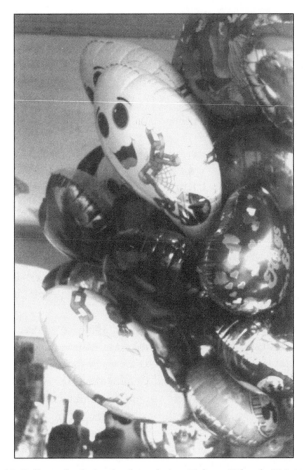

6.2 Balloon depicting broken chains. Toluca, Edo. de México

In Oaxaca, one of Mexico's poorest, most traditional states, I saw many little girls dressed as witches on October 29 and 30. A number of shops were selling mass-produced Hallowe'en paraphernalia: masks, decorative pictures of witches, ghosts, and other U.S.-style toys and accouterments that could be used as parts of costumes or as decorations for a Hallowe'en party. The market stand where I bought calaveras de azúcar* was also selling large cardboard images of witches, goblins, and zombies, all imported from the United States.

A week earlier I had seen a very traditional barbershop near the marketplace in Tepoztlán, Morelos, elaborately decorated with such cardboard

6.3 Barbershop. Tepoztlán, Morelos

images (see Figure 6.3). In all of the traditional markets[3] I visited, I saw industrially produced masks and hollow plastic pumpkins with little handles—perfect for filling with donations. In addition, boutiques and bakeries in middle-class and upper-class neighborhoods tended to be decorated with Hallowe'en motifs, even the old Spanish bakeries,[4] which as late as the early 1980s sported calaveras painted on their windows imaginative rotulistas* and which sold row upon row of sugar calaveras, alphabetized by name, along with the pan de muerto* they continue to produce. In Mexico City's La Merced, the oldest market in America, and in Oaxaca's Mercado Benito Juárez and the market in Toluca, there were mass-produced Hallowe'en costumes of witches, devils, and monsters.

On November 1, 1992, I saw numerous Hallowe'en parties with masked children—sometimes costumed, male and female, between twelve and sixteen years of age—in the streets and plazas of Oaxaca. One group was carrying a boombox and doing jerky dances as the children hopped among the tables of a café, one hand held out to the patrons. Occasionally, one or another asked, "¿No quiere cooperar?" [Would you cooperate?]. I did not see anyone give them coins. I saw another group of young people at around 11:30 at night, running and leaping around in the streets in masks and costumes. This crew did not request a cooperación.

Whereas the children in Mexico City request their "jalogüín" (Hallowe'en), meaning their treats, door to door, those in the provinces and on the margins of the city request their calavera. Whereas the bourgeois children are led by their parents or teachers in this event, the poorer children are the ones who are poaching elements of Hallowe'en that they graft into their celebration. Whereas for the wealthy children only the great quantity of candy they can accumulate by trick-or-treating is out of the ordinary, for poor children the candy they may receive is a rare indulgence. The coins they collect are usually the only money that is entirely theirs to spend as they choose—their earnings, if any, normally go to sustaining the family economy—and they often choose to spend it on candy and small toys.

---

3 I say "traditional market" to distinguish it from the U.S.-style grocery store. Traditional markets in Mexico are usually housed in large, humble buildings designed for them. They consist of numerous stands operated by independent owners who often sell produce they have grown themselves, although some have purchased it from other farmers or, in a few cases, imported it. Merchandise is sold in bulk in such markets, and although merchants provide plastic bags, shoppers must bring their own shopping bags. Besides fruits and vegetables, legumes, grains, and seeds, one can find healing herbs and teas and some foods that have not been sufficiently accepted by the typical grocery-store shopper to be sold outside their Indigenous context. There are booths of freshly prepared local foods. In the provinces, one or two days a week, tradespeople from surrounding areas come to town. Some people call these Indian markets, and in many of them one can see people in Indigenous dress and hear Indigenous languages and dialects.

4 Bakeries were established by Spanish immigrants. By now, the recipes have made the rounds, and many neighborhood bakeries have their own versions of the light, sweet bread many Mexicans favor for breakfast and supper with hot chocolate, café con leche, or atole.*

There is another way in which children in Cuetzalan, Puebla, are carnivalizing Días de muertos.* After the altar with the offering has been prepared, in the most traditional homes—most of which are outside the city proper—a path of cempoaxóchitl* is made from the main road or street to the entrance of the house. When everything is ready, two firecrackers are lighted to announce to the souls of the dead that they should come to enjoy the ofrenda.*

Mischievous children obtain some of the firecrackers and take them into the streets, where they light them to *espantar* (to spook or startle) themselves, each other, and passersby. The firecrackers are an element that exceeds the meaning and control of the semiotic system from which the children "steal" them. Because of their youth, most of them do not feel addressed by that system. Their childhood excludes them from either remembering the dead or considering being dead and visiting their living relatives and friends. Like subordinated or marginalized groups, they are interested in finding their own pleasure during the fiesta.* They do so by taking this one element out of its designated context, out of the sacred space of the threshold that the spirits will cross—into the street, which although it belongs to everyone, belongs to them more in the few square feet they inhabit with their giggles, "lifted" goods, and loud, nerve-wracking games.

At least three groups are pushing the margins of Días de muertos by introducing elements and practices of Hallowe'en. The two youngest of the groups, bourgeois children and poor children, use Hallowe'en as a resource from which they choose what they will to enrich, alter, or build their own culture.[5] For the privileged young, Hallowe'en is an excuse for parties, costumes, too many sweets, and trick-or-treating—a socially sanctioned form of begging that is ordinarily inappropriate for their class. Trick-or-treating has not degenerated into a pretext for vandalism as it has for some youths in the United States. In Mexico, the worst that kids do when they are refused treats is to chant or occasionally write *"codos"* (skinflints) on a wall.

The third group that is experimenting with the two celebrations, adult members of the dominant class, uses Hallowe'en for the "invention of tradition" that Eric Hobsbawm describes and that I introduced in Chapter 3, "Días de muertos and National Identity," as well as for commercial gain.

---

[5] This process fits John Fiske's definition of *excorporation*, "the process by which the subordinate make their own culture out of the resources and commodities provided by the dominant system" (*Understanding Popular Culture* 15).

To incorporate some of the constant changes in popular culture into the system of economic gain is, to some extent, to attempt to contain some of the energy of the humble forgers of popular culture whose creativity and cultural vitality counter the power signified by the dominant culture.[6] Of course, doing so is also profitable.

In 1994 Sanborns,[7] an upscale national chain of gift shops cum restaurants or soda fountains, published ads in newspapers with a photo of an ofrenda* that included calaveras, carnations, daisies, votive candles, tamales,* hot chocolate, cut-paper skulls, and the all-important pan de muerto with copy that read: "Este Día de Muertos, ven a Sanborns y revive nuestra tradición. Prueba el delicioso Pan de Muerto de Sanborns. Una tradición muy mexicana . . . Y que nunca muere" [This Day of the Dead, come to Sanborns and revive our tradition. Taste Sanborns' delicious Pan de Muerto. A very Mexican tradition. . . . And one that never dies]. When, in addition, Sanborns produces and markets skulls, pumpkins, and witches made of milk chocolate, as well as pan de muerto from its own recipe, the company is probably acting strictly from a profit motive. For its typical well-to-do clients, the fact that these chocolates are available there makes it appropriate for them to purchase, give, and enjoy them. The higher price, the Americanized mass-market design, and the endorsement of Sanborns make the items acceptable and allow the buyers to participate in the foreign Hallowe'en or the national Días de muertos in a comfortable and class-appropriate manner. The same people could feel déclassé purchasing, giving, and eating the calaveras from traditional market stands along with their servants.

The other perspective of this practice is that of members of the popular class who see their calaveras, the authentic, original ones, rejected by their social "betters." This can easily be translated as a rejection of popular culture, as well as of its members, widening the already yawning chasm that exists between the rich and the poor. The effects of the presence and sale of Hallowe'en in Mexico reach beyond the Sanborns tills: They alter culture. As George Rabasa has observed, "The classes that are

---

[6] See Fiske, in whose *Understanding Popular Culture* the word *incorporation* refers to the dominant culture's practice of adopting elements of popular culture and commodifying it. A current example in the United States would be the production, promotion, and sale of proportionately enormous pants first worn by some African American boys.

[7] The English name is that of the founder, an Anglo Mexican.

adopting (not adapting) Hallowe'en from the US are the wealthy and urban upper middle classes and in fact not the ones that celebrate Días de muertos. In their case, the adoption is whole because it comes into a vacuum" (Rabasa, personal communication).

Children like Aline Ramiro in Cuetzalan and the merrymakers in Oaxaca are transforming Días de muertos to some small extent by taking up and altering foreign elements that originated in Great Britain, traveled to the United States, and were eventually transported from there to Mexico by U.S. immigrants, Mexican tourists to the United States, and the broadcast media, including Hollywood movies.

Some adults also use Hallowe'en as a cultural resource. Ample evidence of this can be seen in the way many tombs in the Panteón Dolores were festooned when I visited it on November 2, 1993 (see Plate 14). When I asked the celebrants who were either decking the graves of their dead or sitting by those graves about their use of Hallowe'en icons, one woman explained simply, "Es el Jálogüin" [It's Hallowe'en].

Another woman was with her two daughters and a son-in-law. They were inflating orange balloons, pulling the balloon's lowest point through and up to the top of the balloon, tying it to the "navel" to give it the shape of a pumpkin, drawing black jack-o'-lanterns on them, and then threading them on long cords above the sides of the tomb (see Figure 6.4). The widow explained that her husband, at whose grave we were, had loved all kinds of fiestas and that while he was alive, the family had celebrated as many as they knew about.

Neither informant thought it was problematic or unpatriotic to incorporate bits of Hallowe'en; nor did the many people who stopped to admire the most elaborately decorated mausoleum, that of a young girl who had died thirteen years before and whose resting place held as many Hallowe'en as Días de muertos icons. Referring to the adoption of Hallowe'en icons by the celebrants of Días de muertos, Rabasa commented: "It's interesting that the clases populares are not borrowing directly from the US but from the wealthier, urban classes. So in a sense it's a case of imitating the customs of their 'betters,' adding a level of worldliness and stylishness to the altars and *panteón* decorations. A little bit of unconscious class-climbing?" (Rabasa, personal communication). Rabasa also elaborates on the point that the jack-o'-lanterns and black cats are perceived as fashionable by the people who add them to their ofrendas. Hallowe'en, in that sense, modernizes the look of the traditional altar.

6.4 Balloon-festooned grave. Panteón Dolores, México, D.F.

No Threat to Tradition and Identity

Metropoligrama	*Metropolygram*
Que si son desmemoriados	That they have a poor memory
es cosa que no celebro,	in the private schools,
en los planteles privados,	deprived of a good brain,
privados de buen cerebro.	is something I do not celebrate.
—Benito Cienfuegos	

Like most countries in Latin America, Mexico works actively to forge a national identity, although a peculiar historical situation distinguishes it from its southern neighbors. According to Professor René Jara, national identity occurs at the juncture of a permanent conflict between memory and present experience, the former fed by oral cultures and their conservative or conservationist aspect, the latter by the need to bring national economics and politics into harmony with the times. Mexico's peculiarity arises from two variables. One is the more profound assimilation of the conquerors' culture than in the rest of the Hispanic and Luso-Brazilian continent, largely through *mestizaje.** The other is the great importance that

Mexican criollos* have attributed to the Amerindian past as a focus for national identity, especially since the Mexican Revolution of 1910–1920 (Jara, personal communication).

One of the ways in which identity is forged is through attention to and promotion of traditional crafts and fiestas* that arouse or affirm nationalist attitudes in the people. Celebrations on behalf of or in memory of dead ancestors are virtually universal. Although I know of no other Catholic country that refers to All Saints and All Souls' Days as the Days of the Dead, these feasts are kept wherever there is an observant Catholic population. Where American populations were not exterminated or thoroughly assimilated into the European ones, syncretism occurred between Christian and Aboriginal religious or spiritual practices and traditions. This is certainly true in the Andean countries of South America, in most of Central America, and in Mexico. Some places have seasonal practices similar to those in Mexico. For example, I was informed by Consuelo Navarro that in her native Ecuador there are Indigenous groups that on this day eat a sweet bread in the shape of a baby. They drink a red punch called *morado* (purple), because it resembles the color of blood (Navarro, personal communication).

Mexicans are not concerned about fiestas or practices similar to theirs. The celebrants of Días de muertos* are unlikely to know about them, and the promoters of national identity pay little attention to them. What interests them is what happens en su tierra*; that is, where patriotism can be planted, tended, and harvested. I have no interest in making ethnographic comparisons in this book; I am concerned with the signs and functions of the fiesta as it occurs in Mexico.

The one coincident celebration that cannot be ignored because it has been making its presence felt since the early 1950s is the U.S. Hallowe'en. It comes from the country that exports two-thirds of Mexico's imports along with a sizable portion of its musical, televisual, and cinematic programming. It comes from the country whose language many Mexicans learn for work or for leisure, whose fashions they adopt, whose tourist sites they visit. It comes from the northern neighbor that is emulated and avoided, admired and feared, respected and despised. There are some similarities between the two celebrations, especially if one considers the origins and apparent intent of Hallowe'en, but it is the differences that many Mexican nationalists find objectionable.

Carmichael and Sayer cite Luis de Hoyos Sáinz and Nieves Hoyos Sancho to describe the Spanish practice of lighting hollowed-out pumpkins with lamps "to simulate a skull positioned in the open windows of houses, as a more public offering than that which shines in the living room or the kitchen" (Carmichael and Sayer 151). This is identical in effect to the Anglo and Anglo American practice of displaying a jack-o'-lantern to invite trick or treaters. What distinguishes the Spanish custom is that the pumpkin skulls invite disembodied guests to an offering or living guests to view the offering.

Nothing similar is done during Días de muertos in Mexico, but both industrially produced plastic jack-o'-lanterns and hand-carved pumpkin ones are sometimes carried by children who ask passersby either for "their Hallowe'en" or "their calavera." Some children carry nothing, and others carry a shoe box with a cross cut in its top through which one can drop coins. Like so many practices of popular culture, this one has multiple sources; both the local one of *calaverear** and the U.S. one of trick-or-treating are more immediate sources than Spain's pumpkin skulls in a window. Carrying jack-o'-lanterns and dressing up while asking for a calavera are imitative of Hallowe'en customs imported from the United States. A practice that is not borrowed is requesting monetary donations. As Arsacio Vanegas Arroyo said when interviewed by Carmichael and Sayer:

> It was customary, at this time of the year, to ask for donations. As a small boy [in the 1930s or 1940s], I would say *"Calavera . . . Give me my calavera."* We made holes in cardboard boxes and lit candles inside; then we would walk through the streets, asking passersby for money. With the proceeds we bought sweets and small toys. In the old days . . . my grandfather printed delightful rhyming requests. Shoe-cleaners, roadsweepers, barbers, bath-house attendants . . . all used to ask for their *calavera*. They would hand you a printed verse, and expect a coin. (Quoted in Carmichael and Sayer 129)

The significant difference between the requests of Mexican and U.S. children during this season is that originally trick-or-treating was an imitation of the behavior of the spirits of the dead, which explains the costuming, whereas calaverear was intended to set up an offering to the forgotten or unknown dead, which explains the lack of disguise.

Hallowe'en costume parties are common in the United States, and they are another import to Mexico. They are held strictly for the enjoyment of hosts and guests. In Mexico, gatherings for Días de muertos are not held primarily for the pleasure of the hosts, who are not only the immediate household but also close friends and actual and ritual kin; they are for the honor, remembrance, and pleasure of the spirit guests. They are not so much parties with brief chatting, dancing, perhaps drinking, and flirting as the greatest attractions as they are reunions, with long talking, eating, and remembering the dead as the principal activities.

A family could enjoy a costume party on October 31 and one or more meals for the visiting spirits on the day that corresponds to them,[8] or at least on November 2, All Souls' Day. A conflict could occur if a relatively traditional family were expected to celebrate their angelitos* on October 31 but preferred to attend or hold a Hallowe'en party that same night. To the "modern" who identifies completely with Western culture and values, such a consideration might seem trivial and silly, even superstitious. To the members of a mythopoetic community, such a consideration would hardly call for a decision because ritual obligation and sacred time are inviolable.

I do not want to fuel the fires of xenophobia or cultural paranoia, but I would not want to trivialize the cultural impact of the exportation of holiday traditions that, surely inadvertently, serve American interests not only economically but also by cultivating a strong pro-U.S. element that will continue to ensure political and diplomatic harmony between two countries that share a long and porous border. It is not impossible that such an effect is consciously desired by a few powerful people on one or both sides of the Río Bravo. Still, it seems more likely that the cultural impact is a side effect of the principal objective of economic gain.

That said, I will explore some ideas based on a theory about the power of "new traditions." According to Eric Hobsbawm, three classifications of traditions have been invented since the industrial revolution. The first type constitutes and signifies social identity in particular communities, be they actual or imagined. The second type fixes or legitimizes hierarchies or institutions; the third forms the group, indoctrinating the members and instilling in them value systems and acceptable behavior (Hobsbawm 9).

One could hypothesize that the invention or, in this case, the importation of certain foreign traditions was inspired by a ruling group that saw advantages in both imitating and drawing close to the foreign country and its culture. One could also speculate that members of the dominant class in the United States see advantages in inspiring social cohesion between their

---

[8] As discussed previously, in the most traditional communities in Mexico, the manner of death determines when the spirit visits its living family. Dates vary from community to community, but they usually fall between October 28 and November 4. Thus, a family could be ritually obligated to honor the spirits of a relative who died in an accident on October 30, of dead children on October 31, and of people who died of old age on November 2.

own and Mexico's bourgeoisies, which, after all, have more in common with one another than they do with their respective countries' poor. If they could legitimize their presence through what appear to be innocuous secular celebrations, that very presence might soon operate as a model for behavior and for the celebrations as instruments of socialization and the inculcation of beliefs. As I said earlier, the social and political effects of adopting and adapting foreign traditions are probably not a deliberate objective but a secondary and unintentional result of importing and exporting holiday-specific products for financial profit.

The behavior encouraged by the exported Hallowe'en is primarily consumption.[9] Consumers are encouraged to buy greeting cards and gifts and decorations for their homes, especially if they are hosting a Hallowe'en party. People are encouraged to buy masks and costumes for themselves and their children. Although traditional Días de muertos encourages the purchase of mostly ephemeral goods—flowers, incense, candles, ingredients for elaborate meals, candy skulls, and so on—this practice is confined to las clases populares and does not encompass items that are unnecessary for the traditional observation. Manufactured items are indeed bought, but for the most part they are relatively inexpensive and locally made. Some communities offer items of clothing, either old favorites of the deceased or new ones; and some offer favorite or new tools that the deceased used or might have used. After the spirits have left, not only the leftover food but also the new clothes and tools are distributed and enjoyed by their living friends and relations. Although Días de muertos is undoubtedly an occasion for extravagant spending, it does not approach the style of continual consumerism that characterizes U.S. celebrants of Hallowe'en all year-round. What is bought for the dead serves the basic needs of food, dress, and work, along with the humble and practical pleasure that special or new items in these categories afford.[10]

---

[9] Hallowe'en is not the only vehicle for the agendas of invented traditions. In Mexico City one also notes the presence (and pressure to consume) of Valentine's Day and, to a lesser extent, Easter. Mother's, Teachers', Children's, and Father's Days are of local vintage.

[10] In pre-Hispanic times, feasting was less practical and more self-serving than it is now during Días de muertos, although it also represented a redistribution of food and other goods among kin, friends, and neighbors. Inga Clendinnen describes feasts as enormously lavish affairs in which the host showed himself to be superior to his guests by bestowing on them splendid gifts and serving expensive, labor-intensive meals made special by the inclusion of exotic delicacies from different parts of the empire. Such prodigality humiliated the recipients so that feasts were ambivalent, bittersweet events laden with anxiety for the invited. The poor were unable to put on such extravaganzas, which itself helped to mark their social status.

Regarding the inculcation of beliefs, the most important belief the exporters of Hallowe'en wish to inculcate is that the consumption of seasonal, disposable merchandise is acceptable. More specifically to the holiday and more profoundly, it may inculcate a series of superstitions: a fear of and belief in (evil) witches, a fear of black cats, and a belief in ghosts that are cartoonish in the U.S. style. Whereas the second of these superstitions is trivial and perhaps the least likely to take root, the first may begin to gnaw at the edges of the belief in folk medicine, which is practiced in Mexico almost equally by women and men and which, although it may be more widespread and virtually universal in rural areas, also has an important presence in urban centers. Fear of witches may begin to inspire suspicion or fear of those aisles of traditional markets in which herbs, barks, seeds, roots, and desiccated animal parts are sold, as well as of the people who sell them and understand how to use them.

In 1991 there was an exhibition in Mexico City of death-related traditions among the Celts, Mayas, Tarahumaras, Otomíes, and Zapotecs that was organized by the Asociación de Profesores, Profesionistas y Estudiantes Pro Creatividad en la Educación, AC (Association of Pro-Creativity Professors, Education Professionals, and Students) and the Escuela para Trabajadores (School for Laborers). Their spokesperson was quoted in the newspaper *Excélsior* on November 2, 1991, tracing the origins of Hallowe'en to the Celtic witch-hunt.

Los celtas pensaban que ciertas mujeres hacían hechizos para dañar la agricultura y a la gente. Les decían hechiceras o brujas y si descubrían a una la quemaban en público. Por eso los celtas utilizaban calabazas dándoles formas aterradoras para ahuyentar a los malos espíritus de las brujas . . . así es como surgió el "halloween", que nada tiene que ver con los muertos, tradición que fue llevada a la Unión Americana.

The Celts thought certain women cast spells to harm agriculture and people. They called them spell-casters or witches, and if they discovered one, they burned her in public. That is why the Celts used pumpkins, giving them terrifying forms to frighten the evil spirits of the witches . . . that is how Hallowe'en arose, which has nothing to do with the dead; this tradition was taken to the United States.

The accuracy of this history can be questioned.[11] Histories usually have ideological agendas or axes to grind. What is significant is that the spokesperson attributed sinister beginnings to a foreign custom that he deliberately distanced from the local traditions of what he called the Mexican cult of the dead. María Antonieta Sánchez de Escamilla shares these views, which may be based on just such journalism. She compared the two celebrations, saying,

> Halloween, by contrast [to Días de muertos], distorts the image of death. I regard it as an invasion, as something that doesn't belong to us. Halloween is truly frightening for children, because it focuses on witches and witchcraft, sorcerers and devils. It deforms the imagination, and threatens our Indigenous traditions. In the City of Puebla, however, it has gained little ground. . . . Most people honour the beliefs of their forebears; in this city you will find *ofrendas* in roughly eighty-five percent of homes. (quoted in Carmichael and Sayer 119)

Sánchez de Escamilla's words reveal the intellectual labor involved in telling about someone else's traditions in such a way as to make them appear dangerous and inferior to one's own. As a grade-school teacher, she has particular credibility when she expresses concern that Hallowe'en frightens children with its typical icons and that it distorts their imagination. But it is not the children who are frightened by the foreign holiday; their imaginations are strong and may be populated by monsters more terrifying than Hallowe'en's witches, sorcerers, and devils. By drawing, creating, and dressing as these, children may gain control of them and use them for their own construction of meanings. There may be a few cases in which a child faces her or his "dark side" through a Hallowe'en costume or in which the child has a truly numinous experience, but mostly children dress up mirthfully for their own pleasure and play. For most children, witches and ghosts are simply another intellectual toy.

---

[11] November 1 marked the Celtic new year, and as in many agricultural, cyclical celebrations, it included the prophesying of the future, rituals to ensure good in the new year, and visits by supernatural beings and the souls of the dead. Ritually purifying fires were ignited and jumped over, and splinters of burned wood from those fires were preserved as healing devices and to bring good luck until the following new year (Hubbell 82f).

That is not to say that I do not attach significance and importance to the toys that are available to the young. It is possible that the familiarity with and belief in caricaturesque white ghosts, insofar as children believe they exist, may begin to displace the expectation of perceiving the spirits of one's relatives and friends. In Chapter 1, I presented some celebrants' experiences of the presence of their guests of honor. If the celebrants lose their predisposition to acknowledge or identify extrasensory events, those such as Sánchez de Escamilla will soon realize that evaporation does account for the overnight loss of water in the glasses on the offering table.[12] It is adults who perceive Hallowe'en as an invasion that distorts Native images of death and the dead and that threatens Indigenous and local traditions.

It is also adults who play the role of cultural gatekeepers to the best of their ability to attempt to circumscribe the influence of a foreign practice and to defend the practices of their fatherland's ancestors. I do not mean to disregard or diminish Sánchez de Escamilla's concern or her pride in Puebla's maintenance of its own ways. The celebrants of Días de muertos who are challenged by modern secularization will quickly lose the thin filaments of attachment to the poetry of the holiday and their sense that the dead have come to the table so lovingly set for them. What could follow is the loss of a reason to make the offerings and, subsequently, of a reason to celebrate the harvest and the blessings of the previous year even with living relatives, friends, and neighbors. Is this not what Joaquín Herrera (discussed later), Sánchez de Escamilla, and the myriad organizations and individuals who work diligently to preserve the traditions fear?

In comparison to Días de muertos, Hallowe'en as it is practiced today does distort the image of death. As U.S. television journalist Greg Palmer observed in his public television program *Death, the Trip of a Lifetime,* Hallowe'en celebrants have forgotten that they are impersonating the dead or consoling and propitiating them with offerings. He is not alone in believing that the United States distances itself from the reality of death and the dead. In spite of the ugly, grotesque rubber masks produced industrially for costumes, most Hallowe'en images are cute and trivial. They neither remind their viewers of the universality and inevitability of death, permitting greater realism and perhaps a clearer appreciation of the dearness of

---

[12] See her interview in Carmichael and Sayer (p. 21) and in "How People Celebrate" in Chapter 1 of this book.

life, nor call attention to and criticize socially sanctioned hierarchies of wealth and poverty, as do many calaveras.

The concern is not merely a fear of the loss of local color. As we can see in the torn social fabric of certain populations in the United States, a weakening of familial and local ties wears down the structures of a group's identity—its moral values, spiritual vitality, and economic and social viability. Out of a loss of everything the celebrations of Días de muertos entail could come the eventual disintegration of a sense of community between the dead and the living, a loss of communal identification and cohesion, and increased vulnerability to the manipulation of outsiders who have sound political and economic reasons to want to shift loyalty from the local to the national level—not for the sake of the majority of the nationals but to augment class privilege. A disparagement of the entire complex tradition could contribute to the homogenization of Mexico and to its assimilation to the constantly homogenizing culture of the self-named First World. Numerous jokes about Mexico becoming a fifty-first state of the United States reveal anxiety about the latter's magnetism. What Néstor García Canclini has written about the efforts of a centralizing national government also fits the efforts of a country like the United States to spread its own influence to a neighboring state: "Para lograr su hegemonía sobre los grupos étnicos, la dominación externa ha buscado quebrar su unidad y cohesión, deshacer el sentido que los objetos y las prácticas tienen para cada comunidad" (García Canclini 109) [To achieve hegemony over ethnic groups, external domination has sought to break their unity and cohesion, to undo the sense that objects and practices have for each community]. He goes on:

En países multiétnicos la construcción de la hegemonía, además de basarse en la división en clases, se asienta en el manejo de la fragmentación cultural y en la producción de otras divisiones: entre lo económico y lo simbólico, entre la producción, la circulación y el consumo, y entre los individuos y su marco comunitario inmediato. (García Canclini 112)

In multiethnic countries the construction of hegemony, besides being based on the division of classes, depends on the management of cultural fragmentation and the production of other divisions: between the economic and the symbolic; among production, circulation, and consumption; and between individuals and their immediate communitarian framework.

Considering the important role of Días de muertos in the cultivation of communal and national identity, to have it weakened or, in an extreme case, replaced or displaced by Hallowe'en seems as serious as many Mexican officials, educators, and other members of the intelligentsia fear. Joaquín Herrera wrote in *Excélsior* on November 3, 1991, that foreign elements are being introduced to Mixquic's celebration of Días de muertos by the "invasion" of "grupos de curiosidad" (curiosity groups) that influence the decoration of graves and inspire "el comercio desquiciado" (deranged—literally, unhinged—commerce).

Hallowe'en is, or at least is seen as, one among many instruments used by U.S. cultural imperialism, however, this impulse is reified and characterized to disengage Mexicans from all that is Mexican and engage them with all that is "American"—that is, from the United States. At whatever level the U.S. appeal is established, it will likely lead to the paradoxical Mexican defense of foreign interests, even to the detriment of its own. Think of the "austerity" measures that have been imposed under pressure from the International Monetary Fund and the World Bank, which have led during the 1980s and 1990s to the downfall of the lower middle class—which was just starting to rise at the beginning of the 1980s. These measures have led to illness and death among the most vulnerable and to poverty, hunger, suffering, and anxiety among their caretakers and companions. But these same measures have ensured advantages for the upper middle and upper classes and have been favorable to outside investors.

In light of the implementation of the North American Free Trade Agreement following a long history of trade agreements between the United States and Mexico, few of which have been more favorable to the latter than to the former, the Mexican bourgeoisie considers the celebration of Hallowe'en to mean basically two things. One is "Americanization," which is desirable to those who work for or aspire to work for transnational companies. For a second group among the more purely Mexican bourgeoisie, Hallowe'en is something their children are taught to celebrate in school, and the children teach their parents what they have been taught and draw them into the event by requiring costumes and companionship for treat seeking.[13] In this context Hallowe'en is seen entirely as a *fiesta infantil*, the kind

---

[13] A news article by Roberto Garduño Espinosa in *La Jornada* on November 1, 1993, describes a woman driving a new Suburban in Lomas de Echegaray, a well-to-do suburb of Mexico City, watching her children trick-or-treat dressed as Frankenstein, a witch, and Freddy Krugger. She shouted to the reporter, "I brought the costumes from New York; this is easier than setting up an ofrenda."

of party schools and families promote for the stimulation, education, and pleasure of the students.

Two popular expressions in Mexico accuse those to whom they are applied of loving the foreign more than the national. *Malinchismo** is derived from the name of Malintzin or Malinche, the sometime-concubine of Hernán Cortés who bore him a son and worked as his interpreter, thus helping him in his conquest of the Aztec Empire. Malinchismo means a preference for what is foreign, with a connotation of betrayal. *Agringamiento* might be translated as gringoization, and it suggests that one is losing one's "Mexicanness" and gaining instead an "Americanness," becoming like people from the United States. This is obviously a xenophobic notion based on stereotype and generalization.

The adults in this second group of Hallowe'en celebrants would probably bristle if they were accused of malinchismo or agringamiento, but a quietly political element is present in their celebration that does have to do with group identity. It goes something like this: We are the kind of people who (check all that apply):

- love tenderly and shower attention on our children
- are cosmopolitan enough to know about this foreign festivity
- celebrate Hallowe'en rather than Días de muertos because we are
  - not Christian but secular or Jewish
  - not "indios"
  - not Pagans
  - cosmopolitan
  - not superstitious

Members of this group may enjoy pan de muerto* during that time and, in harmony with all of the items in the list that relate to children, may give their children calaveras. They rarely choose the least expensive, most traditional, most elaborate sugar ones but rather those made of chocolate, often the nameless ones from Sanborns. They do not usually bother to give calaveras with the children's names on them.

For both of these privileged groups, Hallowe'en is mainly an event of togetherness between parents and children, an occasion on which the adults have an excuse to indulge their offspring and to enjoy the children's fun. To some extent and in some subcommunities, the event may have a pedagogical dimension. Except for the educational agenda, it hardly differs from the U.S. practice of Hallowe'en as a children's holiday.

A New Cultural Syncretism

I've been told to stick to what's Mexican, yet I enjoy
trying my hand at different things. . . . [In 1979] I added
skulls in pumpkins to my range. Pumpkins are a feature of
Halloween in North America, but I'll make them if I can sell
them, and witches as well! . . .
In truth . . . skulls sell best—they belong to us, to Mexico!
—Rivas Contreras (Quoted in Carmichael and Sayer 115)

In the myriad newspaper articles that appear around Días de muertos,*
concern is often expressed about the preservation of this holiday, which
many think is threatened by the incursion of Hallowe'en. Some articles
deplore the malinchismo* of preferring Hallowe'en parties to the elaborate
celebration of Días de muertos,* considering such a preference a form of
cultural betrayal. One of Carmichael and Sayer's informants, Arsacio Vanegas Arroyo, grandson of the partner of José Guadalupe Posada,* eloquently expressed this point of view. (Note that in colloquial Mexican
speech, both *North American* and *American* are adjectives that refer to the
United States, excluding Canada and Mexico).

We are being infiltrated by North American values: our roots are being
attacked by business interests, and our heritage is being undermined by
advertising and television. American-style stores, such as Woolworth
and Sanborns, are promoting Halloween in an effort to increase sales,
and many Mexicans are being seduced. This process starts with the
well-off, who prefer North American and European culture to their
own. But the effect spreads.
   If we don't take care of our traditions, they will die. Sadly, our government is not doing enough to preserve them. Sometimes you will see
"official" *ofrendas** in schools and government buildings, but these
often include witches and goblins! Mexican festivities and Halloween
are being muddled up together in a totally incoherent way. . . . We will
become like the people of Costa Rica, who live and think like North
Americans! In parts of northern Mexico this is already happening.
(Quoted in Carmichael and Sayer 130)

   Don Arsacio and those who share his concern are only rarely justified in
their fear and accusations. Traditions that are not cared for do disappear,
but can they be preserved by acts of will or legislation? Traditions remain

strong as long as they are relevant in their community. The families and individuals who celebrate the American holiday have not celebrated Días de muertos for at least one full generation. It is no longer their holiday, not having been observed, much less passed on, by their parents or even their grandparents. This is the case in my family of origin and in those of people who fit into the categories listed in the previous section: the Jews and other non-Catholics, the immigrants and their descendants, inter alia. In none of these cases has the Mexican commemoration of the dead been displaced by Hallowe'en. Unlike Días de muertos, which requires the commitment of great devotion and attention, knowledge, financial resources, time, and even identity, Hallowe'en is not perceived as a value-laden, semiotically rich, or culturally charged tradition but rather as a harmless, superficial custom that offers an excuse for costumes, parties, and the indulging of children.

A different objection is raised by INAH* archaeologist and investigator Eduardo Merlo Juárez. In addition to resenting the commercial interests of Hallowe'en, he speaks of "an abundance of objects which refer to death with a grotesque vision, entirely different from the Indians' idea of it" (quoted in Hernández, untitled). This begins to raise a philosophical concern similar to those of María Antonieta Sánchez de Escamilla and Arsacio Vanegas Arroyo. A number of the sources for this chapter see a profoundly important difference in the way death is perceived in the United States and in Mexico, as reflected in Hallowe'en and in Días de muertos. Whereas the former presents a vision of ghouls, monsters, devils, "spooky" skeletons, cute ghosts, and goblins, the latter presents a vision of the dead as simply dead and of skeletons as fairly realistic or humorous or both. An ethical dimension could arise from these representations of the dead and from the kind of behavior that dressing as ugly spooks and devils might inspire. Mexico's dailies reproduce news from the U.S. press about Hallowe'en vandalism, and some people think a young person who lacks well-established social norms could, if protected and perhaps incited by a costume and by models who got their name in the paper or their story on screen, slip into antisocial behavior.

Some articles by Mexican journalists focus on the importance of teaching children about their national traditions so they may continue them in the future. A number report activities designed to do just that in a public forum. I have mentioned, for example, the workshop on the construction of ofrendas* held by the Taller de Artes Plásticas Rufino Tamayo and the public displays of ofrendas typically sponsored by public schools (see Figure 3.1 and Plate 12). The displays can be of original, earnest ofrendas by the students and their teachers; they can be the result of ethnographic research through which the students learn to duplicate the altars typical of a certain community, as in the Coordinación de Educación Tecnológica Industrial High School (CETIS) exhibition (see Plate 15); or they can be original, carnivalesque ofrendas that exhibit the students' aesthetic and technical competence, as in La Esmeralda's in La Alameda Park (see Figure 1.23 and Plate 16).

Every one of these approaches seems pedagogically sound. The young people are taught about the traditions of the fiesta* and in most cases about some version of its history, sometimes through writing reports and often through oral histories or interviews. They are directly involved in the setting and sometimes in the design of the offerings, as well as in the creation of some of the objects, such as cut tissue paper and colored or sculpted calaveras.* They are engaged both intellectually and physically, which perhaps effectively encourages the students to continue the commemoration after graduation. For that to occur, however, I think it would have to be encouraged socially and communally as well. The rural and small-town immigrants to Mexico City generally lose their traditions within one or two generations, attesting to the importance of social support for practices that have as one end the revitalization of communal bonds (without forgetting that such communities include the dead in their immediate circle).

Those who attend public schools are normally instructed in the ways in which Mexicans honor the dead. Outside of school, Hallowe'en is available to a greater or lesser degree, depending on the neighborhood in which the child lives. If the pupil attends private school, as "Metropoligrama," the epigraph for the previous section, laments, her or his knowledge of Días de muertos is up to the parents and society at large.

One of the most frequently voiced concerns of cultural conservatives and conservationists is that of the contamination of Días de muertos by Hallowe'en. Another is that of the seduction of people away from the former toward the latter. The local press around this time rarely publishes hopeful or realistic articles that recognize the power and relevance of an ancient tradition in its home community. Ery Cámara, assistant director of museography at Mexico City's Museo de Artes Populares, said in an interview with Roberto Garduño Espinosa for the Mexico City daily *La Jornada,*

La tradición de la noche de muertos sigue viva, pero se va a ir transformando; a lo mejor en algunos años incorpora elementos del llamado *Halloween,* a lo mejor, como sucede con las bandas, incorpora elementos del rock. Lo que ocurre en Neza[14] con esa incorporación de elementos no será lo mismo que sucede con las prácticas de Santa Fe, Yucatán o Chiapas. (Garduño Espinosa, "Viva la tradición")

The tradition of the night of the dead is still alive, but it will be transformed; perhaps in a few years it will incorporate elements of so-called *Hallowe'en;* perhaps, as occurs with bands, it will incorporate elements of rock. What happens in Neza with this incorporation of elements will not be the same as occurs with the practices in Santa Fe, Yucatán, or Chiapas.

Cámara, like many good intellectuals, is already behind the times. He is right in saying that the tradition is alive and well. His verb tense is off regarding its predicted transformation. As Figures 6.2–6.4, 8.5, and Plates 14, 20, and 21, as well as the examples I have cited show, elements of Hallowe'en have already been incorporated in the ofrendas for the dead in different parts of the country. Such incorporation bespeaks the syncretism that is not only typical but definitive of popular culture. The student of this syncretism is less apt to judge it as a distortion or contamination than is the anthropologist or cultural conservative, whose professional, political, or

---

[14] "Neza," short for Ciudad Nezahualcóyotl, began as an enormous slum in Mexico City. It has developed into a city within the city.

sentimental interest in a "pure" and "authentic" fiesta influences the way she or he thinks about syncretism.[15]

Víctor Fosado Vázquez, a jeweler and gallery owner in Cancún, spoke to Carmichael and Sayer regarding children's exposure to Hallowe'en. His perspective is that of a collector and canny observer of popular culture: "Mexican children seem able, as our ancestors were in the wake of Conquest, to reconcile apparently conflicting notions. They retain the Mexican view of death, yet adopt the most attractive features of Halloween. They may enjoy dressing up as death—death in this case being cheerful, not spooky—yet also buy skulls and skeletons of sugar" (quoted in Carmichael

---

[15] María Estela Palacio Albor, a writer for *El Heraldo,* published this sentimental, if heartfelt, text on October 31, 1993:

Cómo cambiar la sonrisa hueca de la calabaza por la carcajada sarcástica y provocativa de la calavera; cómo olvidar los rituales de nuestra gente que se reúne en estos festejos para recordar, celebrar y esperar.

Cómo enterrar el repique de las campanas anunciando el toque de ánimas en Mixquic, Tonantzintla, Pátzcuaro y Xochimilco, en donde según las creencias, salen los muertos a visitar a los familiares. . . . Cómo olvidar los rezos, los cánticos y alabanzas para los seres queridos, y algunos padrenuestros adicionales por los difuntos olvidados.

Y el compartir la ofrenda con los vecinos, conocidos y hasta desconocidos, siempre en nombre de los que se han ido, pero siguen presentes en nuestra vida como si nunca se hubieran marchado.

De esta forma, la tradición de Día de muertos que encierra la dualidad de la existencia, vive cada año en la necesidad de compartir el pan y el vino; en la comunión de la luz y la sombra, la risa y el llanto . . . la vida y la muerte.

[How to trade the hollow grin of the pumpkin for the sarcastic and provocative laugh of the calavera; how to forget the rituals of our people who come together in these festivities to remember, celebrate, hope, and wait.

How to bury the peal of the bells announcing the call of the souls in Mixquic, Tonantzintla, Pátzcuaro, and Xochimilco, where, according to the beliefs, the dead come out to visit their relatives. . . . How to forget the prayers, the chants, and the praises for the beloved and a few additional "our fathers" for the forgotten dead.

And the sharing of the offering with neighbors, familiar and even unfamiliar, always in the name of those who have gone but who continue to be present in our life as if they had never left.

In this way, the tradition of the Day of the Dead that encloses the duality of existence lives each year in the need to share bread and wine, in the communion of light and shadow, laughter and weeping . . . life and death.]

and Sayer 132). I would extend this acute observation beyond Mexico's children to encompass all creators of popular culture.

The connection Fosado Vázquez makes between contemporary and ancient Mexicans is also perspicacious. Many Indigenous traditions were forced underground by the Spanish conquerors and missionaries, beginning in the sixteenth century. Some practices were able to survive by being observed in the privacy of domestic space, others by being disguised in or blended with Catholic ones—resulting in what I have referred to as transgressive syncretism. It is transgressive because it results not in the substitution and abandonment but in the preservation of the local tradition in the face of pressure to conform to the ways of the conquerors.

I will not suggest that the incorporation of elements of Hallowe'en into Días de muertos participates in that kind of transgression. It may, however, point to the other side of the coin of what many Mexicans consider U.S. cultural imperialism. Instead of Hallowe'en taking the place of Días de muertos, it is being dismembered, some bits discarded, others refashioned to fit the traditional celebration.[16] In this detail, which, small as it seems, is important enough to inspire the intellectual labor of many Mexican thinkers, one of the contemporary conqueror's instruments is pacified and turned into a ploughshare to till the soil in which Días de muertos is deeply rooted.

[16] See my readings of the calaveras "Merienda exquisita" and "Conquista del Jalogüín" in Chapter 9 for two of several examples I have seen in which Hallowe'en icons are incorporated into calaveras but are given a semiotically inferior position.

7

Contemporary Attitudes Toward Death

Death's Intimates

Lo que sí es cierto es que cuando
nace una persona,
desde ese momento también lo
acompaña la muerte.
—Candelario Rivera

What is true is that when a person
is born, from that moment
death also accompanies one.

II
Si en todas partes estás,
en el agua, en la tierra,
en el aire que me encierra
y en el incendio voraz;
y si a todas partes vas

conmigo en el pensamiento,
en el soplo de mi aliento
y en mi sangre confundida,
¿no serás, Muerte, en mi vida,
agua, fuego, polvo y viento?
—Xavier Villaurrutia

II
If you are everywhere:
in water and earth,
in the air that holds me,
and in the voracious blaze;
and if you go every place

with me in my thought,
in the sigh of my breath,
and in my confused blood,
are you not, Death, in my life,
water, fire, dust, wind?

J esús Angel Ochoa Zazueta refers to several pre-Hispanic groups as "el pueblo de la muerte," the people of death. First among them he counts the Mexica*—better known in popular parlance as the Aztecs—along with the Mizquica, the Colhuacanos, the Xochimilcas, the Cholultecas, the Teotihuacanos, and so on, inhabitants of Anáhuac, Tláhuac, Tlapacoya, Tlatilco, and Cuicuilco. Ochoa Zazueta assigns these groups the epithet because they gave so much importance to serving the dead in what he calls a *culto a la muerte* (a cult to death) that participating in it seemed to identify a sacred society in the Náhuatl* culture (Ochoa Zazueta 35). Certainly the number of ceremonies in honor of the dead support him. What did those ceremonies mean to the celebrants?

Journalist Natalí has said they were a time to give thanks to Ipanemo-huani, the Giver of Life, for all his gifts. She wrote in the singular about one celebration, which she did not name.[1] Without giving her sources, she stated that it was an occasion on which the material and spiritual planes were close enough to provide an auspicious medium for positive resolutions, solving conflicts, giving advice, and receiving blessings from the visiting spirits. She said the day belonged to *las almas liberadas,* the liberated souls, and she pointed out that it was very different from the Christian notion of the Feast of All Saints. I have addressed the function of this celebration as, among other things, one of thanksgiving, and I have quoted celebrants who speak of being blessed by the disembodied guests.

Regarding Natalí's other interpretations, since Días de muertos is a time of reunion, it offers opportunities for reconciliation and for sharing wisdom and experiences. These notions about the significance and practice of commemorating the dead persist today; because Mesoamerican* culture is, in significant ways, continuous,[2] contemporary meanings can be attributed to the ancients if we keep in mind that historical, lived experience always alters the way individuals construct meaning in their lives.

When we compare what we know about ancient Mesoamericans' attitudes toward death from their poetry and ritual traditions with contemporary Mexicans' attitudes toward death, we find some significant similarities

---

[1] In "Pre-Hispanic and Peninsular Traces in Días de muertos'" I named several commemorations for the dead that took place at different times of the year. Natalí may be referring to Miccaílhuitl, the fiesta of the dead, which is the name some Nahuas still use for contemporary Días de muertos.

[2] See *México profundo* in Glossary.

that indicate continuity through the centuries, particularly among the people whose culture descends from that of Mexico's early civilizations, as it does among the largely Indigenous, relatively autonomous communities. Significant differences also indicate the influences of Spanish Christian and modern Western cultures, as seen in the simpler cosmology and the linear conception of time in the eschatology they brought.

My first example contrasts feelings about the difficulty of life and the ease of death. In a 1991 interview, José Camacho of Cocula, Jalisco, told me, "No se debe temer a la muerte, al contrario, es la vida a la que se ha de temer" [One should not fear death; on the contrary, life is what one ought to fear]. This belief is commonplace in Mexico. A Mexican proverb says, "¿Por qué he de temer a la muerte si la vida me ha curado de espantos?" [Why should I fear death when life has cured me of frights?] Both Inga Clendinnen and Paul Westheim (*La Calavera*) have analyzed the god Tezcatlipoca (Smoking Mirror or Mirror's Smoke), whose abitrariness matches Don José Camacho's expressed anxiety about life.

Tezcatlipoca is an invisible, omnipresent god known as Nécoc Yáotl (the Sower of Discord), between individuals and between cities or empires. Sahagún has written, "Tenían que cuando andaba en la tierra movía guerras, enemistades y discordias, de donde resultaban muchas fatigas y desasosiegos" (Sahagún Book 1, chapter 3, §1 44) [They held that when (Tezcatlipoca) walked the earth he caused wars, enmities, and discords from which resulted many fatigues and disturbances]. He has total dominion over human fate, and he arbitrarily bestows health and illness, prosperity and poverty, honor and shame, bounty and natural disaster, and every kind of inconvenient change. As Sahagún reports, "El solo daba las prosperidades y riquezas, y que él solo las quitaba cuando se le antojaba" (Sahagún Book 1, chapter 3, §3, 44) [He alone gave prosperities and wealth, and he alone took them away when he felt like it].

Westheim accurately describes this god as "la incertidumbre que envuelve al mañana, la constante amenaza de lo que puede acontecer" (the uncertainty that envelops the future, the constant threat of what could happen), "la pesadilla deificada" (the nightmare deified), and "esa angustia vital . . . que confiere a la existencia del hombre precortesiano, también a su creación artística, el cariz trágico, la tensión y la terrífica hondura" (Westheim, *La calavera*, 17f, 19) [that anxiety of life who confers on the existence of precortesian man, as well as to his artistic creation, a tragic look, tension, and terrific depth]. What is similar to that theology in many contemporary Mexicans' view is what we call *filosofía*, a philosophical acceptance of the ills in life, frequently expressed with a shrug and a sigh of "así lo quiso Dios" [it was God's will].

We find another example of the continuity of ancient and contemporary attitudes toward life and death in Westheim's reference to the Mexican poet Villaurrutia's class and ethnic distinction.

Xavier Villaurrutia, cuya poesía gira en torno a la muerte, escribió alguna vez: "Aquí se tiene una gran facilidad para morir, que es más fuerte en su atracción conforme mayor cantidad de sangre india tenemos en las venas. Mientras más criollo se es, mayor temor tenemos por la muerte, puesto que eso es lo que se nos enseña." La carga psíquica que da un tinte trágico a la existencia del hombre mexicano, hoy como hace 2 y 3 mil años, no es el temor por la muerte, sino la angustia vital, la fatalidad de la vida, la conciencia de estar expuesto, y con insuficientes medios de defensa, a una existencia llena de peligros, llena de esencias demoníacas. (Westheim, *La calavera*, 8f)

Xavier Villaurrutia, whose poetry revolves around death, once wrote: "Here [in Mexico] one has a great facility to die, which is stronger in its attraction according to the quantity of Indian blood in our veins. The more criollo* we are, the more we fear death because that is what we are taught." The psychic charge that gives a tragic tint to the life of the Mexican, today as two and three thousand years ago, is not the fear of death but rather the angst of life, the fatality of life, the consciousness of being exposed with insufficient defenses to an existence full of dangers, full of diabolical essences.

In the words of Zapotec anthropologist Gabriel López Chiñas, whose book was published in 1969, for the Zapotecas of Oaxaca "la vida es trabajo, la muerte es descanso primordial" [life is travail; death is primordial rest] (López Chiñas 6). He describes the old women of the Isthmus of Tehuantepec seeing a funeral procession and saying aloud: "Dichoso tu día. Te vas con Dios, que ha puesto fin a tus trabajos. Ya vas a descansar. Mañana o pasado te seguiremos" (López Chiñas 12f) [Happy day for you. You're going to God who has put an end to your travails. You will rest now. Tomorrow or the day after we shall follow you].

At the funerals of Zapotec children, "todo rastro de dolor desaparece" [every trace of sorrow vanishes] because people expect the child's spirit to go directly to God in heaven with no time in purgatory (López Chiñas 16).

What is considered best about dying so young is that the child has escaped most of the suffering of life. The body is laid on the brightly colored satin (called *el cielo*, [heaven or sky]) of the coffin, referred to as *la cuna* (the cradle) (López Chiñas 13).[3] López Chiñas said that the young people who knew the child were dancing nearby to popular music throughout the ceremonies (López Chiñas 16).

Some verses written on the tomb of a child who died in 1862 echo not only the belief that life promised her sorrow but that, not having lived long enough to sin, she would face no barrier to eternity in heaven:

La tierra tocó apenas con su planta,	She barely touched the earth with
Y viendo las espinas de este suelo	her sole,
Cual cándida paloma se levanta	And seeing the thorns of this soil,
para unirse al creador allá en el cielo.	Like an innocent dove she rises
Tumba de la niña Dolores	To be united to the creator in heaven.
Argüelles y Anaya (1860–1862)	Tomb of the child Dolores
(Quoted by Francisco	Argüelles y Anaya (1860–1862)
Suárez Farías)	

The farewells to the adult dead betray great sorrow among the survivors, but it is important to note the difference between sadness at the death of a loved one and a certain eagerness over the prospect of one's own death. López Chiñas offers these quotations of mourners:

"Adiós, mi pálida azucena, el lucero más grande que brilla dentro de mi casa", despide la madre al hijo amado.—"¿Quién velará mi sueño, con quién hablaré cuando oscurezca la tierra y cuando la noche acabe?" Clama la viuda acongojada.— "¿Dónde iré para encontrate, polvo de oro fino, mi paloma blanca?", dice la entrañable hermana. (López Chiñas 19)	"Goodby, my pale lily, the greatest star that shines inside my house," the mother bids farewell to her beloved son. "Who will watch my sleep, with whom will I talk when the earth darkens and when night ends?" cries the afflicted widow. "Where shall I go to find you, dust of fine gold, my white dove?" says the loving sister.

---

[3] In the case of adults, the coffin is still called *cuna*, but the satin lining is black rather than brightly colored (López Chiñas 16).

The author adds, "Se desea su presencia viva, da dolor su ausencia" (López Chiñas 22) [Their living presence is desired, their absence brings sorrow]. Many Mexicans—like, I would guess, other members of the developing world who have limited access to the cultural and economic resources of their countries—would agree with Gautama the Buddha that life is suffering. Unfamiliar with the tenets and practices of Buddhism, however, and immersed in a worldview of their own, they have distilled culturally fitting philosophies that, among other beliefs, include the sense that one's lack of control over life's circumstances brings sorrow and anxiety that eventually and happily dissolve in death. All life long, death is an intimate and constant companion that promises liberation from suffering. As museologist Ery Cámara of the Museo de Culturas Populares has said:

La muerte es una compañera ineludible de la vida, por eso los mexicanos le dan un carácter más convivencial. Esto sólo puede darse en una civilización cuyo origen pudo haber sido no racional como a la manera occidental, sino en una donde la línea que demarca lo natural y lo sobrenatural no es tan fija ni tan nítida como lo ha hecho la ciencia. (Quoted in Garduño Espinosa, "Ricos y pobres")

Death is an unavoidable companion of life; that's why Mexicans give it a more convivial character. This can only occur in a civilization whose origin was not rational in the Western manner but in which the line that divides the natural and the supernatural is neither as fixed nor as clear as science has made it.

The Zapotecas believe that "cada individuo trae fatalmente su propia muerte" (López Chiñas 6f) [each individual fatally carries her or his own death].[4]

---

[4] Although I do not suggest that Carlos Fuentes holds a similar view, his beautiful and difficult novel *Una familia lejana* [*Distant Relations*] can be understood through a pre-Hispanic theology. In it he deploys, among many others, the wonderful idea that one is born with one's death, that to be born is to die, and another pre-Christian Mexican conceit: death is fertile and brings forth new life.

Philippe Ariès gives Christian sources for a similar philosophy: "Christianity adopted the traditional ideas of ordinary people and Stoic philosophers about the gradual deterioration of the human body from the moment of birth. The statement of Manlius' 'When we are born, we start to die, and the end begins at the beginning' is a commonplace that we find in Saint Bernard and Pierre de Bérulle as well as in Montaigne" (Ariès 95).

For the Zapotecas and many of their compatriots, these beliefs about and attitudes toward death are naturalized by their culture such that they have no self-consciousness or skepticism about them. For city dwellers who live in contact with diverse worldviews, such beliefs and attitudes may also feel completely natural and right, but because they are exposed to groups or individuals who do not share and may challenge them, their beliefs become a resource for the construction of identity. They know themselves to be different from the most modern, most Western residents, tourists, or travelers they encounter in person, in the press, on the radio, in the movies, or in their own travels. And the differences are a source of pride and identification.

"Lo que nos distingue como mexicanos es nuestro trato con la muerte" [What distinguishes us as Mexicans is our relationship with death], wrote Elena Poniatowska, novelist, journalist, intellectual. In her article "El gran Panteón de Dolores," she tells an anecdote that she follows with statements that reveal her pride in the traditions that distinguish us as intimate with death:

Alberto Beltrán le enseñó a un niño una calaverita de azúcar y le preguntó:—¿Qué es eso?

Sin más el niño respondió:—Es lo que todos traemos dentro.

Sí, la muerte la traemos dentro. Lo dicen nuestros ritos funerarios, lo dicen nuestros huesos de azúcar y cartón, lo dicen nuestras costumbres. . . .

En México, cada año nos repetimos: "Mira lo que eres, mira lo que tienes dentro, mira que no eres inmortal, mira que si lo fueras, no cabríamos y le quitaríamos a la tierra su aire, su energía y su espacio y la especie desaparecería del planeta. Mira que debes morirte. Sin tu muerte no puede haber esperanza, ni porvenir. Mira, mírate bien. Cada ser que nace es la mañana del mundo."

Alberto Beltrán showed a child a calaverita de azúcar* and asked him, "What is this?"

With no hesitation the boy replied, "It's what we all have inside."

Yes, we carry death inside. Our funerary rites, our sugar and papier mâché bones, our customs all proclaim it.

In Mexico, every year we repeat to ourselves and to each other, "Look at what you are, look at what you have inside, look, you're not immortal; look, if you were we wouldn't fit, and we'd rob the earth of its air, its energy, and its space, and the species would disappear from the planet. Look, really look at yourself. Each being that is born is the morning of the world."

¡Qué bueno que seamos	How great that we're Mexican
mexicanos y que José Guadalupe	and that José Guadalupe Posada*
Posada* nos haya hecho una	made us an X ray as a gift for life!
radiografía de regalo para toda la	Thanks to him we have an innate
vida! Gracias a él tenemos una	wisdom before death, we live
sabiduría innata frente a la muerte,	with her.
convivimos con ella. (Poniatowska)	

In an art gallery in Oaxaca, Oaxaca, I saw an exhibit of ofrendas* and works of art on the theme of Días de muertos.* The smallest work drew my attention (see Figure 7.1). Laura A. Rojas H. depicted an identity document about the size of a Mexican passport, framed in an unusually large white field. Instead of a photograph of the bearer of the document, there is the bust of a skeleton in a black oval imitative of the format for such documents. It is stamped with the Mexican national seal. The work is entitled "La identificación." It is a testimony to how close Rojas feels to death or to her own skeleton or to Días de muertos, for which skeletons are an icon, or perhaps to how close she considers death, their skeleton, or Días de muertos to be to Mexican citizens. She may also be commenting on what she sees as the fatal bureaucracy of the state. Since the artist exhibits and presumably lives in Oaxaca, she may be familiar with the Zapotec belief that each individual fatally carries her or his own death within, and she surely knows the Christian advice that flows from the former belief: that one is to contemplate one's end every day, remembering that the same death will take the most humble and the greatest, in a shack or in a mansion (López Chiñas 6f).[5] The intimacy between death and life is similar in Poniatowska's article, in "La identificación," and in the Zapotecas' account of death.

The self-identification of many Mexican philosophers, be they of the academy or the marketplace, as intimates of death must be taken seriously, although it would be easy to deconstruct the intellectual labor that goes into it. If cultural sensitivity leads us to respect the way people identify themselves, it is because we recognize that self-identification is more reliable than another's definition of whomever is being described. The myriad

---

[5] A beautiful poem that has been memorized by many generations, including my own college students, was written by Spanish Jorge Manrique in the fifteenth century. It is given in Appendix B.

7.1 *"La identificación" by Laura A. Rojas H. Oaxaca, Oaxaca.*

nicknames Mexicans have for death[6] serve less to identify, qualify, and describe death itself than to identify those who apply them as people who feel they deserve to be considered close and familiar enough to death to invent and use terms of endearment for it.

---

[6] These nicknames include Huesuda (Bony), Pelona (Baldy), Parca (Stingy), Flaca and Tilica (Skinny), Intrusa (Intruder), Calaca (Skull).

Death-Life Masks, Duality

Lloro, por más que la razón me   I weep, though reason repeats to me
advierta   that a cadaver is not a demolished
que un cadáver no es trono   throne,
demolido,   nor a broken altar, but a deserted
ni roto altar, sino prisión desierta.   prison.
—Salvador Díaz Mirón (epitafio)[7]

Considering the place of honor the skull holds in the Mexican imaginary, Días de muertos* can be seen as the axial element in a net of intertexts that include, among others, pre-Hispanic tzompantli,* death-life
masks, sculptures, paintings, and bas-reliefs of skulls; images both literary
and plastic of pre-Hispanic deities; Christian images of death as a "grim
reaper," of skulls as mementi mori;* contemporary calaveras,* and others.
Insofar as some sectors of the population live with death as consciously and
constantly as they live with the body, this fiesta* distills the Janus-faced
unity of life and death. The set of works that represents that unity most literally is that of the life-death masks, the icon of life's vulnerability to death,
if I may be forgiven the pun. They are the logic of the concrete sense some
Mexicans have that the living bear our own death all life long. It takes virtually no effort to make the imaginative connection between that feeling,
knowledge, or belief and the life-death mask, which is more than a dance
mask, more than an artist's abstract or poetic expression. I will analyze
their ancient and contemporary presence in view of how they illustrate a
sense of perspective that underlies some of the humor seen during Días de
muertos and all year round in Mexico.

Pre-Hispanic life-death masks are an eloquent sign of the intimacy
between the two that our Indigenous forebears perceived. One half of the
face is skeletal, the other half, fleshed. Whether the skeletal half is on the left
or on the right seems to have no significance. Although examples exist of
both animal and human masks, I am acquainted with more instances of the
latter; the former that I have seen are one or two of human faces with some
animal characteristics or vice versa. Contemporary mask makers continue to

---

[7] He is buried in Mexico City's Panteón Dolores in La Rotonda de Hombre Ilustres, the
Rotunda of Illustrious Men, where I read his epitaph.

7.2 Life-death mask. Museum of Anthropology, México, D.F.
(Permission given by INAH)

produce their own versions of life-death masks in different parts of Mexico.[8] The masks represent the indissoluble union of death and life and are worn by a living dancer, so their meaning is reinforced with some poignancy.[9]

---

[8] Other duality masks are also made for various dances: male-female, animal-human, good-evil. See Cordry, *Mexican Masks.*

[9] A gruesome representation of the life-death union was seen in Tenochtitlan, the capital of the Aztec empire, before the conquest in the fiesta Tlacaxipeualiztli (the Flaying of Men). To honor the god Xipe Tótec (the Flayed One), a fertility warrior god, sacrificial victims were flayed. In some cases their captor and in other cases a priest of the god wore the skin for as long as a month (twenty days) until it rotted and fell off on its own. The practice, like other human sacrifices, was related to agricultural fertility. The flayed skin represented the verdant "skin" of plants that cover the earth. See Sahagún Book 2, chapter 2.

The life-death duality is characteristic of agricultural metaphysics in which the cycle of the plant serves as the model for the human cycle: The buried seed is transformed into new roots that rise above the ground, flower, and bear more seed, which dies in turn. Patrick Johansson's poetic words recall the Mexica myth of origin:[10]

Para los pueblos precolombinos la vida se gesta dentro de la muerte así como el sol brota de las entrañas de la tierra. . . . La muerte vive en el hombre como la raíz en la flor. Como lo confirman los mitos cosmogónicos, la muerte es matriz de la existencia: Quetzalcóatl baja a . . . Mictlan* para crear al hombre. (Johansson)	For pre-Columbian people, life is gestated in death just as the sun sprouts from the earth's entrails. . . . Death lives in man as the root in the flower. As the cosmogonic myths confirm, death is the womb of existence: Quetzalcóatl descends into . . . Mictlan* to create humankind.

Another aesthetic juxtaposition of life and death can be seen in Náhuatl* poetry from the fifteenth—and perhaps the previous two—through the seventeenth centuries. In this case the juxtaposition feels less like a statement of fact than it does in the unsentimental masks. The tragic ambiance that characterizes the poetry betrays an obsession with death and an intense nostalgia for life, as if the poems were the work of individuals on the brink of dying.[11] From birth, Mexica boys were taught that it was their lot to die in battle or, if they should be captured in war, on the sacrificial stone. The first words uttered by the midwife informed them of what lay ahead: the suffering of a life in which cold and heat, hunger and fatigue afflict the body, and the death the baby could expect once he reached maturity. In spite of this, the literature communicates little relief at the prospect of ending the travails of life, and we should remember that although it was written by warriors whose lives were frequently and repeatedly in danger, Náhuatl poetry is the product of members of the ruling class for whom life was relatively enjoyable. To some extent, the writers' tragic feelings regarding the life-and-death duality and the casual feelings of the mask makers may be attributable to their class difference.

---

[10] Appendix B contains the whole myth.
[11] See Appendix D and Father Garibay's superb *Poesía náhuatl*.

These literary and plastic works of art show that Mexico's Native people seem never to have avoided, but rather insisted on, thinking about death, and it is easy to imagine them formulating lessons for their children similar to those contemporary kindergarten director and teacher María Antonieta Sánchez de Escamilla revealed to Carmichael and Sayer in an interview.

> I tell my pupils to live each day as if it were their last. . . . I don't want children to fear death; I want them to respect life. . . . It's good for children to confront the idea of death, and . . . of their own mortality. Sometimes a child feels squeamish about death . . . skulls and skeletons. When this happens, I tell my pupils to touch themselves. "Why are you afraid?" I ask, "when each of you owns a skull and skeleton. We all carry death within us." They feel themselves, and they say: "Yes it's true, we too are made of bones." (Carmichael and Sayer 119)

She continues the teachings of her distant ancestors: treasure life; be mindful that you will die; know that you are skeletal as well as fleshed, dead as well as living.

Often, when Mexicans speak about our philosophy of death and life, it is with some humor, which reveals the sense of perspective that is at its core. And when we discuss our sense of humor about death, we frequently mention our respect for it and often our respect for life, as Sánchez de Escamilla does. I propose that Mexicans' humor surrounding the subject, taboo in much of the industrialized world, reveals a combination of these ostensibly opposite stances of mockery and respect. The combination is as paradoxical to the outsider and as commonplace to the Mexican as are the dualistic death-life masks. It indicates a virtually constant recollection of the death of oneself and of everybody one loves, along with a bittersweet resignation toward its imminence.[12] For the poor, the sweetness comes from the sense that life is hard, that its changes are often bitter, that the repose of death will be a relief. For everyone, the sweetness may come simply from a sense of closure or fulfillment that life has been accomplished to its predetermined end.

---

[12] Read as illustrations of this point "En ningún tiempo, en ningún tiempo cesará" (At No Time, in No Era), "El árbol florido" (The Flowering Tree), "El enigma de vivir" (The Enigma of Living), and "Angustia del poeta" (Poet's Grief) in Appendix D.

Sorrow or regret at the prospect of dying—tempered by a profound acceptance and virtually unflagging awareness that, distant as it may be, death will arrive—indicates an attitude similar to the one espoused by Albert Camus, who believed existential angst comes from the desire to live being frustrated by the consciousness of certain death.[13] Instead of this awareness debouching in angst, as for the French Camus, for the contemporary Mexican it debouches in humor.

All our great dreams and desires, plans, prospects, and projects are ridiculous, etymologically speaking, worthy of at least a little laughter because they will only be held, lived, and fulfilled as long as death permits us to live—which, at least according to those who are in good health and perhaps those who enjoy a stable economic status, is not long enough. Our lack of control wrests the illusion of self-determination from us and shows that our will to be is meaningless in the face of inexorable, if relatively distant, death. The self-importance and stature that our mental, emotional, spiritual, and physical activities afford us are put into perspective as illusion by the fact that they will be cut short by death. The remembrance of democratizing death does not allow us to take very seriously the class differences, "the oppressor's wrong, the proud man's contumely . . . the law's delay, the insolence of office and the spurns that patient merit of the unworthy takes" (*Hamlet* Act III, Scene 1, 69–74) because, as an equalizer, death renders all this relatively trivial, ludicrous. The Mexican advice, as the merry calaveras teach us and as the centenarian Náhuatl poems suggest, is to keep a sense of humor or perspective and to enjoy the flowers and songs, the poetry of life while we can.

Anita Brenner, the German-Mexican author of *Idols Behind Altars*, overromanticizes Mexicans as artists, but she nicely illustrates the mixture of humor and gravity (as well as the logic of the concrete) when she explains the Mexican obsession with death and the almost ubiquitous representation of the skull.

---

[13] Read in Appendix D "Vida fugaz" (Fleeting Life) and "Elegía por Ayocuan" (Elegy for Ayocuan), which are close to Camus; and "Canto de guerreros, 4" (Warriors' Song, 4) and "Que se abra tu corazón como las flores" (Let Your Heart Open as a Flower), which illustrate both the existentialist position and the doubt about the afterlife. "En memoria de héroe" (In Memory of Hero) reveals doubt about whether the dead visit the living.

It is no mood of futility that broods . . . over death, but rather a concern with death because of the passion for life. It is an artist's mood, his sense of limitation, and his great assertion, the purpose of making—by his own strength—life. The control is achieved in the artist's way, by giving a physical place to a physical fact, making an image of it. The skull is the symbol of the thing which like the rain, the trees, the colors, and the moving birds is caught, controlled, and made into lasting visible life. (Brenner 26)

Whereas Mesoamericans believed there would be life after death and even that one would regularly visit the living after one died, at least for some years, then as now they recognized the loss and the difference that would circumscribe the limited postcorporeal existence.[14] In any case, doubt is an ineludible element of belief, as the poems and some of the quotations I have presented show. Doubt is the shadow of what one had to be taught to believe in.

Patrick Johansson contrasts the Spanish and the Náhuatl conceptions of death. For the former, death is definitive except for Christians who will be resurrected at the end of time. For the latter, death is fertile; it results in new life. For the former, the fate of the dead is determined by how they lived, and eternal torture is an option for the unrepentant. For the latter, the fate of the dead is determined by how they died, and there is no threat of punishment in the afterlife. In *La calavera,* Paul Westheim describes the expectations of Mesoamericans:

El México antiguo no conocía el concepto del infierno. Es posible que en el subconciente de las multitudes, sobre todo de las multitudes indígenas, viva aun el oscuro recuerdo de un más allá que no estaba cerrado ni al pecador. El hecho en sí es el mismo, pero la concepción de la muerte es otra. La imagen del esqueleto con la guadaña, con el reloj de arena como símbolo de lo perecedero, es

Ancient Mexico did not know the concept of hell. It is possible that in the subconscious of the multitudes, especially of the Indigenous multitudes, there still lives the obscure memory of a beyond that was not closed even to the sinner. The fact in itself is the same, but the conception of death is different. The image of the skeleton with scythe and hourglass as a symbol of the perishable is an import

---

14 Read "Elegía" in Appendix D.

| en México importación; en los casos en que se adopta—por ejemplo en la danza macabra—se adapta en seguida, se aclimata, se mexicaniza, como lo vemos en Manilla y Posada. (Westheim 8s) | to Mexico; in the cases in which it is adopted—for example, in the *danse macabre*—it is adapted immediately, acclimatized, Mexicanized, as we see in Manilla and Posada.* |

The numerous Catholic sermons in Náhuatl that violently undermine the Mexican ontology of death bear witness to how difficult it was to impose instead the apocalyptic, finite Christian view of death. Those who continued to commemorate the dead according to their traditions instead of accepting the two Catholic dates were severely punished. To a great extent, the proselytizers were successful in changing Mexicans' view of death as productive and fruitful. Perhaps the evangelizers fought more bitterly against that comforting conception because their continent had just left behind the very same one and their history had shown them that this thanatology led to a less disciplined subject than the one that emerged from the Middle Ages.[15] Fear of death replaced acceptance of death. Avoidance of sin replaced a carpe diem approach to pleasure. There are still Indigenous groups in Mexico whose philosophy has survived—often in camouflage—the onslaught of Christianity. Among them one still finds the belief that death is not to be feared because it is good.[16] Mesoamerican conceptions of death have also continued to be held alongside the Christian ones, some of which they contradict.

Another important difference in the way Mexicans have modified the traditional European view of death that was imported to the New World, blending it with the Aboriginal one, is manifested in their sense of humor. Westheim mentions Manilla and Posada, both of whom drew comical calaveras that contrasted dramatically with the severe and serious European images. Essayist Guillermo Magaña Vázquez published a grave response to his compatriots' humor vis-à-vis death in the daily *El Heraldo*. He considers the pairing of death and laughter unlikely. He thinks death frightens everyone and that no one laughs at the prospect of one's own death or that of one's loved ones. In addition he writes about eating calaveritas de azúcar*:

---

[15] See Bakhtin, *Rabelais and His World*.
[16] See, for example, Gabriel López Chiñas, *El concepto de la muerte entre los zapotecas*.

Nos llevamos el azúcar a la boca, y degustamos aquella muerte cuyo dulzor nos agrada, aunque nos empalague. Es posible, también, que por oculto temor prefiramos quitar de enfrente aquella realidad que algún día, más tarde o más temprano, habrá de llegar para cada uno de nosotros. Y ante este hecho . . . ¿nos planteamos el significado real de la muerte?

Es la muerte del cuerpo, pero también del alma, que sale de este mundo junto con el hombre al que le dio aliento. ¿Dónde quedó aquella belleza? ¿Dónde aquella simpatía, aquel porte, la sabiduría, los conocimientos, la presunción las joyas, bienes y atuendos? Se convirtieron en una triste calavera, en meras oquedades redondas. . . .

El amor a la vida y el respeto a la muerte, se nos inculcan desde pequeños; hay quienes lo entienden al revés y son felices, pero se olvidan que nuestro paso por esta vida es muy breve. . . .

Quienes tenemos fe y profesamos la religión católica, estamos ciertos de que hay una eternidad. . . . Es una simple reflexión para recapacitar en lo que coincide toda la humanidad: la muerte. (Magaña Vázquez)

We place the sugar in our mouth, and we taste that death whose sweetness pleases us, though it is cloying. It is also possible that because of a hidden fear we prefer to remove from our presence that reality which one day, sooner or later, will have to arrive for each of us. And before this fact . . . do we consider the real significance of death?

It is the death of the body but also of the soul, which leaves this world along with the man to whom it gave breath. Where now is that beauty? Where that affability, that stature, that wisdom, the knowledge, the presumption, the jewels, goods, and attire? They've turned into a sad calavera, into mere round hollows. . . .

The love of life and the respect for death are inculcated in us from infancy; there are those who understand the reverse and are happy, but they forget that our passage through this life is brief. . . .

Those of us who have faith and profess the Catholic religion are certain that eternity exists. . . . It is a simple reflection to consider that in which all humanity coincides: death.

In his sober philosophizing, Magaña Vázquez commits an error reminiscent of Octavio Paz's generalizations in *El laberinto de la soledad*—that of attributing to the celebrant of Días de muertos a superficial or limited understanding of what it means to live and to die. As the quotations of

Zapotec mourners and the poetry in Appendix D show, the Indigenous person was and is very aware of what is lost when a beloved dies and of what she or he will lose upon dying.

Can Magaña Vázquez be ignorant of that literature? His third paragraph echoes two lines of the most frequently quoted Náhuatl poem, attributed sometimes to King Nezahualcóyotl of Texcoco:

¿Nada será de mi fama algún día?	Will my fame come to nothing one
¿Nada de mi nombre quedará en la	day?
tierra?[17]	Will nothing of my name remain in
	the world?

Magaña Vázquez also disregards the clear and insistently expressed awareness that both pre-Hispanic Mesoamericans and contemporary Mexicans have of the brevity of life, as well as of an afterlife that has more variations than popular and official Christian conceptions of the afterlife present. Arsacio Vanegas Arroyo also has an answer for Magaña Vázquez:

It is often said that Mexicans have a special relationship with death, because we perceive ourselves in life as the skeletons and skulls we really are. . . .

I don't think they [Mexican artists] are laughing at death. I don't imagine that Posada was laughing at death! I am sure Mexican artists fear death as do the rest of us, but they make death a part of their creation. They have a profound respect for death, because death is a part of life. (Quoted in Carmichael and Sayer 124, 127)

As Sigmund Freud and other psychologists who have considered the nature and functions of humor know, humor is ultimately serious and points to that which is most compelling or most valuable to the humorist.

---

[17] See full text in Appendix D, "Poeta anónimo" [Anonymous Poet].

Three Notes About Catholic Attitudes Toward Días de Muertos

A Note About Literary Irony

In 1792, Fray Joaquín Bolaños, "Predicador Apostolico del Colegio Seminario de Propaganda Fide de MARIA Santisima de Guadalupe extramuros de la muy Noble y Leal Ciudad de Zacatecas en la Nueva Galicia, Exâminador Sinodal del Obispado del Nuevo Reyno de Leon" [apostolic preacher of the propagation seminary Faith of Holy Mary of Guadalupe outside the noble and loyal city of Zacatecas, synodal examiner of the bishopric of Nuevo León], as his name appears on the title page, published a remarkable book whose title is as long and deliberately pedantic as his name. It appears in upper case as LA PORTENTOSA VIDA DE LA MUERTE, EMPERATRIZ DE LOS SEPULCROS, VENGADORA DE LOS AGRAVIOS DEL ALTISIMO, Y MUY SEÑORA DE LA HUMANA NATURALEZA cuya célebre Historia encomienda a los Hombres de buen gusto [The Portentous Life of Death, Empress of Sepulchers, Avenger of Offenses Against the Most High, and the True Lady of Human Nature whose Celebrated History He Recommends to Men of Good Taste].[18]

A picaresque novel disguised as a morality tale, *La portentosa vida de la Muerte* shows the published beginnings of the odd sense of humor that not only unites but sometimes, at least for the sake of humor, confuses life and death. This text could as well be considered a morality tale disguised as a picaresque novel, and the entertainment value of its disguise, as well as its pictorial and verbal sense of humor, seduces the targeted audience into reading it. The novel pretends to teach Christian lessons to doubters, infidels, and backsliders. Bolaños, who has too much fun with Death's outrageous adventures to be taken entirely seriously, especially imparts the Catholic view of death as an ally of sin and the devil as ultimately conquered by Christ whose sacrifice renders death impotent forever. In the following quotation, I have

---

[18] The main reason this text is not considered to be Mexico's first novel is because it is a morality tale. There is something ironic about this because, although it operated in Mexico from 1531 to 1834, the "Holy" Inquisition severely limited the publication and importation of fiction. Bolaños was able to write and publish this work by putting his credentials up front and by titling and positioning the novel as a kind of sermon rather than a humorous work of fiction. Enrique Anderson Imbert has described this text as *prosa novelesca*. He thinks it failed to win readers because they found it to be in bad taste, and priests denounced it as hurting both church teachings and the practice of clean living (Anderson Imbert 164f).

preserved the original archaic spelling and punctuation, as in the title above, but I have not attempted to duplicate them in the translation:

Es preciso que todo hombre a cuyas manos llegare la Portentosa Vida de la Muerte, lleve por delante la idéa de que la Muerte, es una Magestad ridícula pero por otra parte su seriedad infunde mucho respeto. Unas veces será motivo de nuestra risa; pero otras será la causa de nuestro llanto, porque ella es triste como la Muerte; y por otro lado es tan alegre como la Pasqua. . . . Ella habita con freqüencia en los Palacios, sin descuidarse de las mas humildes chozas. (Bolaños, Introducción)

It is necessary that every man into whose hands the Portentous Life of Death falls hold foremost the idea that Death is a ridiculous Majesty, but, on the other hand, her gravity inspires great respect. Sometimes she will be the motive of our laughter; but other times she will be the cause of our weeping, for she is as sad as Death; and on the other hand she is as joyous as Easter. . . . She frequently inhabits Palaces without excluding the humblest shacks.

Bolaños picaresquely combines his ecclesiastical duty to teach the official line about death with his very Mexican sense of humor to make fun of that official line, of death, and of his profession and its obligations. I should comment on my ostensibly essentializing phrase "a very Mexican sense of humor about death." Because Bolaños was Mexican, one can expect him to have shared the cultural values and discourse that train the sense of humor. Popular culture in Spain also reveals a sense of humor about death, which has been apparent for centuries. It is not the same as the humor we see in Mexico, but there is at least a tenuous family resemblance.

We begin to see in Bolaños the tendency to use an anthropomorphized character, Death, to uncover social wrongs on an allegorical level. The didactic nature of the text draws it closer to Spanish religious discourse and European danses macabres than to the kind of political and social critique that emerges in the popular texts of Días de muertos* beginning with Posada* and Manilla at the turn of the twentieth century.

In his *Más allá de la muerte*, Héctor Grimrac comments on some of the differences between Mexican and European uses of death. According to him, in European symbolism death is an "omen" that can have a symbolic sense or a moral teaching but that never unveils social problems, as happens in Mexican popular art, which uses caricature and verse to reform or ridicule a reality that it does not dare to handle seriously. He calls death as it is used and represented in Mexico a "splitting of the personality" because whatever Mexicans do not dare to do themselves they impute to death, so it is always death—the festive skeleton—that is the central character of criticism. Grimrac says that in Mexican depictions, "death makes its presence felt by moving like a malleable character in the most daring circumstances, without fear of reproach, 'as if it enjoyed all exemptions and nothing were forbidden to it.'"[19] I will explore further the impact and meaning of the "festive skeleton" in the next two chapters.

A Note About Liturgical Intolerance

I spent some hours in Mexico City's largest cemetery, Panteón Dolores, on November 2, 1993. It has paths that are named like streets and that converge at several *glorietas,* or roundabouts, where there are fountains from which people take water in buckets to clean the graves. At one of them I witnessed the creation of a temporary church where mass was said.

A flatbed truck arrived with a guitarist, eight priests, and as many acolytes. On the truck was an improvised altar with the figure of the Virgin Mary as the Dolorosa, the mother in black veils, mourning her crucified son. As they approached the area, people crossed themselves regardless of whether they were joining the congregation or just passing through, as many Catholics do in Mexico when they pass a church. About 150 people congregated, many carrying shovels, buckets, and armfuls of flowers. Food vendors kept hawking their wares during the mass.

The homily was an anti-Pagan, anti-Hallowe'en diatribe. The priest said that on this date there was hope that the Lord would tell us that the just are in the presence of God. His words are reminiscent of Magaña Vázquez's, although less measured and graceful. He railed:

¿Para qué sirve comer los taquitos y reírnos encima de los restos de nuestros hermanos? Deberían estar rezando porque tengan descanso.	What good does it do to eat *taquitos* and laugh over the remains of our brothers? You should be praying for their rest.

---

[19] Grimrac put this phrase in quotation marks but gave no attribution.

Dios no es Dios de los muertos sino de los vivos. Tomemos en serio la vida y la muerte porque la vida es para glorificar al Señor y la muerte también.

God is not God of the dead but of the living. Let us take life and death seriously because life is to glorify the Lord and so is death.

The priest showed no tolerance for Días de muertos.* He wanted only All Souls' Day to be commemorated. He objected to the faithful eating and making merry on the graves of their dead, and he did not mention the offerings that were being set out lovingly. His brief homily was disorganized and undisciplined; he jumped from topic to topic. The short text I have quoted betrays a lack of sensitivity to popular culture and to the seriousness of its animation. It makes me suspect that the priest went to Panteón Dolores with certain ideas that were unaltered by an open-eyed tour through the cemetery. I saw many people doing what the padre exhorted them to do: praying on the graves. Some were muttering traditional, set Catholic prayers, occasionally in small groups; some were moving their lips and whispering too softly for a stranger to hear; some, surely, were praying for the rest of the dead or at least for their well-being. The priest's omission, which we saw also in Magaña Vázquez, suggests a prejudice that allows no alteration based on firsthand experience.

The utilitarian attitude apparent in the cleric's initial question, "Para qué sirve" [What use is it], clashes with the enjoyment and delight inherent in a reunion of the family, living and dead. It is matched by his appeal that the congregation take life and death seriously and, for that matter, take the glorification of God seriously, as if seeking pleasure and joy had no place in Catholic practice.

The life-negating condemnation of cheer is out of place in Mexico, especially during a fiesta.* Furthermore, it is out of place in Christianity as well if we remember that, when challenged as to why his disciples did not fast as did those of John the Baptist and the Pharisees, Jesus replied, "Can you expect the bridegroom's friends to fast while the bridegroom is with them?" (Mark 2:19). We remember in addition that Jesus was a fairly jolly fellow with an intelligent sense of humor and a sharp sense of irony who picked ears of corn and healed people on the Sabbath and whose first miracle was to turn water into wine for a wedding feast. We can think of the presence of the disembodied spirits among their living friends and relatives in Mexico's cemeteries as a parallel to the presence of Jesus among his disciples or to a bridegroom among his friends. What should hosts express but mirth? Whereas the people who were visiting their dead—cleaning their graves and adorning them with everything from blooms to balloons, talking to the dead, eating with them, arranging for mariachis to sing to them—might have been missing the dead and mourning their physical absence, few appeared to be grieving. On the days of the dead, the dead are among the living; is it not right for the living to rejoice?

One could even argue with the priest on theological grounds. According to Luke, Jesus did say "God is not God of the dead but of the living," but the rest of his sentence reads "for him all are alive" (Luke 20:38). God, like the traditional Mexican, does not abandon someone who has left the body. Was the preacher calling for the dead to be abandoned? It has long been an observation, if only of individuals outside the church, that many Christians live and believe in ways that have little in common with the example of him whom they purport to follow.

A Note About Ecclesiastical Tolerance

While I was researching this book, I asked a few parish priests in Mexico to comment on Días de muertos.* They were Mexican except for one Spaniard who had lived in Mexico for around thirty years. Most expressed tolerance for the commemoration. The Spaniard was very patronizing, and he discursively distanced himself from the celebrants. He thought it was useless to try to uproot as ancient and beloved a tradition as this one, and he considered it harmless. He talked about Mexico's syncretism, which has ensured the survival of some "Pagan" practices.

A priest in Xochimilco genuinely liked the fiesta,* although he thought it had nothing to do with Catholicism but existed, as it were, in a separate reality. He said that he, too, celebrated Días de muertos with pan de muerto* and calaveras* for his friends. As many Mexicans do, he considered the holiday very Mexican and thought it fostered Mexican identity in a positive way. His opinion was similar to those of others I interviewed.

In the churches of Mixquic and Xochimilco, both officially within Mexico City, and of Cuetzalan, Puebla, elaborate and, in the case of Mixquic, sophisticated ofrendas* had been placed on the steps of the main altar. Considering that many churches were built from the destroyed remains of Indigenous sanctuaries and, therefore, were standing on what the locals might have considered sacred space for many centuries, it seems appropriate that the dead of the community were regaled in what a change of symbols, pantheons, and theologies could not stop from being an axis mundi.*

8

Reading Calaveras

Lively Skeletons: The Subversiveness of an Oxymoron

Naranja dulce,
limón celeste,
dile a María,
que no se acueste.
María, María,
ya se acostó,
vino la muerte
y se la llevó.
Naranja dulce,
limón celeste,
dile a mi amada,
que me conteste.
María, María,
no contestó,
vino la muerte
y se la llevó.
—Traditional (Quoted in
Martel Díaz Cortéz 31f)

Sweet orange,
celestial lime,
tell María
not to lie down.
María, María,
in bed she lay.
Along came death
and took her away.
Sweet orange,
celestial lime,
tell my beloved
to answer me.
María, María
did not reply,
death came 'round
and made her die.

A beholder of calaveras,* the sculptural or graphic scenes of skeletons, might discern the foolishness of the dead—if that is what calaveras really represent—doing anything at all instead of discreetly decomposing in their coffins. Yet the popular artist or artisan depicts them as alive. The calaveras are working, self-reflexively making offerings to the dead, socializing, or displaying themselves.[1] Whatever they are doing, what may be most obvious about these skeletons is that they are not dead. They announce the oxymoronic logic, politics, and poetics of the carnival about which Bakhtin and others have written eloquently and extensively. The lively calaveras open the upside-down world over which they preside to the audience; in that sense the world is constructed very differently from the way it is constructed by the Western mindset, in which the living are only living and the dead stay thoroughly dead, out of sight, and usually out of mind.[2]

If we consider calaveras a site of status reversal during Días de muertos, in which the dead and not the living become the center of attention, Victor Turner's insight about the nature of this reversal is germane:

Status reversal does not mean "anomie" but simply a new perspective from which to observe structure. Its topsy-turviness may even give a humorous warmth to this ritual viewpoint. If the liminality* of life-crisis rites may be, perhaps audaciously, compared to tragedy—for both imply humbling, stripping, and pain—the liminality of status reversal may be compared to comedy, for both involve mockery and inversion, but not destruction, of structural rules and overzealous adherents to them. (Turner 201)

The art of the rotulista* or of the sculptor of calaveras is not revolutionary art bent on overturning the status quo. It does, however, seek and

---

[1] There is a curious similarity to the self-reflexive calavera in Europe. Philippe Ariès mentions seventeenth-century "vanities" that included "sermons on death, meditations on nothingness or the flight of time." He quotes André Chastel ("L'Art et le sentiment de la mort," *Revue du XVIIe siècle*, nos. 36–37 [1957] 288–293) for this description: "They appear in a moralistic context, with explicit inscriptions . . . for example . . . the skeleton meditating upon the skull of his fellow . . . or the skeleton as a gravedigger leaning on his spade" (Ariès 366).

[2] T. S. Eliot wrote in the *Four Quartets* "but that which is only living / Can only die" (Eliot 121). Perhaps it is the poverty suggested in the typically Western "only" living and "only" dying that makes the rich duality celebrated in Días de muertos appealing to certain outsiders.

manage to carve out space and time in which the status quo can be examined and questioned, ridiculed, and put into perspective as an arbitrary human construct that serves the interests of only a few. Out of this kind of exhibition, great changes are not expected, but small changes are perhaps facilitated. The clases populares see images of their work and their culture in public spaces, giving them the sense of power and presence afforded by simple visibility.[3] The dominant classes are given glimpses of, and opportunities to think about, the subordinated people's lives and their own role in that subordination. They are given opportunities to admire the art, the culture, the philosophy, and, of course, the sense of humor of their humble compatriots: the underemployed, the unemployed, the immigrants to urban centers, the campesinos, the *pueblerinos* (town dwellers), the household servants, and the Indians whose Spanish is inflected by Native rhythms and marked by sixteenth-century grammar.

Although Días de muertos seems to exalt the Indigenous and virtually disregard the Spanish and the modern international cultural strands that have also influenced it, we—especially the nationalistic Mexican scholars—might do well to take a cue from the calavera, which witnesses to the absurdity of trying to divide pairs of opposites, our genetic and cultural makeup among them. The animated skeletons seem to ridicule the project of division as hopeless, as, in a sense, dead, truly and definitively dead, while in the very same *carcajada,* the very same peal of laughter, they celebrate the triumphant longevity of the pre-Columbian roots that have not been overwhelmed by Western grafts. In my reading of the bakery calavera "Batman con luchadores" (Batman with Wrestlers),[4] I have found a frank celebration of cultural mixture and in "Merienda exquisita" (Delicious Supper) at least an acknowledgment of a foreign presence.

---

[3] In the United States, festivities such as Gay Pride Days, Juneteenth, the Hmong Soccer Tournament, Cinco de Mayo, and others sponsored by ethnic minorities or immigrant groups can give a taste of what I mean by the sense of power and presence afforded by visibility. The celebrants are not deluded into thinking anything will change as a result of their holidays, but they feel the great pleasure of group importance that comes of being together, of doing something that is their very own, and of drawing some recognition from the majority media and the members of the majority who attend the activities.

[4] I have assigned titles to the calaveras I have chosen for close readings; ordinarily they have none. The legends are not titles but rather advertisements for the pan de muerto* sold in the bakery. Exceptions are Posada's* calaveras, which are all titled.

On the quotidian level, the reader of calaveras can perceive a sharp interrogation of the dominant gender and class roles in the comical depictions, as we will see in readings of "Bellas concursantes" (Beautiful Contestants), "Luchadores" (Wrestlers), and "Gran fandango y francachela de todas las calaveras" (Great Fandango and Wild Party of All the Calaveras). By exposing and ridiculing the roles in which they cast their calaveras, the artists make those roles available for comment, for consideration, and even for possible overturning.

This dynamic of consciousness-waking attention illustrates the struggle for meaning that can be discerned in the calaveras exhibited in government-sponsored museums, shops, and public spaces. Often, the calaveras perform a carnival of mimicry and ridicule of the images of "Mexican folk" held by the dominant class and of people's performance of the roles assigned to them. They still serve, cook for, and entertain the moneyed, but the exaggeration and absurdity of these jobs being carried out by brightly colored skeletons suggest that subservience is interrogated. John Fiske defines popular cultural capital as the discursive resources people use to express their understandings of, not their acquiescence to, their subordination. It involves skills that parallel those admired by the well-off, which allow them to appreciate "high" art (Fiske, *Reading the Popular*, 135).

In several cases, the rotulistas and sculptors have chosen stereotypical images of Mexico and *lo mexicano,* what is Mexican, for the calaveras. With few exceptions—most attributable to two rotulistas—the images in my collection reach toward what the bourgeoisie might call the past. But in fact, considering the unequal, combined development typical of "peripheral" countries, they reach toward the life of the Mexican periphery where marimba bands play in the *zócalo* (the central square), where bread may still be delivered by a cyclist, where women wear their traditional clothing and prepare and serve food in traditional implements. Most of the calaveras I read in detail were photographed in Mexico City, where there are neighborhoods with parks in which balloons are sold, photographs are taken with old-fashioned cameras, and knives are sharpened on home-assembled, portable grindstones (see Figure 1.17, Plate 17).

These representations of popular culture reveal the work of humble semioticians who circulate received meanings but who, in Volosinov's sense, inflect or accent those meanings according to their standards and context. They raise what is most ordinary—courting, selling, cooking—and place it in the center of attention. Because our habitual activities—especially if we are in the working class—are shown performed by skeletons, they are unnaturalized such that we are invited to think about them: What do we do? Why do we do it? For whom? What does our activity mean? When will it change or cease?

The calaveras fill the gaze of the metropolitan audience with caricaturesque images of the humble. The artists cook the images, as Lévi-Strauss might say, until they are boiled down to their most grotesque form. They seem to say to the dominant culture, *You think us quaint? You think us colorful? You think us chronologically anterior and therefore inferior to you? Here is what your stereotypes look like, what they feel like, and they are as dead as the reductionist minds from which they originally came. And as alive. Here they are, stripped down to the bones, having come back to haunt you and bite you back.* As Michel de Certeau put it, *ils remordent*—in Spanish, *remuerden*—the repressed returns surreptitiously and "rebites" secretly, repeatedly, and in disguise (de Certeau, *Heterologies,* 3). The irritation of remorse is punishment for relegating underprivileged compatriots to marginality, subordination, and caricature. And by the way, see the catrín, the catrina?* That's you. You may count on many advantages in life, but under your ample flesh you are skeletal, too, as skeletal as the poorest of the skinny poor.

Where Have All the Calaveras Gone?

When I left Mexico in 1981 to take up residence in Minnesota, virtually all the bakeries in the capital had calaveras* painted on their display windows. Although they all still sell pan de muerto,* only a few bakeries in working-class neighborhoods in the D.F.* and other towns and cities sport calaveras. In the more cosmopolitan, higher-class neighborhoods, the display windows are clean. And in middle-class shops are only icons and images of Hallowe'en, borrowing another bit of U.S. culture with which many members of the bourgeoisie identify.

In some of Mexico's *barrios populares,* people still resist being dragged into the transnational colony. One of their means of resistance is reviving the traditions of Días de muertos* year after year. The fiesta* says no to Hallowe'en and, for the most part, to transnationalism. The rotulistas* choose their own subject matter and are paid by members of their own class to paint the bakeries for visual consumption by their peers. Because they are acting locally and for a limited amount of time—therefore offering a small market—their observance of Días de muertos is not commercialized by outsiders. The artists and their audiences are independent and separate from the ideological apparatus. This exemplifies Fiske's hypothesis that pleasure is a subversive tactic because it is experienced privately, beyond the reach of hegemonic dominion that pretends to know and control every aspect of social life. By raising the possibility of a viable existence that is invisible to and independent of that power, the myth of omnipotence is exposed (Fiske, *Reading the Popular,* 64).

So whereas bakery calaveras once enjoyed the privileged space of wealthy neighborhoods, they are now limited to humbler ones, although they are reappearing in some prestigious spaces. Numerous intellectuals— who are reviving the democratizing impulses of José Guadalupe Posada,* Frida Kahlo, the muralists, and others and are enjoying the vitality, creativity, and sense of humor of the popular art of Días de muertos—are to some extent turning over art galleries, museums, theaters, shops, and parks to that popular art. The University of Puebla held a contest for altares de Días de muertos in 1992; the CETIS* school system and the Museo Nacional de Culturas Populares host displays of ofrendas* from many ethnic groups; university students set out their sometimes outrageous ofrendas where many can see them. Children in the public schools are taught to erect altars and to cut tissue paper and draw calaveras of their own. Children in the private schools, if they are taken to public spaces during Días de muertos, are also able to enjoy some of the ironic calaveras that some xenophile teachers and parents may scorn, and they may (re)learn to enjoy them.

Building on the theories of Michel Foucault, John Fiske has demonstrated that people in subordinated classes sometimes openly resist their subordination and, at other times, skirt it through tactics of evasion. Calaveras are examples of both resisting and evading the dominant culture and its oppression. On the one hand, they are resistant and transgressive, even subversive, insofar as they do their best to take over the attention of the community, obliging all members of society to see and remember the humble people whom the powerful prefer to ignore and forget after giving them orders. Calaveras subvert the most common use of public space, which during the other eleven months of the year exclusively displays images of the dominant class. Instead of staying docilely in the shadows of the margins all year long, during Días de muertos the people take the center of attention and highlight their art, their lives, and their fiesta in a spectacle that cannot be ignored.

Pop star Madonna invites her readers to gaze on her parody of patriarchal images of women.[5] Rabelais virtually forces his readers to gaze on, feel, smell, hear, and almost taste the lower bodily stratum. The discourses of Días de muertos call its readers to take care of the spirits of the dead and to live, work, and ingest for their sake during the celebration's short reign. Calaveras reveal class relations, economic stratification, and gender roles in a way that, in a Foucaultian sense, puts too much attention on the activities and roles depicted to continue to consider them natural. Seeing the grotesque and humorous depictions gives the audience the opportunity to realize how arbitrary those activities and roles are in the first place.

The grotesque is transgressive in and of itself, uniting life and death, displaying the nonbeautiful, nonclassical, unglamorous practices of the subordinated in, no less, the form of nonbeautiful, nonclassical, unglamorous, living skeletons. In addition, making death the center of attention turns the usual order of things upside down and inside out, for the privileged classes prefer to pretend that death is too far in the future to be relevant, feeling protected by their wealth, their access to medical resources, and their generally low-risk lifestyles.

The classical body privileged by the aesthetics of the elite is always fleshed—even when artists represent it in death—but it is usually alive and in the prime of life, generally posing or reposing (signs of leisure and wealth), healthy, and beautiful (Bakhtin, *Rabelais,* 25, 29). The calavera privileged by the popular aesthetics of Días de muertos is always skeletal— even when artists represent it as partly fleshed—and is usually working unless it is a member of the upper class;[6] although it is strong and healthy enough for physical labor, the fact that it is working shows it is not wealthy enough to enjoy leisure. Finally, it is, if ugly is too harsh a word, normally caricaturesque and grotesque.

What is evasive about calaveras is their comical quality. The powerful sense of humor characteristic of them is never simple. Transgressively, instead of expressing self-pity or conformity with the mundane, repetitious tasks and practices of the subordinated and performing those tasks humbly and almost invisibly, the calavera makes fun of them and makes them eminently visible, as well as risible. At the same time it makes manifest the

---

[5] See Fiske, *Reading the Popular,* 95ff.

[6] I have seen one calavera that shows an unusual black Zapata or zapatista sitting in a chair while an *adelita** cooks for him. In this case, the gender hierarchy prevails. Although the male is a laborer, as a revolutionary he is superior to his female companion—a member of his class—who serves him.

class hierarchy that relegates to the poor the most unpleasant, arduous, and dangerous work.

Derision is a way of questioning the value, seriousness, normalcy, and usefulness of some humble occupations. It masks embarrassment or shame at being the ones designated to do these tasks, at being relegated to the margins. But also, the humor in the calaveras exalts the fact that the clases populares find fun and pleasure within, as well as in spite of, their drudgery and relative poverty. As Fiske has said, there is pleasure in following rules and participating cooperatively in social norms, and there is pleasure in making fun of them—in this case by showing them performed by calaveras (Fiske, *Reading the Popular*, 134f).

The humorous nature of the calaveras puts into play another tactic of subversion as it pretends not to care about the deadening, often hard and distasteful tasks and practices the dominant classes demand of the humble in exchange for meager wages. Humor masks the anger and pain of subordination and marginalization, whereas the visibility of the calaveras unmasks and makes central the experience of that way of life. At the same time, because these sculptures and paintings show the people laughing while they work, they question the humanist stereotype of the suffering and long-suffering downtrodden folk. Some members of the dominant classes think pleasure should be entirely theirs. I have seen a well-educated, wealthy woman scoff at her servants' fun and at the fact that they are having fun. Many calaveras flaunt the fact that there is plenty of pleasure to go around.

Readings of Calaveras I

As a symbol, the calavera* is very unlike the serious, dignified skull that symbolizes death for the Westerner. That skull has no sense of humor, it really signifies death, and it is never personalized. The privileged seem to prefer to ignore death, as if they do not quite believe it will happen to them. They do not show the intimacy with death that the subordinated show when they mock it and dress it in their clothes and pose it in the gestures of their livelihood and pleasure.

The calavera is a sign not so much of death or the dead as of Días de muertos* and all it celebrates: the completed but continuing life of the dead; their visit to the living; the continuing life of the living with all its complexity of work and leisure, suffering and delight, and knowledge of a certain future death. Because this holiday puts the interests of the dead foremost, the calavera, with its lipless grin, is a sign of resistance to the usual order of things in which the living look after—and look out for—

8.1 Mother and Child by Posada. (Permission given by Moyer Bell)

themselves. It is a sign of the survival and vitality of pre-Christian and early Christian values, beliefs, and traditions; of the perseverance of the people who embody the fiesta;* and of the self-awareness of the celebrants.

I have chosen a number of calaveras through which to explore the popular construction of death and life during Días de muertos, and I will apply to them some of the theories of semiotics* developed by Roland Barthes, Claude Lévi-Strauss, John Fiske, and René Jara and Nicholas Spadaccini. In calaveras, the dominant ideology is transparent in terms of who does what: Women dance for men; they cook and serve food. Men sell and serve beverages to other men; they take photographs, sharpen knives, sell balloons, play music in public, and deliver bread; they look at and court women. Children are hardly ever depicted in this format, but I found two calaveras in which they appear (Figures 8.1, 8.6). José Guadalupe Posada* and Máximo Urbano both depict humble saleswomen carrying their infant wrapped in a *rebozo,** shawl. The child calaveras are being transported, looking

8.2 Papier mâche Zapata/zapatista y adelita by Linares. Anahuacalli, Mexico, D.F. (Courtesy of Dolores Olmedo Patiño)

quite animated, smiling and peeping out the windows of the school van, probably jostling each other, sitting and standing, then sitting again.

In comparison to the representations of proletarian calaveras, which are all working (except for the revolutionary zapatista who, in a classical *machista* pose, is sitting on a chair, holding his rifle while waiting for his meal; see Figure 8.2), in their inaction the catrinas* and catrines* resemble statues. One catrina has an open jaw, which may indicate speech or laughter if it does not indicate the slackness of death (see Figure 2.2); another catrina is holding a cigarette in her clenched teeth, perhaps to show how she sickened and died (see Plate 7). Both are posed in stillness rather than in motion.

The images of the working-class calaveras are, with few exceptions, ones of merriment.[7] There is no hint of poverty or oppression, although the

---

[7] In Oaxaca a genre of sculpted calavera in clay shows sometimes skeletal women hooded in their rebozos, sitting before a grave or an ofrenda. The rebozos may be black because the community wears black shawls, or they may indicate mourning. The one I have is from Toluca, Estado de México, and the miniature woman is smiling as she sits on the ground before an ofrenda. This is not as merry a calavera as most, but it is also not particularly grim or sorrowful.

means of subordination and control are evident in allusions to commodified labor—especially the preparation and serving of food—and in the school bus calavera, to the educational system. On the one hand, the park photographer is using an antiquated camera, good twentieth-century technology available through transnational capitalism and cared for by a humble owner beyond its expected span of use. The *panaderos ciclistas,* bread deliverers, are riding bicycles; the children are in a bus; the rifle, musical instruments, and balloons are from international sources. On the other hand, the women are cooking and serving in ollas*; the adelita* has used her *molcajete* (mortar and pestle), presumably for a salsa and her *brasero* (portable grill), to cook the tortillas. These are all bits of Indigenous technology that are still used today. They demonstrate the continued coexistence of modern Western and traditional local technologies, which enters the artistic space of the calavera.

"Gran fandango y francachela de todas las calaveras" [Grand Fandango and Wild Party of All the Calaveras]

The photograph of "Gran fandango y francachela de todas las calaveras" was taken in Anahuacalli[8] in 1990 (see Plate 18). Its medium is cartón*, papier mâché, by the famous Plácido Linares and his workshop, inspired by José Guadalupe Posada's* metal engraving broadside of the same title (see Figure 1.22). Not all the original figures are represented by Linares, who shows only one man drinking. Linares has also omitted the second woman, who seems either to be cooking *gorditas* (thick, small tortillas) on a grill or to be serving them. She has been transposed into a calavera with a seated, black zapatista (Figure 8.2). The harp player is to the right of the slack-mouthed man instead of to his left; the two primary figures are also transposed.[9]

---

[8] *Anahuacalli* means House of Anáhuac in Náhuatl. Anáhuac is the name of the Valley of Mexico. Anahuacalli is the name of Diego Rivera's house, which he gave to the country as a museum. It displays his pre-Hispanic collection in one building; the other is for temporary exhibits. Yearly, Dolores Olmedo, executive director of the museum, commissions and displays an elaborate, enormous ofrenda that takes up all of the second building in honor of her deceased friends Frida Kahlo and Diego Rivera.

[9] Anahuacalli has also displayed three-dimensional calaveras of Doña Tomasa, who is represented as an old woman with curvature of the spine, unlike Posada's very erect figure, and of Simón el aguador, Simon the Water Carrier. (See Figures 1.14–15).

8.3 Papier mâché "Gran fandango y francachela de todas las calaveras" by Linares. Anahuacalli, México, D.F. (Courtesy of Dolores Olmedo Patiño)

I will read the calavera displayed in Anahuacalli. There is no indication in that display that Posada inspired some calaveras, nor is Posada's title reproduced.

"Gran fandango" represents a saloon in which the inexpensive alcoholic beverage *pulque* is sold. Posada's original is not a *pulquería* (although it could be set in one), whose primary purpose is commercial, but in the sculptural calavera the legend on the counter or bar indicates a commercial, rather than a strictly social, setting. In the background on the left are two male calaveras at a bar. One is serving a drink from a clay pitcher; the other is drinking from an enormous earthenware vessel. The counter is realistic. The pulquería looks very authentic, from its colors to the two typefaces on its bar.

Pulque is drunk throughout the country; therefore, its presence universalizes the setting, which could be anywhere in Mexico. As cartón* and earthenware are cottage industries for which a neighborhood in Mexico City is known, I consider the capital to be represented in this calavera, as in all of the Anahuacalli display. Another state is indicated by the sarape over the male calavera's shoulder; its pattern is almost indexical for the city of Saltillo in northeastern Nuevo León. The pattern is not discernible in Posada's version. A fourth state represented by Linares's calavera is the Atlantic one of Veracruz, represented by the harp. The small platform on which the foregrounded male calavera is standing is painted with a pattern imitating lacquer work done in Michoacán and Guerrero. The female calavera's skirt afforded another opportunity for a geographical quotation, but instead the garment is fantastical. Its shape recalls that of the *"china poblana"* from Jalisco,[10] but its colors do not conform to any clothing I have seen.

Enough parts of the country are indicated in this calavera to interpret them as standing for the whole. Selling, drinking, dancing, watching, playing, and listening to music go on everywhere.

In the foreground, the female calavera is dancing. Her head is cocked coquettishly toward her right shoulder, a gesture stereotypified in regional folk dance, most of whose dances mimic heterosexual courtship. Her eyelashes are exaggerated as if they were false or painted. Her red gums may pretend to show lipstick; they are different from the lines around the others' mouths. Her fingernails are painted bright red. All of these details are signs either of good grooming—if the beholder does not find them excessive—or of seduction. Her bare torso must not be taken to mean seductive undress but rather calavera-ness, if you will. It may hark back to images of Mictecacíhuatl, Lady of the Realm of the Dead, and of the cihuateteo* (see Figures 5.1, 8.4). Bare bones signify not so much death as Días de muertos when they are depicted in calaveras.

The foregrounded male calavera is not dancing. His knees may be bent because he is keeping a bouncing rhythm to the beat. He may be staggering and trying to keep his balance if he is drunk. He may be crouching a bit like a beast of prey about to pounce on the dancer. It looks that way in the Posada original (see Figure 1.22). Or he may be reeling and trying to regain his balance in the presence of a sexy dancer. In any case, his exaggeratedly big eyes with circles of red, white, and black, and his mouth open in admiration or gluttonous lust give him a quintessential masculinist gaze. The female charms the male with her dance, which he consumes with slack-jawed looking. He almost seems to be drooling. His gaze consumes her as the drinker consumes pulque while the grinning cantinero (bartender) accumulates wealth from the clients' expenditures.

---

[10] The skirt is worn by dancers in *el jarabe tapatío,* known in the United States as "the Mexican hat dance."

8.4 Mictecacíhuatl, Mixquic churchyard

Professor René Jara saw this calavera as representing the voyeur courting death. I pointed out to him that, first, not only for ancient Mexicans but
for many of their successors as well, life and death are as inseparable as two
sides of a coin. Many believe we carry our death in our living body from
the moment we are born. Second, Mexicans hardly ever see themselves as
courting death, a romantic, European notion; finally, this is a calavera,
which by definition must have skeletons as its protagonists.

The scenario is typical. Perhaps the mixing of regional indexes represents
the metropolis, the national capital where raw materials and people come
together to consume and produce culture and goods. Perhaps it means to uni-
versalize the scene for all of Mexico. What is remarkable is its stereotypicity.
This is the Mexico produced by the Department of Tourism, identified primarily with foreign—mostly U.S.—tourists but also, secondarily, with
national tourists of the upper classes. This is the colorful, quaint, musical,
fun-loving, hard-drinking Mexico promised by cartoons and tour guides who
vow they will show you something "veri típico, señor." It seems to be Mexico
packaged and commodified, although no one could deny that such scenes are
probably being enacted at this moment in various parts of the country.

The fact that all of the characters in "Gran fandango" are calaveras
can be read in several ways that may coexist without preference and without excluding alternative readings. It represents Mexico dead and killed,
desiccated, taxidermically arranged in a colorful, desirable package displayed for sale or consumption. It means that in life we carry our death; in
our fleshy bodies we carry our skeletons; our activities in life may be
charming, but we will not be spared death for all our charm and vivacity. It
indicates a conception of an afterlife that is no different from this life.
Commercial and gender roles will be then and there as they are here and
now. The calavera as a whole, or at least the part within the photographic
frame, shows and exaggerates gender and market relations. Sex is commodified along with food and drink. And this is true all over the country, in
death as in life, "on earth as it is in Heaven."

Paz entre Días de muertos y Hallowe'en
Peace Between Days of the Dead and Hallowe'en

In theater, the second most powerful area of the stage after the center is
to the audience's left because in our culture we look left to read, according

8.5 Paz entre Días de muertos y Hallowe'en. Bakery, México, D.F.

to retired director Eliseo Martínez (class lecture 1969). The left panel of this bakery display window is occupied by a white, gray-haired witch who is frowning and pointing left as she emerges from a gigantic jack-o'-lantern. To our right, a cartoon ghost smiles in surprise at seeing the witch as it emerges from the letter "O" in the word *Halloween,* painted in capital letters to look like fire (perhaps the fire of hell). The next panel has only the words "Pan de muerto"* painted in capital letters shaped like bones, with a cross for the T, much larger than those in "HALLOWEEN / SU EXQUISITO Y SABROSO" [Halloween / your exquisite and delicious], which is the phrase "Pan de muerto" completes. The final panel on the right says "2 NOV. UNA OFRENDA TRADICIONAL Y UN REGALO A SU PALADAR! [2 Nov. A traditional offering and a gift for your palate!]. After the legend, a curious calavera* in nightgown and nightcap is kicking up his heels, holding up a big pan de muerto, and whooping, "Yuuuy, Yajay, mi puro gusto!" [My pure delight!].

There is room for both the U.S. and Mexican traditions in this paint-ing. The rotulista* has politely ceded the best place to the newcomers, who represent Hallowe'en. It is true that the witch and the ghost are looking at each other, not at the calavera, and that the calavera is celebrating toward his audience or the world and not regarding the guests. Maybe it is sad because the members of the two cultures are not communicating with each other. I cannot tell to what the witch is pointing; the arm extends in a way that may indicate either the word *Halloween* or the furthest panel with the bread-toting skeleton. This is, after all, an advertisement to entice passersby to buy their pan de muerto in this *panificadora.** In any case, the nonjudg-mental U.S. and Mexican figures share the window in peace.

"Calavera urbana"

"Calavera urbana" was created by the artist who painted "Bellas concur-santes" (see Figure 9.3), "Conquistadores" (see Figure 1.12), "Luchadores,"

8.6 Calavera urbana. Bakery, México, D.F.

and "Batman con luchadores" (see Figures 8.8, 8.9), and "Apoteosis del pan de muerto*" (see Figure 8.7), which is painted on the window next to it. Whereas most rotulistas are content to paint simple calaveras,* perhaps showing a baker holding a pan de muerto, the anonymous creator of these calaveras offers us an idiosyncratic, deliciously complex series of these ephemeral works. His legends are traditional; his graphics are unique, even weird texts that almost demand—and certainly reward—careful reading. Because I was unable to ascertain his identity and because I admire him very much and consider him to be one of the two best urban rotulistas, I will call him Máximo Urbano.

"Calavera urbana" says, "Lleve a Casa lo Tradicional. Pruebelo [*sic*]" [Take Home What Is Traditional. Try it] and below, "El Mejor y mas [*sic*] Rico del Rumbo" [The Best and Most Delicious of the Neighborhood]. On the viewer's right is a "María," a humble woman who is selling a crate of shining pan de muerto on the sidewalk. She is sitting on or in front of a second crate and is wearing a blue gown. She has long, black, braided hair with coquettish curls on her forehead. On her back, in the traditional way of Indigenous women, she has her beaming baby, held in place by a black rebozo. The hair, the rebozo with baby, and the occupation add up to an authentic portrait of a poor resident or immigrant to Mexico City. The woman is gesturing, and her mouth is open as if she were speaking. Both mother and child have skulls for heads.

Just to the right of the center of the painting is a smiling male calavera, unclothed, walking toward the woman. He has a drowsy, distracted, or drunk expression; sports a curious lock of hair on his otherwise bald skull; and is accompanied by a dog. In the dead center of the calavera, if I may, is the only nonskeletal, living thing in the picture: a brown dog that looks a bit like a deer. He seems to be escorting the walker.

A stylized, blue VW van dominates the left side of the painting. It is driven by a chauffeur of uncertain gender with long, black hair and a dour expression. Behind the chauffeur ride fourteen children, represented by small skulls. They look like they are jumping up and down, wriggling, or trying to peer out of the windows toward the viewer.

Finally, on the edge of the picture Máximo Urbano has painted a lamppost from behind which is peering what I interpret to be an adolescent male calavera. All we see of him are a foot and leg, fingers, and his skull, topped by a blue baseball cap. He is looking at the woman, who appears to be addressing him. His expression combines mischievousness, shyness, and sneakiness but no malice.

This is the only contemporary calavera in my collection that shows children and a live animal. Urbano seems to be insisting on the fact that children, too, are vulnerable to death and will die regardless of whether they reach adulthood. Whereas the content of the lesson is not unique, his depiction of the little death heads is oddly disconcerting, even to one who has spent many years contemplating calaveras.

It was while looking at and photographing this painting in 1991 that I felt transformed by a sudden compelling awareness of my own skeleton within me, waiting to be bared of the organs, muscles, tissues, blood, and skin that cover it as clothes cover the body. I believe "Calavera urbana" affected me this profoundly because its realistic urban scene is so common and familiar that in spite of the cartoonish, unrealistic style, it felt like an extension of the sidewalk on which I was standing. Many times a day in many areas of the capital, one is apt to see Marías with their babies, sitting on a sidewalk selling humble wares; vehicles driven by someone aggravated by city traffic and the noise of the children they are transporting; individuals walking with dogs; and youngsters playing around lampposts. The work affected me so strongly that it did not matter that I only encounter and do not engage in any of the activities depicted or that the protagonists are calaveras.

There are mythological echoes in these figures that bear exploring and to which I was clued by the central presence of the nonskeletal dog with whom I will begin. The dog's presence among the human calaveras could be an ironic touch. The creature that is sometimes considered base and lowly by many cultures in the world, including the Mexican, could be considered the most real figure in "Calavera urbana" because he is fully alive. Etymologically, the word *animal* means thing of breath or spirit, whereas the word *human* means thing of soil or dust. It is not necessary for Don Máximo to have consciously deployed this linguistic knowledge, to which he might have access through catechism and the Catholic mass, even if his formal schooling was limited. In any case, as professional readers such as critics and professors of literature have long known, it is the reader who completes a text. So perhaps Don Máximo wished to increase the outrageousness of the upside down world of Días de muertos with the image of the brown dog. He could be exalting the dog by bestowing life, spirit, and moving breath on him alone. He could be excluding the dog from the afterlife of humans, who are shown continuing their life's activities although they are dead. Or he may be representing an ancient Mexican belief.

The mythological allusion of the dog is that newly dead humans must rely on a dog to help them through the series of tests that occur along the four-year journey to Mictlan,* just as the dog-headed god Xólotl opens the way for the sun in its daily journey out of the underworld, to the zenith, and back again. In pre-Hispanic times, a dog was sometimes sacrificed for this reason and buried with a person. Different communities in Mexico have different beliefs about what kind of dog will be helpful. Some think any dog will do. Some favor yellow dogs, some any but black, some any but white, some red. Sahagún has written:

Y más decían [los naturales], que los perros de pelo blanco y negro no podían nadar y pasar el río, porque dizque decía el perro de pelo blanco: yo me lavé; y el perro de pelo negro decía: yo me he manchado de color prieto, y por eso no puedo pasaros. Solamente el perro de pelo bermejo, podía bien pasar a cuestas a los difuntos, y así en este lugar del infierno que se llama *Chiconaumictlan*, se acababan y fenecían los difuntos. (Sahagún Book 3, chapter 1 §23, 296)

[The Natives] also said that the dogs of white or black hair could not swim and cross the river because supposedly the white-haired dog would say "I've washed" and the black-haired dog would say "I've dirtied myself with dark color, and that's why I can't take you across." Only the dog with red hair could take the dead across on his back, and thus in this place of hell named *Chiconaumictlan* (Mictlan of Nine Tests), the dead ended and perished.

Still others prefer dogs with four eyes, which means black dogs that have a yellow spot above each eye, marking the third and fourth eyes; these special "eyes" see well even in the darkness of Mictlan and the nine rivers that must be traversed to reach its shores. Some groups in Mexico are still kind and generous to dogs because they fear the dogs could refuse to help them in the final crossing.[11]

The pedestrian in "Calavera urbana" may be shown with a guide dog on his way to Mictlan. His curious, half-lidded eyes may indicate the disorientation of recent death or the state of being neither alive with wide-open eyes nor entirely dead with eyes closed. Through the curious expression on the pedestrian's face, the artist interprets the road to the final resting place as an ambiguous area of transition.

The van full of child calaveras with their grim driver is reminiscent of souls being ferried across the river Styx to Hades by the grim Charon. In addition to, or instead of, the Greek allusion, Urbano might be making a class distinction and a comment on social mobility through the motion and stillness represented. Thus, on the one hand, we see the privileged children with their mother, father, or professional chauffeur, riding along the city streets, maybe to Mictlan; on the other hand we see the María sitting still on the sidewalk with her baby, going nowhere, and the pedestrian with the dog making his way on foot. In Mexico many people are too poor to own cars.

Finally, we come to the figures that frame the calavera, the boy behind the lamppost and the María selling bread. On the first level of signification, we see a mother calling her son, maybe wanting him to take over the bread stand or change the baby's diaper or get to a job or to school. He could be a shy potential suitor of the attractive young woman, although he seems considerably younger than she, and flirtations between younger men and older women are not common in Mexico. There may be additional mythological references.

Could the humble woman be intended to represent La Muerte,* an ironically Rubenesque incarnation, so to speak, of La Flaca,* enticing passersby to taste her wares and, by so doing, putting money in her pocket and more souls in her realm? Portraying death as a sexy (fertile) young mother is ingenious, and it points to the related beliefs presented in Chapter 5 about birth bringing death and of death being fertile and life-affirming. It

---

[11] A priceless story was told to anthropologist Ochoa Zazueta concerning the consequences of treating dogs badly; I quote it in full in Appendix B. Also see Carmichael and Sayer's *The Skeleton at the Feast* 104.

also parodies images of the omnipotent earth goddess Coatlicue, who dispenses both life and death. The proof is in the skeletal baby, lovingly bound to the skeletal mother's body.

Like the city in which it was conceived and displayed, "Calavera urbana" ingeniously combines the sacred and the profane, the tender and the merciless, seriousness and playfulness, images culled from high and low, national and international culture. It allows Máximo Urbano to be recognized as a consummate forger of popular culture.

"Apoteosis del pan de muerto"

Just to the viewer's left of "Calavera urbana," Máximo Urbano painted what I call "Apoteosis del pan de muerto.*" The text is simple: "El Mejor Pan de Muerto de todo el Mundo. Exquisito Pan de Muerto, Calientito" [The Best Pan de Muerto in the Whole World. Exquisite Pan de Muerto, Nice and Warm.] The graphic is idiosyncratic and bizarrely heretical. The image that dominates the painting is an enormous, stylized pan de muerto on a blue carpet. It is decorated with pink-and-white sugar; a slice has been neatly cut out of it and placed to the right. What is most salient about this loaf, besides its great size, is that it is radiant, with no source of light apparent.

Kneeling to the glorious pan de muerto is a female figure in blue. Her white feet, forearms, and folded, praying hands are skeletal; her head is a skull around which she wears a thin, red ribbon. Her egg-shaped eyes are slightly lidded; she smiles with closed lips. At her feet we see several leafless branches rising out of the ground. They look skeletal also and are reminiscent of the dry bushes or trees sometimes painted behind Jesus in pictures of him praying in the Garden of Gethsemane to be exempted from the bitter trial of crucifixion and death he knew lay ahead of him.

The legend above this picture seems more appropriate than is typical for Máximo Urbano. This does look like the best pan de muerto in the whole world. One could even interpret *world* as including the known universe and still feel secure that one had found the best. Because of the praying figure, the pan de muerto seems deified. The woman has found the holy grail, the bread of life. The fact that it is also the bread of the dead or death makes it appropriate for Días de muertos,* a holiday that celebrates the duality death-life and the life of the dead.

What about "Thou shalt have no other gods before me"? Are we not before an apotheosis of that on which alone man cannot live? Is the kneeling woman not praying to the bread? Because of its radiance and the dry

8.7 Apoteosis del pan de muerto. Bakery, México, D.F.

twigs behind her, this seems the most likely interpretation. But she could also be praying for a pan de muerto, praying in gratitude for having received a portion of the best pan de muerto in the world, or offering it to her dead and praying for their eternal rest. To stretch too far, given that the woman is dressed in her identifying color, it could even be the Virgin Mary offering pan de muerto to her dead son, Jesus, on Días de muertos in Gethsemane, which would explain the dead branches in the picture. Or could it be the dead Mary receiving the best pan de muerto from her "son," John?

I will rest with these readings, which I will not delete from my book, as outrageous as they are, because I think Máximo Urbano's calaveras are suggestive and open enough to allow for the wildest interpretations. Let the reader decide.

To end on a more grounded tone, I will discuss the letter forms Máximo Urbano has used. George Rabasa has observed that there is some attempt at elegance and tradition in the style used at the bottom of the picture (Rabasa, personal communication). The upper style is more straightforward and seems to be better for bragging or shouting. The same holds true for Urbano's other calaveras.

8.8 Luchadores. Bakery, México, D.F.

"Dos calaveras posmodernas"
[Two Postmodern Calaveras]

These two bakery calaveras,* taken in Mexico City, I have entitled "Luchadores" (Wrestlers) (Figure 8.8) and "Batman con luchadores" (Batman With Wrestlers) (Figure 8.9). Their legends are as traditional as they claim the pan de muerto in the bakeries to be. Above "Luchadores" it says "PRUEBE LO TRADICIONAL ... YA LLEGO LO SABROSO Pruebelo [*sic*]" [TASTE TRADITION ... WHAT IS DELICIOUS HAS ARRIVED Taste it].

On the right pane of glass, above the bread, it says "Llevelo [*sic*] a Casa, Delicioso" [Take It Home, Delicious]. Below the loaf of bread on the left pane, it says "Rico Pan de Muerto* pruebelo [*sic*]" [Delicious Pan de Muerto Taste It]. Below the loaf on the right it says "Calientito" [Nice and Warm]. The two images of pan de muerto are fairly typical also, although, as in "Apoteosis del pan de muerto," their scale is proportionately much larger than life-size.

On "Batman con luchadores" the legend is similar: "LLEGO LO TRADICIONAL / Delicioso Pan de Muerto / Pruebelo y . . . / Recuerde / 2 de

Noviembre!!" [WHAT IS TRADITIONAL HAS ARRIVED / Delicious Pan de Muerto / Taste it and . . . / Remember / 2 of November!!]. The only pan de muerto in this calavera is proportionately life-size.

"Luchadores" (Wrestlers)

"Luchadores" shows a pair of wrestlers to the right of the loaf and on its left panel. The one on the left is on the ground, poised on his right knee as if he were falling, trying to rise, or in the process of rising, his right hand extended as if for balance or in supplication. His head, in a typical wrestler's mask, is cocked to the right, possibly in a gesture of submission. Beneath him is a pool of red, orange, and yellow paint that looks like blood; the wrestler's nose is bleeding. The blood is a grotesque element that adds to the tone of the painting. Most of the wrestler's body is underneath a pan de muerto* shown at an angle that follows that of the human figure; it looks as though it is about to fall on him. Perhaps the standing wrestler's tense, thumbs-up gesture is urgent advice to his companion to get out of the bread's way before it is too late.

To the right of this figure is another man whose attire is no less typical of Mexican wrestlers, although it is the full mask, such as the kneeler on the left wears, which has become the identifying uniform of the sport. This man is standing as if in mid-step. He is wearing a partial mask that looks like the Batman bat logo. His mouth and forehead are reminiscent of Frankenstein in their discoloration and deformity. His right hand is elevated with the thumb up, although the signal does not seem particularly triumphant. His body is turning away from the viewer. It is a movement one might read as the relatively closed, opaque nature of the text; he is moving away, further into the text, rather than out toward the audience.

The only true calavera* in this graphic is to the right of a second, larger-than-life-size pan de muerto. Although her head is partially fleshed, the missing nose, cavernous mouth—slightly smiling—and visible facial bones are enough to identify the figure as a calavera, although her body is not only fleshed but has very well-developed muscles. She is wearing a discreet blue brassiere and competition briefs that allow us to see her washboard abdomen and mighty pectorals. The positioning of her arms helps to show off the definition of her muscles.

The bodybuilder's right biceps is perpendicular to her torso, with the fist holding the final "o" of "Delicioso." With this last gesture, it seems that she, as an athlete, as a woman, or as Death, is establishing her primacy over the written words. She is strong enough to take hold of them all. She stands steadily in unrealistic balance, with her heels slightly elevated. Unlike the other two figures, this one has no ground beneath her feet. This gives her a superhuman weightlessness compared with the two wrestlers, and it is similar to Batman's groundlessness in "Batman con luchadores." This calavera has fairly long black hair that is given great volume, but it is unbrushed and ragged. Her face, like that of the standing wrestler, is reminiscent of Frankenstein's. It is cartoonish with heavily lidded, oversized, egg-shaped eyes framed by exaggerated eyelashes and plucked eyebrows. She is by far the largest and strongest-looking of the three human figures. Perhaps with her superior size and fitness, Máximo Urbano is indicating her supremacy as the only calavera. We could read this to signify the power of La Muerte, La Calaca (Death, Skull)—nicknames for the always female Mexican personifications of death. I prefer not to make much of the femaleness of death; *muerte* is a feminine noun, as are most nouns denoting abstractions in Spanish.

The looming female presence challenges the (stereo)typical absence of women in Mexico's professional and amateur sports scenes. It goes against gender type except in the use of makeup. Even in this aspect, the painting is unique in Mexican published images of women, which are more apt to eroticize women's bodies than their faces. The weightlifter's body is too muscular to be sexy, and her clothing is clearly designed to focus attention on her strength rather than on her erotic appeal. If we consider the excess fat of the prone figure, the woman looks even mightier in contrast.

In addition, she is the only one of the three human images that is looking, if a bit foggily, out of the text at the viewer. She is not only the connection to Días de muertos;* she is perhaps the connection between the reader and the artist. Her gaze invites our self-conscious attention, and the "o" in her hand invites our deconstructive recognition of the presence of a writer and painter, of his deliberate combination of written and pictorial elements—in a word, of his intelligent artistry.

"Batman con luchadores" (Batman With Wrestlers)

"Batman con luchadores" contains only one, mostly hidden skeleton. It is a symmetrical composition with standing figures on the left and the right of the legend, almost in the position of opening and closing parentheses. They frame two more or less prostrate figures facing the standing ones, their bodies underneath and, as it were, inside the text.

On the right, the standing figure is appareled in an ocher-colored wrestling costume. His mouth is cavernous and black, his teeth visible beneath the skin of his upper lip, enough to denote him as the calavera* in the painting. He has an odd fringe around his lower jaw, like whiskers of yarn or string from his mask. His torso and arms are quite muscular; his buttocks are fairly pronounced. His arms and legs are less muscular than those of the female calavera in "Luchadores"; they look almost feminine in their rounded smoothness. His left hand is clenched in a fist at his side. His right hand is extended, pointing at the words "Delicioso Pan de Muerto*" or raised in a matter-of-fact gesture. He does not appear to acknowledge the other wrestler.

The figure beneath him is almost identical to the prostrate wrestler in "Luchadores." Instead of his left hand being on the ground, it is raised in a fist toward the other wrestler's abdomen in an ambiguous gesture: a curse, a threat, an expression of pain, supplication, or surrender. We see no blood. The ground underneath the two figures is a slick of off-white color behind which the standing wrestler's right foot is toeing off.

The standing figure on the left is Batman, fully fleshed, smiling slightly, in full regalia, his left leg invisible. He has, so to speak, no ground to stand

8.9 Batman con luchadores. Bakery, México, D.F.

on. He is holding a pan de muerto as if offering it to the kneeling wrestler before him. Batman appears somewhere between neutral and kind, not aggressive in the least.

The kneeling wrestler looks identical to the standing wrestler in "Luchadores," who might have met his match in Batman after succeeding over the paunchy wrestler in the other calavera. His hands, palms together in an attitude of prayer, are held just under his chin. His gaze is downward; his lips are parted. This polysemic pose could indicate that the kneeler is about to receive the pan de muerto from Batman's hands as he would a host from the hands of a priest, that he is praying to Batman for pan de muerto, that he is praying for pan de muerto and Batman is answering his prayer or that through Batman his prayer is being answered, or that he is as deeply grateful for the proffered pan de muerto as if it were holy. He could be receiving the loaf as a consolation prize for having lost to Batman in a wrestling match or for having lost to the ochre-clad wrestler. He could be receiving it as a prize after beating the fully masked wrestler whose posture could indicate deeper defeat than the prayer's. Batman could simply be giving him the pan de muerto because it is Días de muertos* season. The kneeler could be a visiting spirit receiving an offering. The reader can continue to multiply possible meanings.

These calaveras are in different neighborhoods—"Batman con lucha-dores" in a residential, upper-middle-class area, "Luchadores" in a busy, noisy, mixed light-industrial and residential lower-middle-class one. Because they are far apart, I have no reason to think Máximo Urbano imagined the two calaveras would be seen by the same audience, but it is possible he privately imagined some connection between them.

Unlike most calaveras, which are relatively willing to surrender their meanings, these two, like Urbano's other ones, seem fairly resistant. The images do not appear to have anything to do with the traditional text. In each case there is only one calavera, and there is no discernible reason for the other figures to be fleshed. Nor do the images ostensibly have anything to do with Días de muertos. I refer to them as postmodern because both paintings are rich in intertextuality, showing that the creator has appropri-ated elements from certain contemporary, popular-cultural discourses to produce his curious bricolages: We may have quotations and parodies of *lucha libre* (Mexican professional wrestling), prayer, communion, body-building, sado-masochistic power play—possibly (homo)sexual—U.S. Superhero comic books, maybe Superbarrio,[12] Hollywood film and televi-sion, and Días de muertos. Not all the figures represented have obvious connections among themselves, and we see nothing that indicates an anec-dote or a sequence. They present us with one of the hallmarks of postmod-ernism in that the texts offer no possibility for closure. The appropriation of various images is common to products in a capitalist society. The juxta-position of graphics and phrases from widely divergent contexts underlines the artist's great imagination and betrays his minimal interest in linear thinking, in didactic clarity, in consistency of style or sense. Máximo Urbano tenders to his readers polysemic texts full of fissures into which we can fit our own production of sense.

We can try to read in these calaveras the illustrator's vision of Días de muertos, although I would argue that the written words could have been mandated by his employer, the bakery manager or owner. In that case, we cannot assume that a brush-for-hire is the only author.

What is important in these paintings? "Lo tradicional," that which is traditional, that which is tasty, the pan de muerto itself, embodying what

---

[12] Superbarrio is a social activist in Mexico City who wears a costume inspired by those of pro-fessional wrestlers when he leads demonstrations and makes public appearances on behalf of the poor, the homeless, the victims of earthquakes and AIDS, and other disenfranchised people.

is traditional and tasty, representing what is for sale, and that is glorified
and given great size and importance in "Luchadores" and seems to be an
object of worship in "Batman con luchadores" in a way reminiscent of
"Apoteosis del pan de muerto." The bodybuilder seems very important as
the largest of all the human figures in the two paintings, the only female,
and the clearest calavera. She may reveal the rotulista's* challenging of
traditional Mexican gender roles. His inclusion of all-American Batman,
superhero of a city that has some similarities to Mexico City—a national
and international commercial and cultural center with a multicultural,
concentrated population with its concomitant problems of class; national,
ethnic, and religious differences; traffic; and crime—internationalizes his
vision by incorporating a bit of U.S. popular culture.

Paradoxically, Batman is shown as the bearer of a pan de muerto, that
which is most Mexican and most typical of Días de muertos in this picture.
Although I have not seen other calaveras with luchadores, they are one
more Mexican métier, one more group that probably enjoys pan de muerto
and celebrates Días de muertos according to familial and communal traditions. Their representation is in the line of other fighters: boxers, conquerors, revolutionaries, the last of which includes *soldaderas* or adelitas* (see
Figures 1.12, 1.16, 4.4–4.6, 4.16).

In summary, these two calaveras show how one artist envisions this
holiday as a palimpsest open enough to display old and new elements of
Mexico's constantly changing culture, as if there were layers of the traditional past in the pan de muerto, the text, and the calaveras; of the contemporary present in the luchadores and Batman; and of the future in the
powerful woman. He has rendered these relatively short-lived works such
that his viewers may enjoy puzzling over and figuring out the unusual texts,
recognizing fragments of popular intertexts, and enjoying their admiration
and awareness of a fellow who has published a personal vision of popular
culture on this occasion.

"Árboles de la muerte" (Trees of Death])

The town of Metepec, Estado* de México, is famous for its earthenware ceramics. In addition to sets of dishes, ollas,* candleholders, traditional and zoomorphic flowerpots, and decorative knickknacks, ceramists
in Metepec create fantastical "árboles de la vida" (trees of life).

The classical tree of life shows the creation of the earth according to
Genesis 1 (see Figure 8.10). At the top of the roughly diamond-shaped

8.10 Árbol de la vida. Metepec, Edo. de México

configuration is God, often accompanied by a dove representing the Holy
Spirit, sometimes surrounded by angels. In the bottom center is the much
maligned serpent who invited Eve to taste the fruit of the tree of knowledge, which would open her eyes so she would be like God, "knowing
good and evil" (Genesis 3:5). To the viewer's left is Eve, to the right is
Adam. Connecting and surrounding these figures is a mass of flowers and
small animals, showing the various objects God created: plants, fish,
birds, and mammals.

For Días de muertos,* the artists of Metepec produce *árboles de la muerte* (trees of death) as a parody of the árboles de la vida. The form of the parodies is more or less that of árboles de la vida, a diamond or an oval, but instead of displaying fat cherubs and fleshy human figures, they sport skeletons. The parody is not literal. One does not necessarily see the same configuration of characters, as if God, Eve, Adam, and the creatures were all calaveras.*

One I call "Árbol de la muerte, Gólgota" (Figure 8.11) seems to contain a parody of the Crucifixion of Christ. The enormous central figure in this life-size árbol de la muerte has its forearms extended at about a forty-degree angle from its upper arms, suggesting the position of Christ's arms on the cross. Its legs form a rather undignified diamond. Its feet rest on the skull of Adam, which gave the name to the Hill of Golgotha, positioned to be redeemed by the blood of Christ, even in death. Instead of being surrounded by the fruits of God's seven-day creation, this central figure is surrounded by smaller, grinning skulls and skeletons and a plethora of flowers, specifically stylized cempoaxóchitl.*

The second photo shows two árboles de la muerte. The smaller, unglazed one, which I call "Árbol de la muerte: malhechor," has as its central figure a calavera who might be a *cacique,* a landowner who also wields political power in the local government (see Figure 8.12). He is wearing a smart hat and a belt with two pistols. This figure could be a *malhechor,* an evildoer, or he could be a legitimate and innocent rancher—but why then is he wearing nothing but a hat and a belt with holsters? Maybe he is a U.S. cowboy, known from Westerns to prefer violence as a means of solving problems. The figure looks sinister to me because the facial expression is grim and the four calaveras at the level of his elbows and knees are skulls and crossbones. This last detail in ancient Mexica* art is indicative of certain female deities, the sinister cihuateteo* who are related to the life-taking Xólotl (Earth Monster). The depicted malhechor might have killed the bodiless four himself. This árbol de la muerte, like the others, contains numerous flowers, some of them stylized cempoaxóchitl that reemphasize death.

The second árbol de la muerte in this photo has two tiers (Figure 8.12). We see two weddings: The top tier holds a catrín and catrina* bride and groom, skeletal, of course; the lower tier holds a peasant bride and groom. I call it "Árbol de la boda" (Wedding Tree). The two couples are surrounded by musicians, flowers, and leaves. The humor of this árbol is especially ironic. Whereas the true árbol de la vida shows the first human

8.11 Árbol de la muerte, Gólgota. Metepec, Edo. de México

couple, according to Judeo-Christian mythology, now separated by the snake and, if you will, by their sin of disobedience, "Árbol de la boda" shows two human couples. They are just being united in, presumably, a Christian sacrament. They are not surrounded by creatures but by human musicians to show their secure integration into society through the rite of

8.12 *Árbol de la muerte, malhechor. Metepec, Edo. de México*

passage. They are surrounded by enormous blooms whose crowns are as big as the humans' chests. In weddings, flowers are a sign of fertility, as well as a symbol of love, life, youth, and beauty; in this case, the large size emphasizes the meanings, working as an iconic exclamation mark.

So, instead of being cast out of the Garden of Eden, marking an end to innocence and harmony with God and nature, the skeletal couples are drawn into society and earthly happiness, marking a beginning of their life as full adults—especially if we give in to the vulgar focus some wedding guests adopt and think lasciviously about the wedding night and the first time the couple can legitimately engage in sexual intercourse. But how ironic that the wedding parties are skeletal and the wedding flowers are alive. Indigenous philosophy never gave the human being dominion over the earth; nor did it promise us life longer than that of a flower.

The other thread of irony is the placement of the couples, emphasizing their class status. The calaveras catrinas are at the top, belonging as they do to *la clase alta,* the upper class; the calaveras campesinas are below, as behooves those of *la clase baja* (the lower class).

Thus, "Árbol de la boda" parodies at least three socially significant matters vis-à-vis árboles de la vida. It shows harmony between humans and nature, possibly attributable to the death of the men and women, in contrast to imminent disharmony among humans, nature, and God near the beginning of human life on earth. It emphasizes the happiness of skeletal, married partners compared with the unhappiness that ensued for Adam and Eve after they became fully conscious, in fact, self-conscious beings. And it makes evident the unequal relations of catrines and campesinos. Harmony may exist among the members of each social class, but harmony between social classes depends on the hierarchy being maintained.

9

Feasting on Skeletons

Estaba la muerte seca,
sentada en un muladar,
comiendo tortilla dura,
pa'ver si podía engordar.

Dry death
was sitting on a dump
eating hard tortillas
to see if she could grow plump.

Estaba la muerte seca,
sentada en un carrizal,
comiendo tortilla dura,
y frijolitos sin sal.

Dry death
was sitting among the reeds
eating hard tortillas
and unsalted little beans.

—Traditional
(Quoted in Martel Díaz Cortés 34f)

Our epistemology of scientific rationalism expects food to nurture life, and it expects the living—never the dead—to be the preparers and ingesters of food. On another level that does not accord with this rationalism, Western culture—at least as it is manifested in metropolitan Mexico and the United States—seems to lull us with business, consumerism, and programmed leisure into considering death very distant and personally irrelevant. In a grotesque inversion of such cultural expectations, which are shared to a great extent with the cosmopolitan upper classes I dare say, of the whole modern world but certainly of Mexico, Días de muertos* proliferates calaveras (comical images of skeletons) that depict calaveras* (skeleton characters) preparing, selling, or serving food in a parody of what living people do every day. They not only parody these acts by the living for the living, but, because this is Días de muertos, they also parody the preparation of elaborate feasts on behalf of the dead. By their skeletal nature, they remind the living of the reality and imminence of the death of their loved ones, as well as of their own. They also allow their audience to question their beliefs and assumptions about the festival and about life and death in general.

A remarkable number of the calaveras I have seen or photographed show food and food-related activities. As food is a central element of any human life and culture, it is not surprising to find it as a central element of cultural production. And, as food is equated with life, why not expect it to be part of life after death? In contrast to this popular art, food is rarely present in the art of high culture, except for still lifes, the Last Supper, the serendipitous child with fruit, and the occasional banquet or picnic scene.

Normally, the upper classes take the preparation and selling of food very much for granted. In Mexico, that work is ordinarily performed by servants, as is the buying of food for the household. The well-off are never plagued, as are the poor, by concerns that they may not have enough money to purchase the food they need or want or that the harvests are insufficient; money can always buy imported or transported food. Furthermore, the privileged do not have to practice ingenuity to stretch small food supplies or make leftovers interesting or create variety out of the same few staples the poor can afford or grow themselves. Given all this, it is understandable that popular texts feature food more often than "high" cultural texts. "For the hungry," as Caroline Bynum has written, "food forces itself forward as an insistent fact, an insistent symbol" (Bynum, *Holy Feast and Holy Fast*, 1). And since members of the power bloc may own and manage supermarkets, bars, and restaurants but not sell and prepare food themselves as we see done in the calaveras, it is not surprising that high-culture artists do not depict their peers performing these tasks.

Cooking signifies civilization and culture for Lévi-Strauss. I have not purposely collected food-related calaveras. In four years of going to Mexico for Días de muertos, I photographed all the calaveras I saw, and I have sometimes traveled the streets of Mexico City's barrios populares specifically to scout out calaveras to see and to capture on film. It has been impossible not to notice how many of them center on preparing, selling, and serving food, although only two in my collection show the enjoyment of food. Food is an apt sign for a fiesta* that is a long meditation on life and death, on how they are related, and on how one gives way to another. It is especially apt in a culture that has a memory of ancient cannibalism and the experience of the Catholic mass, during which a host is transubstantiated into the body of Christ to be consumed by the communicants.[1] As Caroline Bynum has perspicaciously observed:

> Like [the] body, food must be broken and spilled forth in order to give life. Macerated by teeth before it can be assimilated to sustain life, food mirrors and recapitulates both suffering and fertility. Thus food, by what it is, seems to symbolize sacrifice and service. And, in Christian doctrine, the suffering, broken, crucified body on the cross, from which springs humankind's salvation, *is* food. (Bynum, *Holy Feast and Holy Fast*, 30).

Plants are harvested and animals slaughtered to become food for humans, who die and become earth in which plants grow, which can feed animals and humans, ad infinitum. Calaveras depict skeletons consuming bread in an absurd staging of that which cannot happen. Food may come from the dead, both because they fertilize the soil and because, as spirits or semidivine beings, they can influence divine powers to grant good harvests, sufficiently remunerative work, and laden tables for the living. So the living give back a little of that bounty to their dead in gratitude and celebration. The spirit thus enjoys the spirit of food.

In a more down-to-earth context, the creators of calaveras portray members of their class doing what they do in public and for the well-to-do. Many earn a living by cooking and selling food, sometimes from an improvised sidewalk stand as shown in Figure 1.24. The bread vendor in "Calavera urbana" (see Figure 8.6) carries her calaverita baby on her back. No husband-father provides for them while they stay home and he goes out to work. One figure is shown selling sweet potatoes from a humble cart in the papier mâché sculpture of Plate 17.[2] In "Gran fandango y francachela de

---

[1] Writing about late-medieval women mystics who had graphic visions, among others, of eating the baby Jesus in the host or of the host becoming meat in the mouth, Bynum has said: "Eating is a central metaphor not merely because the eucharist is the place in Christian ritual in which God is most intimately received but also because *to eat* and *to be eaten* express that interpenetration and mutual engulfing, that fusion of fleshly humanness with fleshly humanness . . . necessary for uniting with a God-who-is-man" (Bynum, *Holy Feast and Holy Fast*, 156).

todas las calaveras" we see a neighborhood pulquería, a very humble sort of pub in which not food but pulque is sold and in which may be music for dancing (see Plate 18, Figure 1.22).

Another curious scene is depicted in Figure 9.1, which is not really a calavera. A homemade skeleton puppet with a cigarette between its teeth invites passersby with a waving left (sinister) hand to enjoy a home-cooked meal in the patio of this middle-class household. This is a service to a few of the 2 million visitors to Mixquic and is also a way to integrate some of the outsiders' pesos into the local economy.[3]

Figures 1.24, 4.12, and 8.2 show historical references to zapatistas or to Zapata and adelitas. The adelitas were the wives or companions of the revolutionary soldiers; a few were soldiers themselves, but usually they went along to fill the fighters' hygienic, nutritional, and sexual needs. In Figures 1.24 and 8.2, the adelita is separating a bit of dough to pat into a tortilla such as the one she is grilling along with what looks like a chunk of meat for the resting zapatista. Her grinding stone is to the right of the grill. The smaller adelita in Figure 1.24 offers up a cooked sope, much thicker than a tortilla, while she tends three more.

Only the earthenware Figure 9.2 shows banqueting skeletons. A large group of male and female friends sits along three sides of a sumptuously laden table. Some are holding tacos, one is taking food to its mouth, others are talking, embracing, and listening. Their disposition around the table is so like that in representations of the Last Supper that when I first spotted this work, I counted to see if there were thirteen figures. There are more, but even with the difference in the number of diners, the cultic event is parodied.

This calavera is unique because it shows the acts of sitting at a table and eating. Is it not significant that the subordinate are usually shown preparing, selling, and serving food but not enjoying the literal fruits of their labor? Here, the fact that the females' hair is stylishly cut in bobs indicates that they are members of well-to-do classes. The men are dressed like *rancheros*, who own land and livestock.

---

[2] These carts have a big metal barrel that produces steam by which sweet potatoes and plantains are cooked to be sold on squares of brown paper, served with salt and chile or with sweetened condensed milk.

[3] In 1991, more than 2 million people visited Mixquic in a three-day period, 1.2 million on November 2 alone.

9.1 Comida casera. Mixquic

9.2 The Last Supper. Metepec, Edo. de México

I close this introduction to a second series of readings by reflecting on the fact that all of these cooks, vendors, deliverers, servers, and eaters are skeletons. Calaveras are open texts that require the collaboration of an active reader to complete them, and there is no definitive answer to the questions they toss to their audience. Are the calaveras dead because they consumed that particular bakery's bread or part of their own wares? Do they somehow deserve death, as if their very existence were a sin? Are we all dead or dying because we consume food, because to live is to spend life, which is to die?

If there are lessons, lectures, and consumable, comprehensible readings in the calaveras, perhaps one goes like this: Since all bread eaters will die and stay dead, as have all the bread eaters who have preceded us, clearly death dwells in life, survives life, and hence should be seen as even more natural to the human body than life. Días de muertos with its calaveras tells its readers:

You can enter this fiesta by taking flowers to the graves of your dead. You can interpret this fiesta* by designing, painting, and sculpting calaveras. You can discern some of the meanings of the fiesta while driving to Mixquic in your VW bug or your new Chevrolet, while eating pan de muerto* and sugar calaveras. You can open yourself to the holiday's lessons while gawking at and videotaping our exotic practices and understanding something of them, although you have not bothered to learn our language. You can meditate on life and death as this fiesta expresses them while coming home from your northern residence to pay your respects and to turn your favorite holiday into intellectual labor. You can read this fiesta reading an expatriate's book. You can read Días de muertos. You can laugh at calaveras. Know what it is you hold in your eyebeams. Know you are seeing yourself. Are you still laughing?

9.3 Bellas concursantes. Bakery, México, D.F.

Readings II

"Bellas concursantes" (Beautiful Contestants), or How the Bread Was Won

We recognize the style of rotulista* Máximo Urbano. The simple legend, translated, reads: "Delicious pan de muerto, the best of the neighborhood in quality and flavor." The calavera* shows three women posed identically, each holding up a pan de muerto.* What makes them calaveras is that although their bodies are fleshed, their heads are skulls. All three wear only bathing suits and high-heeled shoes and have prominent bottoms; one has large breasts. They stand on little numbered platforms: Number 1 is for the one with the largest breasts and red hair, number 2 is for the one with the longest eyelashes and black hair, number 3 is for another with black hair. It is perhaps significant that number 1's hair, because of its color, looks the most Northern European or "American" (from the United States). Autochthonous Mexicans typically have black hair. One must recognize that most Olympic swimmers come from the bourgeoisie. Who else in Mexico has access to training?

How shall we read this calavera? Three contestants participate in an Olympics, perhaps as swimmers, and their prize is pan de muerto. Or is this a contest for the most desirable sort of woman who is willing to be seen in public wearing a swimming suit because she wants to please the male, because she likes how she looks in a swimming suit, because she is not in Mexico City where this calavera is displayed but on a beach where a swimming suit is the most appropriate, comfortable, and practical attire? In the matter of the contest, pan de muerto is the prize, along with the "place"—first, second, or third—which means recognition and status and visibility (so much for evading the panoptical gaze). Or perhaps pan de muerto was baked by the contestants, who hoped to present the winning loaf, although this does not solve the problem of (un)dress. During Días de muertos,* baking contests for pan de muerto are held in numerous communities, sponsored by groups that want to promulgate "nuestras tradiciones mexicanas" (our Mexican traditions).[4]

In any case, the reader is allowed to think that the women and the bread are prizes she or he[5] can consume with her or his gaze and body; that beauty deserves or creates the best bread; that good bread is good nutrition for Olympic athletes; and that, like the bread in the bakery behind the calavera, the woman who values the best bread in the neighborhood is also the most desirable and the best woman in the neighborhood.

Or we could read it like this: The winner of this contest must smile as she serves the best pan de muerto in the neighborhood, which she bakes for the bakery; she buys at the bakery; she wins in an athletic contest; she brings from heaven to earth, which explains how delicious the bread is; or which she has received from her living relatives as an ofrenda* on Días de muertos and is taking home to share with her disembodied friends and relations. Since these contestants are calaveras, this last option could include any of the possibilities of how the bread was won.

In the right panel of "Bellas concursantes" we have, as in the eponymous calavera read in the last chapter, a kind of apotheosis of pan de muerto in a loaf that is very nicely browned and sparkling with sprinkled sugar, typical of Máximo Urbano's calaveras. The three contestants are paying tribute to it with their humbler, smaller loaves. Perhaps they have been inspired to win or buy their own to participate in the essence and glory of Pan de Muerto-ness. As winners in athletics or aesthetics or baking, they are

---

[4] As one example, according to *Excélsior,* a Mexico City newspaper, the county of Miguel Hidalgo held such a contest for housewives and bakeries on November 1, 1991. They were to submit loaves of pan de muerto weighing 500 grams and reveal their recipes. The best three were to receive "reconocimiento y útiles regalos" (recognition and useful gifts).

[5] I insist on being nonsexist and nonheterosexist, although I recognize that the intended audience of this calavera is male. Heterosexual or lesbian women are unlikely to have been considered potential readers.

part of a cult of desirable, consumable female persons and are participants in the adoration of the perfect, hallowed Pan in the sky, so to speak.

If the swimming-suited calaveras signify desirable female nature, we cannot dismiss the task of reading the pan de muerto itself. First, this bread signifies Días de muertos. Local versions are offered in most communities that celebrate the fiesta. It is favored because, considering its use value, it is sweet and light and tasty and a good source of carbohydrates. Considering its exchange value, it is commercially produced, which means it must be purchased; it is rarely baked in the typical urban home. In this sense it also signifies modernity, in part because it is Spanish, leavened, wheat bread, not a Native staple. It also signifies the capitalist economy, which teaches us to value that which is advertised and which we need to purchase with coin to satisfy our needs and our whims and to do our part to keep the economy moving, as well as to keep up with the Joneses. Or the Pérezes.

The bread is highly valued in this calavera by its much larger-than-life image on the right and by its importance as the only object on the left. The calaveras wear very little, stand on very little, have empty right hands, and hold high the pan de muerto in their left hands. They appear to love this object. It was as important as their bodies' strength or beauty in obtaining their prizes, even as bread—the staff of life—is essential to giving life and strength to our bodies, leaving aside that we cannot live by bread alone.

The loaf in each contestant's hand is about the size of the platform she stands on, so we can read that the bread is as fundamental as the ground. It is the ground of being or baking or winning or athletic prowess or (female) goodness or (female) beauty or all of these things. And because of the ambiguity of the contest rules, we can (but do not have to) assume that the beautiful contestants and the pan de muerto are identified with each other. There is an implication that both are desirable, both can be judged hierarchically—good, better, best—and both can be bought and consumed. Because bread is the staff of life, the identification of bread and woman suggests that strong, sexy women are as essential (to male and perhaps lesbian readers) as bread is. Bread and women can be consumed with the gaze, they can be eaten or cannibalized, they can be purchased or sold.

We still should contend with the fact that the beautiful, bread-bearing, skin-baring contestants are calaveras. Like Madonna, Máximo Urbano parodies patriarchal values. What Fiske has written about the popular star could be extended to apply to the rotulista.*

Parody can be an effective device for interrogating the dominant ideology. It takes the defining features of its object, exaggerates and mocks them, and thus mocks those who "fall" for its ideological effect. But Madonna's parody goes further than this: she parodies not just the stereotypes, but the way in which they are made. She represents herself as one who is in control of her own image and of the process of making it. This, at the reading end of the semiotic process, allows the reader similar control over her own meanings. (Fiske, *Reading the Popular*, 105)

The contestant calaveras are not in control of their own image; they are images. Urbano has given us a producerly text with enough gaps for a feminist reading, among others. Sexy, Olympic-star skeletons are ludicrous. Eroticizing the body is ludicrous. Eroticizing the skeleton is more so. Believing that life and death are separate, that eating protects us from death, is as ludicrous as eroticizing bodies, whether skeletal or fleshed. Contests and the processes of elaborating and maintaining hierarchies are ludicrous. Giving time and attention to trying to win contests or to rise in a hierarchy that will reward us with nothing but a loaf of bread, however delicious, is ludicrous—not the least because it puts us naked in full view of whoever is guarding the panopticon. This reading has at least one possible moral: Let us live our lives and find our pleasures as much as we can outside of the system whose pleasures and prizes are too fleeting and trivial to be worth our time—that is, our life.

"Panaderos* ciclistas" (Cyclist Bakers)

In "Panaderos ciclistas" we see cut tissue paper with mirror images of two cyclists delivering bread—more specifically, two calavera* cyclists delivering pan de muerto.* Both this calavera and the following one, "Soñando pan de muerto," were displayed and photographed in Mexico City: the paper one in the rather exclusive popular-art market known as Bazar Sábado, the painted one in a middle-class residential area. I have not seen this form of delivery since around the mid-1960s, but this was how bread used to be delivered from the place at which it was baked in large quantities to where it was sold in neighborhood bread shops that did not have their own kitchens.

"Panaderos ciclistas" is especially pleasing because it shows baskets of bread so full that second, smaller baskets are added to the bike racks and that loaves are falling off the top hat baskets, more typical of that mode of

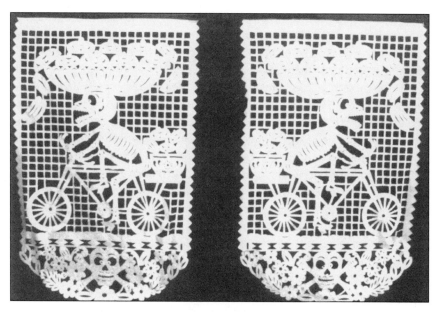

9.4 Panaderos ciclistas. Bazar Sábado, México, D.F.

delivery. The two cyclists have open mouths that can be read as the slackness of death; as speech; as panting from hard, fast cycling; as salivating for the pan de muertos; as exclaiming on seeing the loaves falling; or even as trying irrationally, the way we sometimes do when we drop something, to catch the loaves in their mouths. Bakhtin gives another possibility: "The gaping mouth is related to the image of swallowing, this most ancient symbol of death and destruction. At the same time, a series of banquet images are also linked to the mouth" (Bakhtin, *Rabelais*, 325).

Applying this interpretation of a European medievalist, the cyclists and most calaveras—not only those with open mouths—can be considered signifiers of death, not only, as I claimed previously, for Días de muertos. But ironically, they can also signify life in a typically grotesque inversion within a carnivalesque discourse. In any time, medieval or modern, the mouth is the threshold of the body, the border between me and not-me. It is where half of mutual sexual contacts—that is, those enjoyed simultaneously by both partners rather than performed by one and received by the other—occur, through kissing; and therein is an association of fertility and reproduction, new life, as of love and pure pleasure. The mouth is where both food and breath enter the body and where the last breath of life leaves it. In this sense, the mouth signifies both life and death. One of the things calaveras do is show and remind the readers that they are no closer to life than to death, to food and breath than to expiration. They cannot separate themselves from their mouths or close them to keep from expiring, sooner or later.

All of these readings, plus more that other readers could provide, are mildly humorous in their grotesqueness, but they are also anxiety provoking. The reader of "Panaderos ciclistas" wants to help the cyclist deliver his load complete. The reader hopes the loaves are not counted and that the cyclist will not have to pay for the fallen ones with which probably not he but his supervisor overloaded the baskets. The reader experiences negative empathy based on times when she or he has also dropped, broken, lost, or ruined valuable items. The reader is disgusted, wondering if the cyclist will retrieve the fallen loaves, which may end up on the reader's table—grime and all—bearing germs, maybe illness and death, instead of health and life. (Adult Mexicans, unlike some Europeans, have little tolerance for bread handled in a less than sanitary manner.) The calavera's wide-open eyes, the nervous checkered pattern all around the cyclist, the lightning-shaped cut-outs below the surface of the road he travels, and the clear spokes of the bicycle wheels all lend to the anxiety of the entire scene.

In addition, in each of the two panels we see a skull and crossbones below the pedals. They are symbols of death, imported from pre-Hispanic or European imagery to play a part in Días de muertos iconography. The skulls' eyes are crossed, subtracting from their dignity and danger, indicating confusion or a sense of feeling overwhelmed, driven crazy by the job of delivering too much bread in too small a basket with too short a deadline.

The skull may also be thinking the image of the panadero ciclista: it may be the cyclist himself anticipating his work if he is alive or remembering it if he is dead. It may be his dead or to-be-dead *patrón,* or boss, thinking about him. It may be a prediction of his future, possibly early death from overwork and too much stress. It may be a spirit remembering the good old days in which bread was delivered by cyclists (himself before death?). For a few more possibilities, see the next section, "Soñando pan de muerto."

In any case, the falling bread signifies excess, and the excess of meaning that can be harvested from this and many calaveras makes it a producerly text that gives its reader great pleasure.

9.5 Soñando pan de muerto. Bakery, México, D.F.

"Soñando pan de muerto" (Dreaming of pan de muerto)

"Soñando pan de muerto" was painted on a bakery's display case with the figure of a skull and crossbones thinking about a pan de muerto* in a cartoon thought-bubble. The small figure can be read in several ways, none of which excludes the others.

It represents a spirit looking forward to Días de muertos* when its relatives will offer it pan de muerto, its favorite food. It represents the cyclist longing for his (all cyclist panaderos were men) own pan de muerto, which (1) he cannot afford or (2) he will purchase or (3) steal or (4) be served at home at the end of his day's work. The cyclist is longing for or remembering bread he recently purchased, stole, or was served. He represents the panadero, who may be thinking how nice it will be to be dead, at which time his relatives will provide him with pan de muerto.[6] I

9.6 Merienda de pilón. Bakery, México, D.F.

enjoy the vertigo that results from this last reading, considering that the daydreamer is already a calavera.*

"Merienda de pilón" (Supper Plus)

In "Merienda de pilón" the caption reads: "Pan de muerto* con pilón . . . que es calidad y finura" [Bread of the dead with something extra . . . quality and excellence]. *Pilón* is the extra item of merchandise traditionally tossed into the buyer's bag to attract loyalty. Whereas it was common into the 1960s to receive a pilón in markets, small shops, and sidewalk stands, the custom has largely died out in Mexico City, where most merchants do not expect to see the same buyers repeatedly.

The joke in this legend is that in this bakery the buyer will not receive an extra roll or cookie that would be a typical pilón; instead, she or he can count on the bread purchased being excellent. The typically carnivalesque humor cuts both ways. By reminding the reader of how times have changed, how people have become less generous, neighborhoods less neighborly, and

---

6 See the epigraph for Chapter 1, "A Family Reunion, National Affirmation."

the economy more constraining, the artist makes fun of the baker who is too poor, unwise, greedy, or stingy to give a real pilón and perhaps too unscrupulous to guarantee the quality of the product without trying to receive extra remuneration, or at least recognition, for doing so. At the same time, the artist, Carlos Oznaya,[7] makes fun of the buyer who is always on the lookout for a bargain or for a little extra something for nothing. The buyer's attention is caught by the promise of a pilón, only to catch the joke—in small lettering—that all she or he can expect is what she or he already expects: bread of fine quality.

These meanings could raise consciousness regarding the rather poor economic situation that has resulted for a great many people because of the financial policies of the last two regimes under which subsidies for staple foods, including bread, have been cut. The calavera's reference to el pilón and the sense of abundance and generosity it once conveyed could inspire nostalgia that, if the customers relate the good old days with good, fresh pan de muerto, should result in sales.

The painting confronts us with repeated images of death and the dead. For the excess and redundance we expect of carnival humor, the words *Pan de muerto* are written in letters that resemble bones. So we have bone letters, the name *pan de muerto*, the image of the bread with its parodied skull and bones, and the two skeletal figures. We remember the quotation from Bakhtin about the open mouth being another signifier of death, particularly since these two figures are partly skeletal. The irony we cannot ignore is that the mouth may as easily signify breath, which indicates life; speech, which means communication, which indicates life; eating, which indicates life; or kissing, which indicates sexual arousal, which once again indicates life. Chapter 7 contains examples of the imbrication of life and death. We can consider that imbrication to be a permanent carnivalesque element that has the potential to disturb the expectations of Mexico's Western-identified bourgeoisie.

At the center of "Merienda de pilón," a table is almost entirely covered by a disproportionately large, steaming pan de muerto that dwarfs the cups

---

[7] Calaveras are unsigned, anonymous works. Although I tried to learn the name of the rotulista* I have called Máximo Urbano and to contact both him and Oznaya, it was impossible to do so. Oznaya has no telephone and can only be contacted in person at one of the bakeries he paints during the first or last few days of some months. I was unable to meet him, as the last days of October and the first days of November were holidays during which he did not work because he had already painted the calaveras on the bakeries.

and coffeepot, which are also steaming. The presence of a coffeepot suggests that the two figures are drinking *café americano* (U.S.-style coffee), weak enough to drink until the pot is empty, rather than the drinks more typical of a *merienda*, or light supper—hot chocolate or *café con leche*, of which no one is likely to drink more than one cup at a meal. Since a taste for unsweetened black coffee is rare in the popular classes, the café americano can be taken as a sign of the privileged ranks or a parody of them.

A gesticulating male calavera (nick)named Gordo,[8] on the viewer's right, is seated on the only chair. His clothing is odd for a member of Mexico City's middle class: a cropped turtleneck with an even shorter black vest over it. Beneath his exposed navel and below table level, he is wearing bright pink shorts with tiny black polka dots. His socks are striped black and pink; there are holes in their heels (see Plate 19).

El Gordo's outfit is grotesque and comical. His upper body is dressed well enough for public appearance, including at a supper table, but his lower body gives signs of private space. The patterns of the socks and shorts are clownish; the lack of proper public footwear, including the holes in the socks, denotes comicity or intimacy. The lower part of his body intrigues the viewer because of its impropriety. It gives us reason to suspect readiness for bed, whether he has just emerged from it or is just getting ready to retire.

The male calavera's head is skeletal, although there is flesh on his bony limbs, and his belly and buttocks are round, which also draws our attention to the lower body; we remember that Bakhtin interprets such emphasis as humorous by itself and as indicating the fertility of carnival humor. El Gordo's left leg has a fringe of long black hair. Its strangeness and location draw attention to the part of his thigh we do not see under his shorts.

The calavera is speaking to his female companion, who seems to be speaking to him at the same time. He looks animated and excited. His wide-open mouth indicates eagerness to chat energetically, to consume the gargantuan pan de muerto, or, for that matter, somehow to consume the female partner, to whom we now turn.

On the viewer's left is the gesticulating, speaking female calavera, Viky, in a flamingo pose, her raised ankle just above her locked knee. She sports a miniskirt so mini that one can glimpse her bright pink underwear

---

[8] *Gordo* (or *Gorda*, feminine) is a common term of endearment, although it literally means Fatty. See note 10 in this chapter.

where the skirt splits between her parted thighs. She wears high-heeled shoes to match her cropped tank top, which says "Hola" across her chest. The pink on Viky's clothes is precisely the shade of el Gordo's underwear. This similarity seems to attract the two pinks to each other, shoes to socks, underwear to underwear, as the exposed middles similarly attract each other—navel to navel.[9]

Viky wears bangles and a bead necklace, and her hair looks suspiciously like an orange wig, although it may be intended to be her natural hair or it may be dyed. The fact that it is the same color as the removable jewelry signifies artificiality, whether because of the use of dye or because of wearing a wig. Her eyelashes are disproportionately long and thick. The color and short cut of the hair, the makeup, and the fashion join the beverage to indicate the bourgeoisie or its parody or imitation by members of a lower class. The coffeepot is on her side of the table, so Viky is serving el Gordo; although she also has a cup, she has no chair. The two calaveras could be spouses, lovers, or, as I intend to show, prostitute and john. Viky's hair, jewelry, and seductive dress could indicate that métier. The "Hola" on her blouse could almost be her breasts speaking. The minuscule glimpse of lingerie could seem seductive. The situation seems very homey—el Gordo may be a regular customer; their conversation belies familiarity (the punctuation is idiosyncratic).

—Pa que veas Gordo yo doy pilón	"So you see, Gordo, I give 'pilón.'"
—Qué barbaro Viky . . . ahora sí te	"Wow, Viky . . . you outdid
echaste un 8 y de rebote pasta	yourself this time and, to top it off,
con Pilón	pastry with 'Pilón.'"

To what pilón is Viky referring? To what principal merchandise? Have they just had sex, the main purchase? Viky seems eager to please el Gordo; she not only gives him a pilón, she also draws his attention to it, as the baker not only sells us high-quality bread but draws our attention to its excellence. The disrespectful parallel of baker and prostitute is not lost on the reader, as if Oznaya were imputing some immorality to commerce.

---

[9] A common joke in Mexico is evoked by the two crop-tops. The boss says to the secretary, "If anyone calls, say that I'm at a meeting," and under his breath he adds, "of navels," unless the secretary is the one to add the quip once his back is turned.

El Gordo's compliment could refer to a sexual performance, and the phrase "y de rebote"—literally, on the bounce-back—contextually, "and besides" or "on top of that" could allude to bouncing on, in, or out of bed. Mexican popular speech is very creative, and this phrase is an example of situational polysemy. In any case, pan de muerto with coffee would be a good postcoital snack—the complex carbohydrates of the bread replenishing expended energy, the caffeine dispelling lingering drowsiness and inertia.

It is unusual to have such a suggestive cartoon in a very public place where men and women, young and old, the prudish, proper, and promiscuous of all social classes can see it. When I photographed it, glancing only casually at the print, it looked like an innocent, domestic merienda scene. I do not remember reading the calaveras' speech when I took it, and as the reader can see, it is virtually illegible, almost invisible, so it was not until writing these pages that I took the quotations—under a magnifying glass—into account.

Like certain examples of high art, some popular art delights in its ability to épater la bourgeoisie (shock the middle class). Carlos Oznaya has deployed the politics and poetics of transgression, to use Stallybrass and White's phrase, by using public space for a private and suggestive scene. He has not acted very differently from the art directors who design the images for billboards and printed ads. In Mexico, such ads are even more sexist than in the United States, presenting women in suggestive clothing and seductive postures to entice the (presumably male) reader's attention and purchase. But Oznaya has gone further by depicting prostitution, which does not figure large in the domain of polite public discourse in Mexico. Given a space and an assignment to paint a calavera on that space, the artist has dared to allow the possibility that the bakery's female patrons could also link sex and supper. Viky's words show pride in that link, and readers of commercials are used to being pressured to look and behave like the models in ads. In "Merienda de pilón" Oznaya has exploited his parody of an unpretentious supper very creatively.

Finally, as to the possible meaning of these characters being skeletal, I would add to my suggestions about the open mouths that some popular expressions link sex and death. And there are other similarities: Both are usually situations of vulnerability, abandon, a lack of self-consciousness, and intimacy. Both are moments in which the boundaries of the body are transgressed or transcended. Both are relatively welcomed by Mexicans.

As with all these readings, this one does not pretend to be definitive. I believe the true pilón received not only by those who buy bread at this bakery but by all passersby is the provocative painted calavera.

"Merienda exquisita" (Delicious Supper)

"Merienda exquisita" is a calavera by Carlos Oznaya, the artist who created "Merienda de pilón." The two are similar in style and subject, both representing one male and one female calavera* facing each other, gesticulating, and talking across a table that holds an enormous pan de muerto.* The most important graphic differences are in the female calaveras and in the seats. Although both dialogues are intimate, the one in "Merienda exquisita" focuses on language and relies on double entendre for its humor, whereas the one in "Merienda de pilón" focuses more on sartorial conventions and the situation.

The female calavera in "Merienda exquisita" is seated. Like her partner, she wears blue and has one foot bare (see Plate 20). (Their shoes rest symmetrically on the bonelike, uppercase letters that spell [PAN DE] MUERTO.) She is blond and wears a blue ribbon. Although her face is skeletal and her limbs are bony, her bottom is as round as el Gordo's in "Merienda de pilón," and her breasts are more prominent than Viky's. Her skirt is as short as Viky's, but it reveals no underwear. Her bangles and necklaces look like they may be gold, whereas Viky's resemble costume jewelry. This last detail, the more discrete clothing, the fact that she shares the table with her companion, and her cheeky style of addressing him all indicate a higher-class status than Viky enjoys. It seems safe to assume that la Gordis,[10] as the male calavera calls her, is his wife or partner. I'll refer to him as el Hablador, the Talker, the reason for which is revealed in the words of la Gordis.

Three things are interesting about the seating arrangement. The first is the equal status conveyed by the fact that both figures are sitting and in virtually identical positions. Unlike Viky, la Gordis is not serving el Hablador; in fact, she has a steaming cup and saucer on her knee, while he has none.

---

[10] *Gordis* literally means Fatty, but it is a term of endearment that has nothing to do with the weight of the interlocutor. We can only guess as to whether the writer meant to be ironic in applying it to the calavera who, by being female, could be read as an incarnation (so to speak) of La Muerte,* who is referred to in popular Mexican speech as, among other things, La Flaca (Skinny) or La Huesuda (Bony).

9.7 Merienda exquisita. Bakery, México, D.F.

The second is that el Hablador's stool is at an angle and a distance from his body that indicate a highly precarious situation, if the pun can be pardoned. Is he about to fall? Does he have no need of secure footing because he is a spirit? Like la Gordis, he has bony limbs and a skeletal head, but in contrast to her and el Gordo, his body is very skinny and has no eroticized parts that draw attention to his sexuality. His instability and rather child-like features, plus the fact that he is a bit smaller than la Gordis, emphasize that he is the underdog in the calavera. Counting only the two humans, la

Gordis has the last word, and it is a word that silences el Hablador and gives him a command with a sexual innuendo. Here is the whole dialogue, read curiously from right to left, with its inconsistent capitalization, spelling, and punctuation intact.

Hablador: Gordis, no puedo creer que tú hayas traido está Exquisites . . . de Pan de Muerto . . . pa' chuparse los dedos pa' REPETIR 1-2-3-4 y las que sean . . .
Gordis: Para tú coche. y como dijiste chúpate esta RICURA y no eches tanto verbo. Simplemente di ARRIBA . . . ABAJO . . . y pa' Dentro[11] . . . YA . . .
Calabazota: No se adornen tanto[12] . . . y denme mi parte . . .
Calabacita: yo también Quiero Quiero

Male calavera: Gordis, I can't believe you brought this Exquisiteness . . . which is this Pan de Muerto . . . finger lickin' good enough to REPEAT 1-2-3-4 and as many as may be . . .
Female calavera: Stop your car, and as you said lick this DELICIOUSNESS and don't lay out so much verbiage. Simply say UP . . . DOWN . . . and in . . . ENOUGH . . .
Large jack-o'-lantern: Stop being self-important . . . and give me my part
Small jack-o'-lantern: me too I want some I want some

In the eyes of la Gordis and the two jack-o'-lanterns that literally and literarily support her, el Hablador talks too much. The three females (*calabaza*, pumpkin, is a feminine noun) are more interested in eating the pan de muerto than in praising it or in hearing the male praise it and la Gordis for having brought it home. Do we detect on the writer's part a sexual stereotype typical of Western anthropology in the association of women with materiality and men with words—that is, with intellectuality or spirituality? Do we detect a fear of nagging, of female solidarity, of female power to spend money independently and to surprise, delight, and enchant with her purchase? Do we detect a fear of a male being unbalanced and unseated, as well as silenced, by his female partner's discourse?

---

[11] "*Arriba, abajo y para dentro,*" literally *upward, downward, and inward,* is a common drinking formula that indicates motions made with glasses of alcoholic beverages, *up* into the center of the table or circle of friends, *down* into the center, and *into* the drinkers' mouths.
[12] Literally, *don't adorn yourselves* (with language) *so much.*

Or is there a quasi-feminist attitude in this calavera? El Hablador talks too much, and the value he places on praising la Gordis and on talking about the wonderful bread is ridiculed vis-à-vis the females' much more sensible (in every sense) preference for the pleasure of eating. Perhaps his slipping stool is meant to make him the butt of the entire calavera, as well as of his mate's disdain for his verbiage. The two pumpkins are in unstable positions also, if one imagines a three-dimensional situation, but in the calavera they are balanced. La Gordis sits on them firmly, and their smiles betray no derision or penchant for mischief.

Here is the lascivious double entendre. Whereas el Hablador's reference to finger licking is relatively innocent, as one would expect from such a boyish figure, the way la Gordis has phrased her command to "lick this [emphatically capitalized] DELICIOUSNESS" seems decidedly salacious, especially followed by the set phrase "arriba, abajo y pa' dentro"; its first word could mean something like "get it up," its second word could be indicating the lowering of bodies to a horizontal position ("get down"), and its third word could suggest sexual penetration. More innocently, the expression could indicate, first, the up-and-down movement of the jaws as the bread is chewed ("arriba, abajo") and, second, the act of gulping the food down ("y pa' dentro").

I said earlier that three things interested me about the seating in this calavera, and I come now to the third. Given the hot debate that takes place each year in the country's major newspapers, most of which attack Hallowe'en as a sign of U.S. cultural imperialism attempting to undermine the Mexican tradition of Días de muertos,* I find it significant that la Gordis is sitting on two U.S.-style jack-o'-lanterns. As with any popular text, as John Fiske describes and discusses, this one is incomplete; it reveals no clear message, permits no single authoritative interpretation. The first words of the large jack-o'-lantern, "Stop being self-important," echo the words of la Gordis and also address el Hablador. In her second phrase, she competes with him in demanding her share of the bread. Remember that el Hablador indicated, albeit ungrammatically, that he would keep "repeating"—in other words, serving himself—one, two, three, four times or as many times as it would take to finish the loaf. Given his likely plan to eat the entire pan de muerto, there will be nothing left for either the large jack-o'-lantern or the small one, who childishly echoes the former's request with "me too I want some I want some."

Since both calaveras completely fail to acknowledge the presence or the speech of the jack-o'-lanterns and since la Gordis basically tells el Hablador to shut up and eat (although the direct object is playfully uncertain), we have no reason to think the jack-o'-lanterns will be fed. They are not calaveras;[13] this is not their holiday. Although they may be trying to usurp the place of real spirits, both in this calavera and in Mexico's Días de muertos in general, as the artist makes clear, they play a literally lowly, supporting role; they have no voice. La Muerte mexicana (Mexican Death) sits on them, putting Hallowe'en in its place. It is as if the artist were granting the U.S. holiday a minor part in Días de muertos, but although the jack-o'-lantern icon is present and the jack-o'-lanterns speak, they are not heard, and they are emphatically not fed as invited guests would be, as are la Gordis and el Hablador and all the bodiless relatives and friends who are called and accompanied and regaled during these days.

As a seat for la Gordis, the jack-o'-lanterns serve La Flaca.* Hallowe'en and its U.S. celebrants are allowed to witness the feast because they are neighbors, because they are among us, but the creator of this calavera dictates that the foreign sign will remain below the true event and will not undermine it. So, as I read it, a calavera that on first impression appears to be a light-hearted domestic scene develops both a strong sexuality and a political consciousness with admirable economy.

"Conquista del jalogüín" (Hallowe'en Conquered)

Tiny earthenware skeletons stuck firmly into green-tinted marzipan jack-o'lanterns were being sold one November in the best sweet shop in the world, Mexico City's Dulcería de Celaya (see Plate 21). The little collages caught my attention because I had already photographed the bakery painting "Merienda exquisita" in which a female calavera* was perched on two jack-o'-lanterns who were requesting their share of the pan de muerto* the calavera couple was preparing to eat.

Despite my title for this edible piece, the calaveritas sit in a relaxed manner, and their faces do not look the least bit aggressive. Their conquest was assured long enough ago that their demeanor betrays neither the danger of the fray nor any effort to protect it. But here is a sign that immigrant Hallowe'en, represented by the jack-o'-lantern, has been conquered in the popular culture: Its constitutive elements are taking their place within the

---

[13] That is, they are not real, authentic Mexican calaveras, although they are carved to resemble skulls, if roughly. I daresay relatively few celebrants of Hallowe'en recognize that fact, and it is possible that no celebrants of Días de muertos do, either.

9.8 Conquista del jalogüín. Bakery, México, D.F.

dominant host culture. The winner can do anything she or he likes with the booty. She or he is free to deracinate it from its original context and plant it where it will bring the sweetest fruit. So instead of finding itself surrounded by sinister bats, wart-nosed witches, spitting black cats, and smiling ghosts, as it might in its country of origin, this jack-o'-lantern serves as a seat for a Mexican calaca.*

More than a seat, the pumpkin also held a marzipan tombstone and a paper rose, as if it were the graveyard in which the skeleton had been buried. There are echoes here of the Mexica* belief in the fertile ground of death that nurtures new life. It is as if the pumpkin had already decomposed and become one with the earth or as if the candy jack-o'-lantern had already been digested by and united with the eater, who had died and become earth and was prepared to receive a tomb, a body, an offering of flowers. Like the contemporary Mexican feeling that because we are destined to die we are already dead, the jack-o'-lantern, destined to decompose, is already earth.

There are both Maya and Mexica bas-reliefs or codices that represent a warrior or god standing or sitting on a human being, for example, a captive from a battle. The depictions emphasize the superiority of the winner, if not of his entire city and culture. Sitting on a person underlines the fact that he has lost. He is humiliated and forced to render a service that is normal only for inanimate objects. It is unrealistic to attribute causation to an artist or a candy maker and idle to speculate as to whether pre-Hispanic art inspired a contemporary artifact. It is the duty and pleasure of the semiotician to identify units of signification. It is enough to juxtapose objects that are similar in productive, interesting ways.

"Conquista del Jalogüín" is a delicious cultural tidbit that illustrates the cool demeanor of the winning calavera that, hours earlier, might have battled mightily and perhaps xenophobically against the jack-o'-lantern, as did the one that illustrates the beginning of Chapter 6, "Días de muertos Versus Hallowe'en: A Fight to the Death?" In one sense it is a fight to the death, for the foreign contestant in the boxing match has only a skull and crossbones—signifying death—in its thought balloon. And in the figure from Dulcería de Celaya, once it is bought, the foreign jack-o'-lantern is destined to be consumed entirely, disappearing to supply energy to the eater, who will still have a little clay calavera like a trophy that will last long after the *mazapán* has been eaten and its energy transformed beyond recognition.

"Allegados son iguales"[14] (Having Arrived, They Are Equal)

This is a truly democratic calavera* (see Figure 9.9). Cartoon characters, both animal and human, share the same universe as a revolutionary—perhaps Emiliano Zapata himself—and a skeletal baker. One of the three little pigs cavorts fearlessly behind Zapata, whose foot rests on a skull, presumably that of a dead enemy, while from between the letters of the word *pasteles* (cakes) peer *el Ratón Miguel* (Mickey Mouse), *el Pato Dónald* (Donald Duck), Popeye, *Tribilín* (Goofy), and *la Pantera Rosa* (the Pink Panther). The multipurpose painting includes a big outlined heart for *Día de las madres* (Mother's Day), and the motif that dominates the left panel: a skeletal baker holding aloft a pan de muerto* that he seems to be carrying to a grave labeled "Pan de muerto."

---

[14] This is the beginning of the last line of Jorge Manrique's famous "Nuestras vidas son los ríos"; the complete text appears in Appendix B.

9.9 "Allegados son iguales." Bakery, México, D.F.

Will the peeping 'toons eventually come down from the heights to take over the space of the Días de muertos figures? Does the rotulista* predict the death of pan de muerto and its replacement with generic pasteles that can be served on any occasion and not just during a few weeks of the year? Is that why Pan de Muerto lies dead and buried? Does the fact that the baker is a skeleton suggest that only the dead bake(d) the holiday bread, that only the dead remember the dead?

More likely, this is a postmodern calavera in the same category as "Batman con luchadores" (see Figure 8.9) and another painted by Carlos Oznaya, which shows the Pantera Rosa proudly carrying a pan de muerto. It is another expression of the multiculturalism of a city where children hear "Los tres cochinitos" (*The Three Little Pigs*) read to them in Spanish and English, where locally published and imported comic books feature Popeye and the Disney characters, where time-honored traditions are still comforting and relevant. In this world, as in the kingdom of death, "allegados son iguales" (once they have arrived, all are equal), whether they came for children or adults, whether they are foreign or national, old or

new, traditional or trendy. On the sidewalk in front of the display window, a grandmother with a young girl, a man watching the photographer, and a young woman selling boiled corn and pancakes all remind us of the audience intended by the rotulista: all those who eat bread, all those who (remember they) will be dead.

❮10❯

Last Words, Last Rites

Bajo nuestra piel vive una hermana entrañable que se da cuenta de nuestras desventuras, de nuestros amoríos, y de la cual no hemos de separarnos hasta que toda nuestra carne y sangre vuelen alegremente por los aires, convertidas en un puntito de energía entre el esmog. La hermosa calaca, recordatorio de nuestra muerte siempre presente, es el invitado especial a las festividades.

Under our skin lives a dear, dear sister who is aware of our misadventures, of our loves, and from whom we will never be separated until all our flesh and blood fly happily through the air, turned into a tiny point of energy in the smog. The beautiful calavera, reminder of our ever-present death, is the special guest at the festivities.

—*Tiempo Libre,*
October 20–26, 1994, p. 2

In its folk aspects, Días de muertos* is a celebration that continues ancient practices, altered by the celebrants according to their interests, understanding, capabilities, needs, and resources. There is no reason to believe this holiday will disappear from rural areas and small towns, as certain anthropologists fear when they see it has changed since they first witnessed or read about it. Although it may be threatened in urban settings, where it has ceased to be relevant to the third and fourth generations of immigrants to the cities, it will continue to be observed because it serves cultural interests of profound importance to the communities in which it is held. It is a family reunion of the living and the dead, an extended expression of gratitude for the good enjoyed in the previous year, a dramatized prayer for blessings in the following year, and an affirmation of cultural identity and of communal solidarity and values (see Figure 1.10).

In its popular aspects, this holiday not only shares characteristics and motivation with the folk aspects, but it also serves as an arena for political expression. Visibility is a political act by members of subordinated groups who are usually invisible to the dominant classes, and some set offerings in public places or create calaveras that make their presence known and felt. The sense of humor patent in many of these works is complex, containing threads of bitterness and suffering along with stoicism and pleasure. It reveals a sense of perspective from the margins of society.

One of the functions of Días de muertos is to stimulate national identity. Because its roots lie in pre-Hispanic practices and it has been enriched by Spanish, Catholic elements, this fiesta* exemplifies the syncretism that characterizes Mexican culture; there are enough varied elements to appeal to virtually everyone in the country. Many national tourists who visit sites where Días de muertos is celebrated describe the fiesta as "very Mexican," and they feel "more Mexican" by witnessing the decoration of graves or a long graveyard vigil. These feelings are encouraged by many members of the intelligentsia and by government officials such as those in the Ministry of Education—the former because they find the celebration valuable in itself as a kind of national treasure and the latter because they hope that a nationalistic citizenry is a law-abiding, docile citizenry. And since the support of the upper classes is essential to any government, the Ministry of Tourism encourages members of that group to seek out places where they might be inspired to identify with their compatriots and their country.

The introduction and adaptation of Hallowe'en into Mexico's popular culture works, in an odd way, to draw the privileged—who are frequently foreign identified—into celebrating something tenuously related to Días de muertos in the same season. The latter might never have been part of this group's festive calendar, and the former is adopted to fill a void. As in the United States, Hallowe'en in Mexico is promoted by the merchants of its paraphernalia. To many nationalists, it feels like an imperialistic set of cultural practices that discourages patriotism and encourages malinchismo,* thereby colonizing Mexicans' consciousness. Numerous defenders of Días

10.1 Cookie graveyard. Dulcería de Celaya, México, D.F.

de muertos fear that the U.S. holiday will displace the Mexican one. I see no evidence that this will happen. Some celebrants of Days of the Dead do incorporate Hallowe'en icons into their ofrendas,* but many others do not. Those who do have no impulse to abandon or betray their practices, only to vary them, as if with a new dish. Mexico is expert in syncretism and in the adaptation of bits of foreign cultures such that they are "Mexicanized" harmoniously.

In Mexico City and other parts of the country, the most popular and prevalent icon during Días de muertos is the calavera,* which is formed in many media. Images of death in Mexico are embraced or eaten with an enthusiasm that has been known to disconcert foreigners (Figure 10.1). Part of Mexicans' self-image is that of intimates of death. We see ourselves as people who face our fear of death courageously and who regard death with equanimity. This attitude is not universal; it prevails among the poor but is shared by members of all social classes. My compatriots are conscious of the fact that living entails dying, and in pondering that we are destined to die, we arrive at the conclusion that we are, in a sense, already dead. Both popular and formally trained artists multiply images that illustrate this belief. It is as if life were deconstructed by means of the Days of the Dead.

Imagining a Sociology in Días de muertos

During this celebration there is a realism so radical that—at least during this time of the year for those who are able to entertain its humorous, serious implications—it explodes the illusion of immortality that underlies many hopes and plans, much security in our physical and psychological well-being, and our secret sense of triumph at having outlived others. Because of this realism, it seems perfectly appropriate that most ofrendas for the dead are ephemeral. They serve as signs of ephemeral life: Flowers quickly wilt; food quickly cools, soon spoils, and is consumed in a fraction of the time it took to prepare it; beverages evaporate; candles melt; incense burns; cigarettes go up in smoke; sugar skulls dissolve much sooner than bone ones.

As we have seen, along with the insistent reminder of death, during Días de muertos the usual hierarchy that puts the interests of the living celebrants before those of the dead is turned upside down. For this time the living organize their economic means, imagination, time, schedules, and energy around the dead, whom they remember, honor, and serve.

Kent and Valencia reported an anecdote that clearly exemplifies this point. An old woman, Doña Cheva, has been pressed to teach the Yaqui chief's Anglo wife how to cook properly for the spirits of the ancestors. Doña Cheva arrives during breakfast, saying: "No time to lose. This soup takes all day. We can't make the ancestors wait just because we've been drinking coffee" (Kent and Valencia 219). A little later, the apprentice would like to take a break, but Doña Cheva forbids it.

"No!" she said, looking at me as if I were a barbarian. "We have soup to stir. Until it is done. If we leave now the ancestors will think it is finished. They will believe we have no respect for them if we give them meat that is not properly cooked. . . . The ancestors are waiting to taste what we have done. This food is not for us, Elena. It is for them. It is for the ancestors. It must be perfect." (Kent and Valencia 219)

Días de muertos, more than any other time of the year, rejects social atomization by including the dead in its communal embrace. It confronts and challenges immortality-affirming consumerism, the illusion of being able to work for infinite wealth, of being able to purchase ever-increasing comfort. It points its white phalanges and laughs, if sarcastically, at the materialism that currently dictates the misdistribution of wealth and power in Mexico, as in most of the world. During these days in October and November, the awareness of death and the deployment of humor bring wealth and poverty and the divisions among classes, among ethnically and geographically distinct groups, and between the dead and the living into perspective. Through its paraphernalia and activities, this fiesta shows La Pelona* living within everyone.

During the festival, the Mexicans who live the most traditional lives enjoy the "powers of the weak" that Victor Turner associated with "liminal* entities," usually those who are undergoing a rite of passage or other ritual. The celebrants of Días de muertos fit this category insofar as they are entering and, for its duration, residing in the ambiguous time that permits contact between the living and the dead, that dissolves the differences between past and present. Turner explained the powers of the weak as "the permanently or transiently sacred attributes of low status or position" (Turner 109). He said the "communitas" enjoyed by marginal or liminal persons is considered sacred precisely because it disregards the hierarchies and norms of institutionalized relationships and results in powerful experiences (Turner 128) such as profound recollections, revived closeness with the family or community of origin, or deep reconsideration of a personal, communal, or national past.

Many people in Mexico are assigned low status by the dominant classes because of their relative poverty; because of their limited opportunities to participate in the processes of political, cultural, and economic production; and because their education and values—in a word, their culture—differ substantially from the hegemonic ones. But as the people in power value certain folk or popular traditions and express nostalgia for them, they recognize that their modest compatriots are valuable for keeping traditions alive.[1] Turner observed that "mystical and moral powers are wielded

---

[1] I am giving the upper classes the benefit of the doubt, although Néstor García Canclini believes Mexican Indians are preserved as living museums that attract tourism and, thus, contribute to the gross national product.

by subjugated autochtones over the total welfare of societies whose political frame is constituted by the lineage or territorial organization of incoming conquerors" (Turner 109). This recognition manifests in *la gente pudiente* (the people of economic, political, and cultural power) as a certain sense of guilt about the poverty of the Mexican people, their gross exploitation, and the lowly status assigned to them. As keepers of cultures that, in most cases, have been lost or transformed beyond recognition by conquest, colonization, and rural-to-urban migration, the marginalized are valued during ritual occasions as the true and only keepers of the soul of the true Mexico. During Días de muertos, traditional towns and neighborhoods are visited, photographed, written about, and remembered in public forums with great respect by the hegemonic class. Turner wrote, "In closed or structured societies, it is the marginal or 'inferior' person or the 'outsider' who often comes to symbolize what David Hume has called 'the sentiment for humanity,' which in its turn relates to the model we have termed 'communitas'" (Turner 111).

Because the value of Mexico's liminal entities is recognized during Días de muertos, a certain role reversal takes place in which the humble are at the pinnacle of attention and regard, at least in the intellectual and artistic circles that esteem the fiesta. Some cosmopolites, upon visiting Mixquic or Janitzio or any public ofrendas, find the differences between them and their other are accentuated and reconfirmed, and the wall of alterity* is reinforced. Only limited role reversal occurs for them; they do not relinquish their central position, and they are willing only briefly to concede the limelight to those they consider second-class citizens. For such individuals, the quick tour into the national, cultural margins serves as a kind of sling that shoots them back to their secure positions in the hierarchy and to their institutionalized relationships.

Other cosmopolites reaffirm or discover a solidarity with the celebrants. For them, the status reversal is renewing and invigorating, resulting in new insights about themselves and the celebrants. For some, the familiar hierarchy is recognized as an instrument that serves those on top; in their personal relations they can enjoy its weakening and partial dissolution. For those who experience reverent traditions without resisting them, there can be an exhilarating sense of having touched or been touched by something of great potency and value, something precious precisely because it is other, our other, what Guillermo Bonfil Batalla called el México profundo.* The experience can be strong enough to purify participants of the burden of class-based guilt, enabling them to establish interethnic, interclass, intercultural relationships on a more equal footing.

The humble art of the event quietly and indirectly criticizes the political and socioeconomic status quo, as did the medieval European danses macabres. This art imagines alternatives to the way things are, the way people relate, the way we conceive of ourselves and each other. Some of these visions are presented through the preparations, ofrendas, and graveyard visits; some through jocose earthenware, paper, and candy calaveras. The good-naturedness, equanimity, and beauty of the gifts and of the arrangements on the tombs and altars, the grace and humor of the calaveras serve to hide—if not erase—the boundary between life and death, the living and the dead.

Through their commemoration those who observe Días de muertos produce a sociology of solidarity in oppression—solidarity with the dead, who are also marginalized by the bourgeoisie, and solidarity with those who still love their dead as they love and stand with each other and their progeny, including those who will live in future generations and whom they will never know (see Plates 22, 23). Society is not arbitrarily confined to those who live and breathe today. This sociology is inflected by the popular tendency to tolerate the tension between belief and disbelief, and perhaps it leans toward belief as in the words of the Catholic creed, "I believe in all things seen and unseen." This anecdote typifies that tension.

Ante la candorosa pregunta de un periodista, rigurosamente típico, dirigida a esclarecer la cuestión de si, en la creencia de estos hombres huérfanos de una cultura cimera, las ofrendas y las "luminarias" convocaban "realmente" la presencia de los espíritus, un robusto auxiliar de las autoridades del panteón nos espetó tajante: — ¿Y ustedes creen que todos nosotros nacimos de una mujer llamada Eva que fue fabricada con la costilla que le arrancaron a Adán? (Cáceres Carenzo 18f)

To the artless question of a journalist, rigorously typical, which intended to clarify the matter as to whether, in the beliefs of these orphans of high culture, the offerings and the luminarias "really" convoked the presence of the spirits, a robust assistant of the cemetery's authorities spat out cuttingly, "And do you believe we all were born from a woman named Eve, who was made from the rib torn out of Adam?"

✦

Gabriel García Márquez, born and bred in Colombia, has said repeatedly that he does not write fiction; he merely writes about life as he observes it. A Western reader may dismiss this as yet another fiction, but the reader who is steeped in the culture of a Latin American (perhaps of any "developing") country senses the truth in his outrageous claim while perhaps failing to defend it to the satisfaction of an interlocutor from the "developed" world. The statement of this highly sophisticated novelist points to a relationship with reality and truth that is more poetic, less literalistic, less singular and Cartesian than that of a majority of people from industrialized societies. It points to different ways of knowing that, in turn, witness to different relationships with people and with the world than those constructed by the dominant classes. As Rolly Kent and Heather Valencia put it, "I should have known that a culture for whom the dead live can have no story with a beginning, middle, and end" (Kent and Valencia 181).

In Gabriel García Márquez's *Cien años de soledad* (*One Hundred Years of Solitude*), several characters continue to act in the physical world of the living after they have left their gross bodies.[2] Neither the writers nor the celebrants of Días de muertos harbor a childlike ability to confuse fantasy and reality or to have imaginary friends. But their philosophy admits, more readily than that of most members of the dominant classes, to feeling the presence and continuing to relate to dead people to whom they were close. To quote the Yaquis' spiritual leader, Anselmo Valencia, "The dead are always among us. My people have never created any false barriers of the mind between themselves on earth and those who are no longer on earth. There is no permanent death for us" (Kent and Valencia 235). As he explains, the Yaqui, who live in northwestern Mexico and the southwestern United States, believe that when a person dies she or he lives "in eternity" for one year, after which she or he reincarnates again until she or he has served the world to the point that she or he is tired and, in effect, is finished with the work of life. The Yaqui hold a special fiesta on the first anniversary of a person's death to celebrate the new incarnation.[3]

The point that determines whether a relationship is maintained or suspended is not the point at which the alter in the relationship dies. The point

---

[2] This phenomenon can be seen in fiction by other Latin American writers, including Isabel Allende from Chile and Elena Garro, Elena Poniatowska, and Juan Rulfo from Mexico.

[3] Some of these beliefs and practices are ancient and, with variations, remain widespread to this day in Mesoamerican* culture.

is the weakening of memory, the gradual dissolution of the bond between the two, and the incorporation of the alter in the self's life and mind. I do not want to equate the bond with the sentimental love that chooses companions who mirror the ego. That kind of love is not particularly relevant in the committed relationships of Mexico's traditional communities. Of course, there is abundant love. But the basis of the bond is solidarity, unity, something akin to, but much less onerous than, responsibility as the bourgeoisie understands it. The foundation of a committed relationship is not sympathy or antipathy, reciprocity of gifts, favors, aid, or love, although all of these are proffered. Neither is the nexus determined by whether the body of the alter is fleshed or skeletal. What is important is that alter is still somehow part of self's life.

And self's life is not felt to be atomistic, independent of the social body that constitutes its extended family and community. The physical body is not the private property of its owner with the array of rights to privacy and individualism and the independence from relations, friends, and neighbors the body of the typical "first worlder" claims. People are felt to be connected radically.

There is no mysticism in this theory, as if families were reincarnated soul mates or as if "blood" made one of several. Rather, there is fellowship, identification, and intimacy that result in part from poverty because too many people share too little space. There is intimacy that results from the hard fact that the best way to survive is to pool energy, resources, and creativity, and the only way survival is worthwhile is as part of a whole. There is the identification and togetherness that arise from mutual need, mutual help, the recognition of being in the same situation of deprivation and oppression. There is the connectedness of an anthropology, a sociology, and an epistemology different from those of the national and international hegemonic classes.

And just as individuals exist and act with and for their families and communities, they also extend their care to those who have left their tangible bodies behind. Those people's spirits are still part of the unit of the living. There is no question about their desert to be humored, fed, entertained, and regaled on dates of remembrance. Those who live with this understanding know existentially that no one is an island.

An Anthropology in Días de muertos

The fact that people earnestly celebrate Días de muertos implies that, explicitly or not, they postulate a theory about the nature of the human being, whether deceased or living. The fiesta's raison d'être—the relationship between the living and the dead—indicates a belief that a person does not require a body to maintain integrity, to preserve the personality that was developed while she or he did have a body, or to sustain allegiances and retain memory and taste. The spirit's "body" is not considered exactly physical, but it does quasi-physically enjoy the spirit of food and drink and other gifts. It is not normally believed to haunt or agitate or do tricks in the world, as a poltergeist might.

The disembodied person obtains some privilege that the bodied person does not share. It is believed to have some supernatural *palanca* (literally, lever), some influence with God and the saints, who are believed to have power over human life and destiny. Pre-Hispanic Mesoamericans referred to the dead as *teotl* (gods). Contemporary Mexicans think that the spirits can effectively intercede on behalf of their living friends and relations to convince the saints to grant good weather, good harvests, good fortune in life's ventures, good health, and everything else that is good. Luis Sierra Martínez quotes Salvador Cruz Montalvo, the chronicler of Tehuacán, Puebla, who describes an aspect of Días de muertos in the municipality of San Gabriel Chilac where "la celebración tiene una característica peculiar, porque ahí existe la creencia de que 'si los vivos no ofrendan a sus muertos, éstos no pueden estar en contacto con ellos para protegerlos'" [the celebration has a peculiar characteristic because the belief is held there that "if the living do not give offerings to their dead, the latter cannot be in contact with them to protect them"].

In this light, the commemoration takes on a certain functional nuance shared by other celebrants, as we saw in Chapter 1. If the living take care of the dead, which they can do because of the nature of the physical body and the physical world, the dead take care of the living, which they can do because of the nature of their numinous existence in a hierarchically structured cosmos.

Still, the dead are not thought to have power over their superiors in the afterworld, which explains the misfortunes they are unable to deflect with their prayers. The living quietly resign themselves to accidents of fortune and fate, those ancient forces embodied in Tezcatlipoca, which have not been banished from life by the Christian pantheon.

I will close this section by mentioning a contradiction between a commonplace of Días de muertos and the relatively common, year-round experience. It is often said that spirits are only allowed to visit their living during those few days of the year named after them (the use of the passive voice eludes saying by whom or what). But many people talk to the dead and feel their presence, love, and influence in spite of that supposed restriction on their movement. We remember the tenacious human ability to harbor contradictory beliefs simultaneously.

The Politics and Poetics of Días de muertos

What are the effects of seeing human society as Días de muertos represents it, of seeing depictions of members of society going about their daily business with casual strength and humor but skeletal, dead? I am inclined less toward an existentialist interpretation of the absurdity of life in which "*Il faut imaginer Sisyphe heureux*"[4] than toward the Hindu notion that all the world is *līlā* cosmic play, and that we have no option but to play. That seems to me to approximate the philosophy of life I discern in the discourse of members of the Mexican *clases populares* among whom there is a strong element of fatalism, the fatalism of the subordinated.

Many individuals experience in their own lives, in their own flesh, the futility of trying to apply the strategies that help members of the ruling classes to advance: self-improvement, education, persistence, hard work. Most find they are cut out of educational opportunities because dire poverty necessitates finding food and shelter first, even though by law Mexicans are required to go through the sixth grade. Hard work and consistent effort are often rewarded with less than the insufficient minimum wage, just as efforts are often exerted in the informal economy—for example, on the streets, where no driver has contracted to pay for having the windshield washed at a stoplight or for being pitifully entertained by a fire eater or a juggler. Even highly developed skills, such as weaving and embroidering textiles, are often rewarded by unfair, heartless bargaining. The women sell their laboriously crafted goods for a pittance because any coin will buy more food than no coin. And, as any traveler to Mexico City can attest, some have given up any pretense of working; they only beg.

---

[4] "We must imagine Sisyphus happy" (Camus).

Contemporary Mexican fatalism is not entirely unlike the fatalism of pre-Hispanic astrology, which predicted good or ill according to one's birth date. In Anáhuac, the Valley of Mexico, midwives and parents welcomed infants into the world by warning them that they would suffer, that life would be hard. In Mexico, birth still determines the future. If one is born poor in the developing world, what, realistically, are the chances that opportunities will be found for rising out of poverty?

Another influence in Latin America, if not in all of Christianity, is the fatalism taught by most Catholic priests, excluding the hopeful praxis and preaching of theologians of liberation. The most commonly heard lesson promises that all ills and injustices will be redressed in Heaven. It promulgates the prayer, "Thy will be done." In the face of every problem, injury, injustice, and tragedy, the faithful are taught to repeat those words of cold comfort, which might first have been heard from a priest, "Así lo quiso Dios" [It was God's will]. Like Hinduism, Catholicism is a religion that contains pockets that help to maintain a caste system that collaborates with capitalism to keep a fraction of the population wealthy, secure, and healthy, while the majority remain poor and insecure and live in unsanitary, sickly conditions.

With all of this in the background, we can better appreciate the sharp irony of the pictorial, sculpted, and edible calaveras* of Días de muertos. Everyone who finds herself or himself in a body, physical and social, must play in this life and by the rules that predate her or him. The calaveras present a philosophy that witnesses to a will to make the best of a frequently miserable lot, a philosophy that focuses on the beauty, love, and fun that can be enjoyed within strict economic, social, and political limits. There is, as it turns out, plenty of pleasure, even for the subordinated. One of its results is a rich culture.

Representing society as consisting of skeletons mocks the illusion of immortality that seems centrally important to capitalism. On that illusion depend the notions of perfectibility and attainable total happiness that inspire self-discipline, self-improvement, labor, and consumption. The bourgeoisie acts as if it thought itself immortal. There is no end to its optimistic buying and planning for an increasingly comfortable future.

The calaveras act as mementi mori,* albeit more mirthfully than do the sober skull and crossbones and Angels of Death that more lugubrious Christians have depicted. More than that, Días de muertos naturalizes death to the point that at least I came to feel, after years of gazing on calaveras, that I am a skeleton in some essential sense. That alteration in my consciousness inspired the author photo for this publication. Largely as a result of working on this topic, life has come to feel transitory, nearly momentary, to the point of seeming almost trivial in comparison to the length of death. All the details of my life—beginning with my body and my mind, my work, thoughts, feelings, health and wealth, social status, fun and leisure—all seem as thin as clothes that must wear out and be tossed off, sooner or later. How can I know what other scholars and members of the bourgeoisie experience? Most, I suspect, defend themselves fairly effectively against Días de muertos by laughing it off as humorous, exotic, quaint, antiquated, lowbrow—as, first and foremost, other. To respond dismissively is much safer than to open up to the impact of the popular culture that claims public spaces, time, and many kinds of resources for a few days in October and November; much safer than to feel compelled to work toward changing what in society destroys others' health, freedom, and happiness.

If "nature is cooked into culture because all human societies negotiate their relationship with culture" (Fiske, personal communication), we can begin to see how, in a second process, the artists of Días de muertos cook selected elements of the dominant culture into a discursive stew palatable to their tastes and needs, in close accord with their social location. And what does it mean that many calaveras are eating, dreaming of eating, or cooking? Is it merely a reflection of the hunger experienced by too many people in the subordinated classes? Without dismissing that possibility, I adduce what Lévi-Strauss has pointed out: that eating crosses the boundary of the body and turns the not-me into me, literally.

By eating, the calaveras do not sustain life, as living people do when we eat. Rather, they sustain death by incorporating life into death. This is a fine example of what Stallybrass and White called the politics and poetics of transgression. It reflects the experience of the humble that society consumes them, demanding their sacrifice. It is an image that turns the world upside down, inside out. It erases the difference between being alive and being dead, and that erasure permits a hope in some continuing existence after life and in some continuing relationship with the dead who were dear to us. It permits a hope of transcending the suffering and the sorrow of subordinated life, including through hope itself.

Resisting Homogeneity

From the time of Caesar, ecumenizing tendencies have been present in the Western world, as John Fiske pointed out in a conversation. The emperor wanted to Romanize the world; Christians wanted to Christianize it; in our time capitalists insist that the world must follow their politics, economics, ethics, philosophy, and religion. All of these movements have been successful until they have met the stubborn resistance of local culture embodied in people whose own politics, economics, ethics, philosophy, and religion do not allow room for the radical changes the outsiders try to impose. The resistance need not be conscious; it is existential, fully lived. It results from a worldview that does not understand the foreign one because the native one is very well suited to local life.

Even as, historically, syncretisms have adapted new elements to local culture, disguising the old in the clothing of the new or taking in enough of the new to enjoy a fresh resource and enrich the tradition, Días de muertos shows its celebrants defending what is meaningful to them, what they have produced, what they enjoy against the ecumenism of transnational capitalism with its homogenizing and thinning culture and values.

In the end, this may be the most important aspect of reading a fiesta that exalts ancient practices and beliefs, preserved against and within all conquests and colonizations. From it we can learn how to defend the particular against the universalizing. In a time in which the U.S. academy is recognizing—and, predictably, institutionalizing—the value and importance of cultural diversity, scholars will do well to support pockets of living, local culture with our skills, our attention, and, often, our admiration.

Setting Ofrendas, A Conversion Experience

After a lecture about the Days of the Dead that I had given to a group of high school teachers in spring 1994, one of them asked me why I had never set an ofrenda. My internal response was something close to shock because until that discussion settled into my consciousness and the teacher's strong advice to honor my dead like my compatriots took hold, it had never occurred to me to do so. My family did not celebrate Días de muertos; people in my social location did not do so, either. My external response did not own up to everything that underlay my private reaction, but I did not answer the question with my usual academic aplomb. I felt more as though I was making excuses than as though I was confronting the matter honestly. Other members of the audience joined in encouraging me to transcend my hesitation and set an offering that year.

On November 3, 1994, George Rabasa and I spent several hours in the Riverview Branch Library in St. Paul, building an altar and arranging on it books, miniature figures, cut paper, photographs, foods, and other items we

thought would please my childhood nana,* Rosa Ortiz Torres; my grandmother, Dolores Villalpando de García Godoy; and my great aunt, Xóchitl
Garciagodoy de González Guerrero (see Plate 24). The occasion was one of
a series of lectures cum concerts of ethnic and national music in the Twin
Cities called "Gathering at the River." I gave a brief, illustrated lesson
about Días de muertos and explained the ofrenda, and then a group of
mariachis regaled the living and the dead with traditional Mexican songs.

It was a transforming experience. From the time I began to contemplate it, I felt a closeness with the three women that brought back the love
that binds me to them and that intensified, along with my sorrow at their
absence, into what felt like a burning in my consciousness. Choosing what
to offer them involved remembering and imagining their tastes, consulting
my mother for suggestions, and talking about them. Gathering and preparing the things and the foods, I was never without a feeling of their presence.
Setting the offering, I was never distracted from the three I was honoring. It
was a profoundly contemplative process.

And when the ofrenda had been prepared, all I wanted to do was sit in
the front row of the small auditorium, look at the beautiful altar, and be
with Abue, Xochi, and Chita, as I had called them from my infancy.
Despite my sophistication, agnosticism, and skepticism; despite having
been raised with little reference to the dead, I was certain my guests were
pleased with the gifts, happy to see my excellent marriage, and proud of
who I had become—thanks, in part, to them.

About a dozen ofrendas were set in the Macalester College chapel on
November 1, 1995, by students, faculty, and staff. Relatives and friends
were remembered and regaled, along with Latin American novelists and
revolutionaries, religious martyrs, Jerry Garcia, and el ánima sola* (see
Plates 25 and 26). Many of those who visited the display expressed deter-
mination to honor their dead in following years, and some, in fact, did so.
Some of the participants articulated feelings of love, joy, sadness, and communion with the spirits, as well as with the spirits' community.

As long as Days of the Dead is about the dead, it seems fitting for people
foreign to Mexico's folk tradition to join the celebration. It is important to
respect it and to respect those whose ancestors have kept and elaborated the
commemoration. I do not agree with the artists who produce aesthetically
accomplished works that glorify themselves more than they do the putative
honored. I am troubled by groups in the United States using the fiesta to
exalt their identity with parades and elaborate skeletal costumes but with
little thought for the primary purpose of the event. I am not disturbed by a

"Hungarian ofrenda" that has no Mexican item on it because the person for whom it was set had no experience with Mexico.

I harbor a fantasy that people, especially those who wield little power in their society, will discover new aspects of their generosity and tenderness through setting offerings for their dead. I imagine them glowing in the pleasure of renewed connection with relations and companions. I imagine them spreading their goodwill in all of their contacts. Strength and magnanimity are generated by the practice of giving freely, thoughtfully, and lovingly. Why not revive a festival of liberality—gathering beloved spirits, thanking them for their positive influence on our life, living in their memory for days or weeks or months, recognizing the preciousness of life, and nurturing our relationships with the living in the awareness that we will all be joining the dead?

Glossary

Words in the glossary are followed by an asterisk the first time they appear in a section.

adelita: wife or companion of a revolutionary soldier. She might have been a soldier herself or have accompanied a soldier to fill his hygienic, nutritional, or sexual needs.

alfeñique: figures molded in sugar that are included as part of the offering for the dead in some communities. The most typical figure is the lamb, a reference to Jesus as the lamb of God. For greater detail about alfeñique, see Carmichael and Sayer 108ff.

alter: the other.

alterity: otherness, from Latin *alter,* other.

angelitos: literally, little angels; that is, the spirits of those who died as infants or children.

ánima sola: solitary soul or spirit who has no relatives or friends to care for it or who died far from home.

atole: a sweet, hot drink made either from cooked, ground, dissolved, boiled corn or from flavored cornstarch.

axis mundi: Latin. The axis of the world, considered by mythopoetic people to be a powerful supernatural space that allows communication among different realms of existence. Despite the fact that the word is singular, every "sacred space" is an axis mundi.

calaca: synonym for calavera. Skull, in popular speech.

La Calaca: literally, the skull. A name for personified (female) Death.

calavera: literally, skull. During Días de muertos the word takes on multiple meanings: rhymed, humorous pseudo epitaphs; skeletons made of different materials ranging from lead to plastic; skeletons depicted on various surfaces; graphic cartoons or plastic scenes with skeleton characters; a (small) monetary contribution requested by children. Diminutive form: **calaverita.**

calavera de azúcar: sugar skull. Diminutive form: **calaverita.**

calaverear: traditional practice in which a group of elders appointed to take care of one or more ritual aspects of a fiesta goes from house to house requesting items from people's ofrendas to set up an offering for the ánima sola. See **ánima sola.**

cartón: cardboard or papier mâché; always papier mâché in references in this book.

catrín, catrina: masculine and feminine for dandy. José Guadalupe Posada drew the first Calavera Catrina (ca. 1900), which has been reproduced during Días de muertos ever since. See **Posada.**

cempoaxóchitl: Náhuatl. Marigold, *Tagetes erecta* and *Tagetes lucida,* the traditional flower for commemorating the dead in Mexico since pre-Columbian times. Cempoaxóchitl literally means flower (*xóchitl*) of twenty petals (twenty connotes *many* in Náhuatl). In much of Mexico it is simply called *flor de muertos,* flower of the dead. Also called *cempasúchil* or *cempasuchi,* with various spellings.

CETIS: Coordinación de Educación Technológica Industrial (Coordination of Industrial Technological Education), a high school in Mexico City.

Chinampa: raft covered with dirt, planted with vegetables, and anchored in lake; prehispanic in origin.

cihuateteo: Náhuatl. Literally god-women, these are the spirits of women who died in their first childbirth and who accompany the sun on its daily journey from the zenith to the nadir. They sometimes steal children at crossroads or afflict them with disease.

comadre, compadre: literally, co-mother and co-father. They are the god-parents of one's children. This relationship is more serious and often closer in Mexico than in the United States. It is a great honor to be chosen to be a godparent, as it reveals a trust and a hope that, should the natural parent(s) die, the comadre or compadre (who may be from different families) will care for their ahijados. It is also a term of endearment toward a friend, even if there is no formal compadrazgo to indicate great intimacy.

copal: incense made from the resin of tropical trees in Mexico and parts of Central America.

criollo: In Mexico, the term was used during the colonial period to desig-nate the Mexican-born offspring of two Spaniards. It has largely fallen out of use except in references to that period.

D.F.: Distrito Federal, Federal District; Mexico City.

Días de muertos: Days of the Dead, celebrated in most of Mexico at least on November 1 or 2 but any time from October 18 until November 30, depending on the traditions of the community.

en su tierra: in their land. Tierra means earth, soil, land. This is the most common expression for "home" among the popular classes, many mem-bers of which have been forced to find work outside their communities because of limited access to arable land and jobs. It carries the same nostal-gic connotation as "back home" in English.

Estado de: State of. Several states in Mexico have the same name as their capital city. Whereas only Estado de México contains three words in its name, I write the state name as *Estado de* ——— to distinguish it from the capital's name.

fiesta: not only party; also a festival, a feast day, the observation or celebra-tion of a religious or ritually significant time or event.

La Flaca: literally, Skinny (feminine). A name for personified (female) Death.

INAH: Instituto Nacional de Antropología e Historia (National Institute of Anthropology and History).

itzcuintli or **xolotlitzcuintli:** Náhuatl. The medium-sized "Mexican hair-less" dog with gray skin and a few wiry hairs on its head. Generally, itz-cuintle-itzcuintli means any dog. In some communities the belief has subsisted since pre-Hispanic times that a dog must help the dead to cross the River Chiconauapan (Seven Tests) to Mictlan, the land of the dead.

Xolotlitzcuintle: monster dog.

liminality: from Latin *limen,* threshold. The state of being on a border, threshold, or margin.

malinchismo: preference for the foreign over the national. For a complete explanation of the term, please see "No Threat to Tradition and Identity" in Chapter 6.

memento mori: Latin, reminder of death. Plural: **mementi.**

Mesoamerican: Bonfil Batalla defines this word as describing one who con-tinues pre-Hispanic traditions. Geographically, Mesoamerica is the area that extends more or less from the Valley of Mexico to Guatemala. It is characterized by its significant Indigenous and mixed Indian-European population.

mestizo/mestizaje: person of mixed heritage: native Mexican and European (originally Spanish). Mixture of "races," miscegenation.

Mexica: the people of preconquest "Mexico" who inhabited the Valley of Mexico, spoke Náhuatl, and included the Aztecs.

México profundo: includes the Indigenous people who identify themselves as such and a less clear category of Mexicans who live aspects of Native traditions but do not identify with any particular Indian group.

Miccaílhuitl: Náhuatl. One of the pre-Hispanic festivals for the dead, trans-lated by Diego Durán as either "la fiesta grande de los muertos" (the big fiesta of the dead) or "la fiesta de los muertos grandes" (the fiesta of the adult dead) to distinguish it from **Miccailhuitontli,** the little fiesta or the fiesta for the "little" dead. The term is still used to refer to Días de muertos in some communities, such as Cuetzalan, Estado de Puebla.

Mictlan: for pre-Hispanic Mesoamericans, the place of the dead, the domain of the fleshless, "el lugar de misterio," the place or kingdom of mystery. It is described in terms similar to Sheol or Hades: a place of dark-ness where the dead barely live, "donde de alguna manera se existe" (where one somehow exists), as some Náhuatl poems put it in a fixed phrase. Mictlan is sometimes identified as located in the north, sometimes as below the earth. It is ruled by **Mictlantecuhtli** and **Mictecacíhuatl,** the lord and lady of Mictlan. See Appendix D for other ideas about the word.

La Muerte: literally, death. A name for personified (female) Death.

muertitos: literally, the little dead. The diminutive is used in Mexico not to patronize but to express endearment or respect. Náhuatl does the same.

Náhuatl: the language spoken in central Mexico before the conquest. It is still spoken by millions of people who are likely to be bilingual. The speakers of Náhuatl are **nahuas** or **nahuatlacas.** Although there was no Náhuatl nation as such, the nahuas did and do share common cultural elements. Written in Spanish, the diacritical accent indicates a practice that is always true of Náhuatl words: The penultimate syllable is stressed. Often, the accent is not written but is understood (Garibay, *Historia*; León-Portilla, *Visión*). Also, member of nahuatlaca culture.

nana: nanny.

ofrenda: offering, with a ritual or religious connotation.

olla: earthenware cooking pot.

padrino: godfather.

pan de muerto: bread of the dead, a sweet, light yeast bread fashioned into a stylized human form, into a round with stylized skull and crossbones on top, or into animal shapes, according to the community's traditions. Plural form: **panes.**

panadero: baker or one who sells bread.

panificadora: bakery.

La Parca: literally, Stingy (feminine) or Parsimonious. A nickname for personified (female) Death. It may double as "fate" through its Latin etymology.

La Pelona: literally, Baldy (feminine). Another nickname for personified Death.

peso: Mexico's currency, which has been floating since around 1980.

petate: a woven reed mat that may be used for sleeping or as a floor covering. It was also used traditionally to wrap corpses for burial, a practice continued today by some communities.

Posada, José Guadalupe (1852–1913): printer, designer, and engraver who popularized calaveras and is credited with initiating the Mexican "renaissance" by distilling Mexican and Spanish aesthetics and subjects to produce Mexican popular art. See Chapter 4, "Posada: X Rays of Fin de Siècle Mexico" and its selection of reproductions of his prints.

rebozo: rectangular shawl, approximately six feet long. It can be made of various materials: wool, cotton, artificial fibers. In addition to its basic function of providing warmth, it is used to cover the head in church and for carrying something on the back, often a baby. Rebozos are only worn by women, usually Indigenous women, although they are fashionable items, especially silk rebozos, for a limited number of bourgeois women.

rotulista: poster artist or designer of lettering. In Mexico, rotulistas are the artists who paint display windows for bakeries and other shops year-round, not only for Días de muertos.

semiotics: the study of *semes,* signs.

stellar eye: stylized star represented on deities associated with death and funerary rites. It may look like a double circle, one inside the other, and may even be shaped out of bread in the form of a thin doughnut in offerings, especially in Xochimilco and Mixquic. It may look like a small, very fat single or double circle.

tamal: cornmeal cakes steamed in corn husks. They bear a slight resemblance to Italian polenta. They may be sweet, prepared with *piloncillo,* unrefined sugar (honey, in ancient times), or savory, with a bit of chile and vegetable or meat in the center. Plural: **tamales.**

tehuana: a woman from the Isthmus of Tehuantepec in the state of Oaxaca, southern Mexico. Tehuanas continue to dress in traditional costume on special occasions.

Todos Santos: All Saints, that is, the Catholic Feast of All Saints, one of the Días de muertos, celebrated on November 1.

tzompantli: Náhuatl. Literally, rack of skulls. On the original tzompantli, the detached heads of sacrificial victims were pierced through the temples and slipped onto poles like beads on an abacus (Figure 5.6). Stone tzompantli sculpted in low or high relief can be seen in many archaeological sites in el Valle de Anáhuac, the Valley of Mexico, including Templo Mayor, Mexico City, and Tula, Hidalgo.

Appendix A: Literary calaveras*

Contents

---

[1] I use the first line as a title for untitled calaveras.

The writer of this calavera,* a fifteen-year-old immigrant to Mexico City from Tehuantepec, Oaxaca, gave me a copy, illustrated by a skeleton in crayon. She wrote it as a homework assignment.

A mí amada maestra	To My Beloved Teacher
Lorena Martínez Castillejos[2]	Lorena Martínez Castillejos
Cómo me acuerdo de usted	Oh, how I remember you
La muerte se la llevó	Death took you
y buen recuerdo nos dejó	and left us a sweet memory
con sus lecciones de amor	with your lessons of love
la calaca por amor	The calaca* out of love
de sus huesos se adueñó;	took possession of your bones
La Flaca[3] murmuró	Skinny murmured
como late mi corazón,	how my heart beats
porque ella nos dará	for she will give us
muchas tundas[4] con amor.	many slaps on the wrist with love.

The next three calaveras are written by students in a high school in the neighborhood of Coyoacán, Mexico, D.F. They were part of a contest for ofrendas and literary calaveras in 1993 sponsored by Dirección General de Educación Tecnológica Industrial, Coordinación de Educación Tecnológica Industrial, Primer concurso de ofrendas y calaveritas.

---

[2] I reproduce the spelling and punctuation of the originals, idiosyncratic as they may be. The first group consists of calaveras written by students. In my translations I seek clarity of comprehension of the original, not improvement of the text. I make minimal attempts to reproduce rhyme, but I do imitate the register of language in the original. The spelling in English is standard, but the punctuation follows the Spanish calavera. Capitalization follows the original, including the first word of each line.

[3] Nickname for (female) Death. Literally, Skinny.

[4] Physical punishment of any kind is rare in schools, but a few instances may occur. This may be a vestige from the anecdotes of older generations.

Mario Moreno "Cantinflas"[5]
Enrique Rodríguez P.

Mario Moreno "Cantinflas"
Enrique Rodríguez P.

YA MURIO CANTINFLAS
YA LO LLEVARON A ENTERRAR
ENTRE TODA LA GENTE
QUE HIZO CARCAJEAR

CANTINFLAS HAS DIED
ALL TOGETHER THE PEOPLE
WHOM HE MADE LAUGH ALOUD
HAVE TAKEN HIM TO BE BURIED

A LA MUERTE CON SUS CHISTES
LA HIZO CARCAJEAR
CON SU FORMA DE EXPRESARSE
Y SU MODO DE CANTINFLEAR.[6]

WITH HIS JOKES HE MADE
DEATH LAUGH ALOUD
BECAUSE OF HIS STYLE OF EXPRESSION
AND THE WAY HE CANTINFLATES.

YA SE ESTABA ARREPINTIENDO LA
MUERTE
DE QUERERSELO LLEVAR
PERO TODOS TENEMOS UN LIMITE
Y LE TUVIMOS QUE LLORAR.

DEATH BEGAN TO CHANGE HER
MIND
ABOUT WANTING TO TAKE HIM OFF
BUT WE ALL HAVE A LIMIT
AND WE HAD TO MOURN FOR HIM.

TODOS ESTAN MUY TRISTES
PORQUE CON NOSOTROS YA NO VA A
ESTAR
PERO AL VER SUS PELICULAS
SIEMPRE LO VAMOS A RECORDAR.

EVERYONE IS VERY SAD
HE'S NO LONGER AMONG US
BUT WHEN WE SEE HIS MOVIES
WE WILL ALWAYS REMEMBER HIM.

---

[5] Mexican actor and comedian (1911–1993) best known in the United States for his role in *Around the World in 80 Days*.

[6] *Cantinflear*, a verb that comes from the name Cantinflas, means to clown in his style: wittily, politically, suggestively, in the character of a poor and (officially) uneducated young man from Mexico City.

Salinas de Gortari[7]

En un sillón muy sentada
hoy Peposa la huesitos,[8]
pues esta muy ocupada
escuchando a Don Carlitos
El ha dicho cinco informes
a todita la nación
más la flaca* ya anda "sobres"
pa' jalarselo al panteon

Ya dejó de resollar
¿Que le pasó? no lo sé
más ya no va a disfrutar
del mentado "Te,Le,Ce."
Ni modo así es la muerte
nos llega de un sopetón
y pa' nuestra mala suerte
se nos "pelo" un gran pelón.

Salinas de Gortari

Today Bony Peposa[9]
is seated deep in an easy chair;
she is very busy
listening to Don Carlitos
He has given five state-of-the-union
reports
to the whole entire nation
but Skinny is after him now
to pull him to the cemetery

He has stopped breathing
What happened to him? I don't know
but he will no longer enjoy
the famous NAFTA.
Too bad, that's death
it comes to us suddenly
and for our bad luck
she peeled off a great baldy.

---

[7] Carlos Salinas de Gortari (called "Don Carlitos" by the writer of this calavera) was president of Mexico from 1988 to 1994, best known for establishing the North American Free Trade Agreement (*Tratado de Libre Comercio*, to which the writer refers as *Te, Le, Ce*) with Canada and the United States and for being in office during the January 1994 armed rebellion in Chiapas by the Ejército Zapatista de Liberación Nacional. He was president when this anonymous calavera was written. The writer refers to Salinas's baldness, calling him *pelón*.

[8] Nickname for personified (female) Death.

[9] See footnote 8.

Doña Frida,[10] bendita sea   Doña Frida, Bless Her Soul
Alma Rosa Castillo R.   Alma Rosa Castillo R.

DOÑA FRIDA, BENDITA SEA,   DOÑA FRIDA, BLESS HER SOUL,
UN LAMENTO NUNCA EXHALÓ,   NEVER EXHALED A COMPLAINT,
PUES DE NIÑA, COMO MUÑECA,   FOR AS A CHILD, SHE PLAYED
CON LA MUERTE SIEMPRE JUGÓ.   WITH DEATH AS WITH A DOLL.

MUJER REVOLUCIONARIA,   REVOLUTIONARY WOMAN,
ROJILLA DIRÍAN ALGUNOS,   RED SYMPATHIZER, SOME WOULD SAY,
MARIPOSA CON ALAS ROTAS,   BUTTERFLY WITH BROKEN WINGS,
TODOS LOS SUEÑOS HICISTE TUYOS.   YOU MADE ALL DREAMS YOUR OWN.

MAS NADA TOMABA EN SERIO,   YET SHE TOOK NOTHING SERIOUSLY,
NI ACCIDENTE, NI ABORTO ALGUNO,   NEITHER ACCIDENT NOR MISCARRIAGE,
SENTÍAS PARTE DEL CUADRO,   YOU FELT PART OF THE PAINTING,
SURREALISMO TAN PROFUNDO.   PROFOUND SURREALISM.

CONVIRTIO A LA CALAVERA   SHE TURNED LA CALAVERA
EN UN ANGEL DE LA GUARDA,   INTO A GUARDIAN ANGEL,
ATRAVESO SOLA LA NOCHE,   SHE CROSSED THE NIGHT ALONE,
¡QUE COMO ANTORCHA ARDA!   MAY SHE BURN ON LIKE A TORCH!

---

[10] Frida Kahlo (1907–1954), Mexican painter and Communist activist best known for her frank self-portraits.

Templo Mayor, México, D.F., November 2, 1993. This calavera was part of an ofrenda* set outside the entrance of the archaeological site that was the central sanctuary of the Aztecs and destroyed by Hernán Cortés in 1521.

Esta pobre calavera

ESTA POBRE CALAVERA
QUE AL TEMPLO MAYOR REMABA,
SE PUSO MUY ENOJADA
AL VER LA PUERTA CERRADA:
QUE ME IMPORTAN LOS
INFORMES,[11]
LA MUERTE NO ESPERA NADA!

This Poor Calavera

THIS POOR CALAVERA
WHO WAS ROWING TO THE TEMPLO MAYOR
BECAME VERY ANGRY
UPON SEEING THE DOOR CLOSED:
WHAT DO I CARE ABOUT STATE-OF-THE-UNION ADDRESSES,
DEATH WAITS FOR NOTHING!

The following three calaveras were culled from various newspapers. I will put their source before their title.

Oaxaca, Oaxaca, *Sur,* November 1, 1992

La Poli[12]
Nikito Nipongo[13]

Unas veces asalta por gacha,
otras más por obligación;
y siempre anda con la facha
no de protector, sino de hampón.
Pero la Calaca ya se cansó
de tanta y tanta majadería
y torturándola ayer mató
a la reverendísima policía.

The Police

Sometimes they assault you
because they're cruel,
other times it's their duty;
and they always patrol in the guise
not of protectors but of scamps.
But la Calaca* got tired of so-and-so much abuse
and by torture yesterday she killed
the reverend Police Department.

---

[11] Former President Salinas de Gortari delivered the State-of-the-Union Address on November 1, coinciding and competing with one of the Days of the Dead. November 1 is a national holiday, and the calavera complains that because of it, there is no admittance today to the Templo Mayor archaeological site and museum it wanted to visit.

[12] Mexican slang for *la policía,* the police.

[13] Pseudonym of Raúl Prieto that means *I neither take away nor add.*

Mexico, D.F.: "Calaveras de La Jornada," *La Jornada,* November 2, 1993

Michael Jackson
Miguel Luna Pimentel

Ya es puro tornillo y tuerca
éste que fue negro congo,
y se mueve todo oblongo
como lombriz de agua puerca.

Hoy ya no come mondongo,
plato de negro vulgar
come nada más caviar
entre brinquito y rezongo.

Y por su afán de lograr
de la bemba disimulo
ya puede ver con el culo,
tanto se ha hecho restirar.

La Parca* dice, a este chulo
tan embarrado de yeso
ya hasta parece de hueso,
de mi lista yo lo anulo.

Michael Jackson
Miguel Luna Pimentel

Now nothing but screws and sprockets,
he who was a congo black man,
moves completely oblong
like a worm in filthy water.

He no longer eats fried chicken,
the dish of an ordinary black;
he eats nothing but caviar
between whimpers and jumping
jacks.

And through his zeal to hide
the fullness of his lips,
he can see with his ass
because of being surgically stretched.

La Parca* says this cutie
so smeared with plaster
already looks like bone;
I'm crossing him off my list.

México, D.F., *Excelsior,* November 1, 1992

Carlos Fuentes[14]
La culta polaca

Carlos Fuentes
(The cultured [female] Pole)

Ahora sí descansa en Paz[15]	Now he rests in Paz,[15]
el que más guerra le dio,	he who gave him the most trouble,
el mexicano fugaz	the transient Mexican
que allá en extranjía vivió.	who lived far away abroad.
Entre verbos y aforismos	Among verbs and aphorisms
quedó por fin sepultado	he was finally interred,
y, en acto de narcisismo,	in an act of narcissism,
junto a un espejo enterrado.	next to a buried mirror.

The following three calaveras appeared in Mexico City's daily *El Día* in the "Metrópoli" section on November 1, 1992. Together they are "Las calaveras de Heras."

Modernización
Heras

Modernization
Heras

En la "moder",[16]	"They've clobbered us,"
decía la calavera	said the calavera.
la que nos espera	"What's in store for us
con la modernización.	with modernization.

---

[14] Prolific Mexican novelist (1928–) and essayist who has spent many years abroad, including childhood in Washington, D.C., ambassadorships, and several semesters of teaching at Harvard. A recent nonfiction work, also televised, is *El espejo enterrado (The Buried Mirror).*

[15] A pun is made on *paz,* meaning peace, and Paz, meaning Nobel literature prize winner Octavio Paz. Fun is made of a rivalry between the two writers, who both served as diplomats and ambassadors for Mexico, taught at Harvard, and have international reputation.

[16] Lector hispanoparlante, éste es un juego de palabras por modernización y *mother* pronunciado en castellano. La expresión "en la madre" significa que algo está violentamente echado a perder o atacado. [Hispanophone reader, this is a pun on *modernización* and *mother* pronounced in Spanish. The expression "en la madre" means something that is violently ruined or attacked.]

No iremos a llorar,
muertos al panteón,
el inglés hay que hablar
y entrarle al jalogüín.
No hay velorio
de café con peluquín,
ora[17] puro tecnócrata
con celular.

We won't go to weep
for the dead in the cemetery,
we have to speak English
and get into Hallowe'en.
There's no wake
with spiked coffee,
now just technocrats
with cellular phones.

Calaveras v. Halloween
Heras

Calaveras v. Hallowe'en
Heras

La tradición del "Día de muertos"
muy festejada,
la quieren enterrar,
los comerciantes
nos quieren embuchacar
el jalogüín . . . pura gringada.
Las maestras de jardines
y primarias, muy acomplejadas
atareadas con los chiquitines
a enseñarles tales pen . . .
samientos.[19]

Salespeople want to bury
our very celebrated "Day of the
dead" tradition
and force-feed us
Hallowe'en . . . nothing but a
gringada.[18]
Neurotic kindergarten and grade-
school teachers
driven crazy by the little ones
teach nothing but idio . . .
syncrasies.

---

[17] Ahora, en "mexicano" (Now, in "Mexican").

[18] *Gringada* could refer to anything done or created by an American from the United States but especially something that would identify the actor as stereotypically American.

[19] The ellipsis after "pen" allows the Mexican reader to finish the rhyme and the word with "-*dejadas.*" *Pendejada* is a vulgar term that means something stupid. *Pensamientos* means thoughts.

El pueblo mexicano[20]
Heras

Al panteón lo acompañó,
el TLC nos cayó,
ora pa' decir tortillas
se dice hot-cakes
y tener voluntad,
¡many eggs!

The next six calaveras were published in *Excélsior* on November 2, 1993.
They are by Eduardo Camacho Suárez.

Jackson
Eduardo Camacho Suárez

En hotel de cinco estrellas
a Michael lo velan como blanco.
No hizo temblar a las bellas;
sí, a los niños de Polanco.[21]

Jackson
Eduardo Camacho Suárez

In a five-star hotel
Michael's vigil is that of a white man.
He did not turn on the beauties;
only the boys of Polanco.

Halloween
Eduardo Camacho Suárez

Fiesta sangrienta y mezquina,
en México, un desacierto.
¡Que en la panadería de la esquina
nunca vendan Pay de Muerto!

Hallowe'en
Eduardo Camacho Suárez

Bloody and tight-fisted fiesta,
in Mexico, so misled.
I hope that the corner bakery
never sells Pie of the Dead.

---

[20] I will not attempt to translate "The Mexican People," as it depends too much on Mexican slang to be effective in a translation.
[21] Polanco is a well-established, fairly wealthy neighborhood in Mexico City where Michael Jackson went shopping during his 1993 concert tour.

Laura Esquível[22]
Eduardo Camacho Suárez

La muerte bate que bate
un puré de buen sabor.
Laurita, de tanto calor,
está como agua para chocolate.

Vargas Llosa[24]
Eduardo Camacho Suárez

Como líder, de los peores;
en política fue maleta.
Como autor, de los mejores,
se llevó el Premio Planeta.[25]

Dyllan Thomas
Eduardo Camacho Suárez

Insaciable bebedor
una noche en Nueva York
se bebió toda
la poesía del mundo.

Whitman
Eduardo Camacho Suárez

En su barba de hierba amarilla
el gusano repta
pero brilla.

Laura Esquível
Eduardo Camacho Suárez

Death whips and whips
a purée of good flavor.
Laurita from so much heat,
is like water for chocolate.[23]

Vargas Llosa
Eduardo Camacho Suárez

As a leader, among the worst;
in politics he bombed out.
As an author, among the first,
he won the Premio Planeta.

Dylan Thomas
Eduardo Camacho Suárez

Insatiable drinker
one night in New York
he drank up all
the poetry of the world.

Whitman
Eduardo Camacho Suárez

In his beard of yellow grass
the worm crawls,
but glowing.

---

[22] Author of the bestselling novel *Como agua para chocolate (Like Water for Chocolate)*.

[23] This expression means as ready as she/he/it will ever be.

[24] Mario Vargas Llosa (1936–), politically conservative Peruvian novelist and essayist who lost a presidential election.

[25] A prestigious literary prize for Latin American writers.

The following series by Otto-Raúl González, from *Excélsior,* November 1, 1991, is called "Calaveras de azúcar." A second part of the same series of calaveras is signed by González Martínez, Tablada, Paz Paredes.

Posada[26]

Yo diría así de pasada
que el inventor
de los rayos equis
fue Posada.

Posada

I'd say this in passing
that the inventor
of X rays
was Posada.

Rivera[27]
González Martínez, Tablada,
Paz Paredes

Rivera
González Martínez, Tablada,
Paz Paredes

En los murales
de Rivera
se enrosca la eternidad
como una enredadera.

In the murals
of Rivera
eternity winds itself
like ivy.

---

[26] José Guadalupe Posada (1852–1913), Mexican engraver and printer, who popularized the humorous, often ironic calavera.

[27] Diego Rivera (1886–1957), Mexican muralist married to Frida Kahlo. He painted Mexico's history and also romanticized the Indian.

N.B.: These lines are not a calavera proper because they are not a faux epitaph but a verse that was written above a tzompantli* consisting of sugar skulls set near the entrance of the Templo Mayor Museum in downtown Mexico City in November 1993.

Tlatzotzompantli[28]   Tlatzotzompantli

NADA EN ESTE MUNDO DURA   NOTHING IN THIS WORLD LASTS
FENECEN BIENES Y MALES   GOOD AND BAD THINGS DIE
UNA TRISTE SEPULTURA   A SAD SEPULCHRE
A TODOS NOS HACE IGUALES   MAKES ALL OF US EQUAL

N.B.: The following lines are not a calavera proper but a parody of a grammar lesson to conjugate verbs. This was part of an otherwise serious and formal Oaxaca-style ofrenda displayed in Coyoacán's municipal headquarters in 1993.

Yo muero   I die

Tú falleces   You perish
El sucumbe   He succumbs
Nosotros expiramos   We expire
Vosotros os petateais   You kick the bucket
Ellos se pelan   They check out
Y todos felpamos   And we all bite the dust

---

[28] Sweet tzompantli or rack of skulls.

N.B.: This verse is not a calavera proper but a criticism of private schools' tendency to celebrate Hallowe'en instead of Días de muertos. I include the whole text, taken from the newspaper *El Día* on November 2, 1993.

Metropolígrama
Benito Cienfuegos

Metropolygram
Benito Cienfuegos

Halloween en escuelas privadas;
ofrendas en escuelas oficiales.
Choque cultural, con la celebración
de colegios particulares a la
"americana."

Hallowe'en in private schools;
offerings in official schools.
Cultural shock with the
"American"-style celebration of
private schools.

Que si son desmemoriados
es cosa que no celebro,
en los planteles privados,
privados de buen cerebro.

That they are forgetful
is something I do not celebrate,
on private campuses
deprived of a good brain.

Appendix B:
Two Mexican Stories and
a Spanish Poem

Contents*

---

* Terms marked with astericks can be found in Glossary.

Mexican Myth of Anthropogony Retold by the Author

A council of the gods came together and asked, "Who will inhabit the earth? The sky has been created, the earth has been created, but who, oh gods, will inhabit the earth?" Without replying, Quetzalcóatl stood up, left the council, and went to Mictlan,* the Land of the Dead. He called Mictlantecuhtli* and Mictlancíhuatl,* the lord and lady of Mictlan, and announced, "I have come in quest of the precious bones you keep; I have come to take them away."

Mictlantecuhtli asked, "What will you do with them, Quetzalcóatl?"

"The gods need someone to inhabit the earth."

Mictlantecuhtli replied, "All right, sound my conch and walk four times around my precious circle."

But Quetzalcóatl saw that the conch had no openings, so he called on the worms to make openings, and then he called on the bees to go into the new openings and sound the conch.

When Mictlantecuhtli heard it, he said again, "All right, take the bones." But then he turned to his servants and said, "People of Mictlan, go tell Quetzalcóatl he cannot have our precious bones; he must leave them here where they belong." Quetzalcóatl replied, "No, Mictlantecuhtli, I am taking them now."

So Quetzalcóatl gathered up the precious bones. The bones of man were in one place, and the bones of woman were in another, and Quetzalcóatl made a bundle of all the bones.

Once more Mictlantecuhtli addressed his servants. "Gods, is Quetzalcóatl really going to take the precious bones? Gods, make him fall!" Then the people of Mictlan quickly made a hole, and Quetzalcóatl tripped and fell into it. He fell dead, and the precious bones were scattered, and quails flew down to peck and gnaw them.

Then Quetzalcóatl was resurrected. In consternation he asked his spirit, "What shall I do, oh my spirit?" And his spirit, his *nahual,* answered, "Things turned out badly. We're at the mercy of fate."

Quetzalcóatl gathered up the bones once more, bundled them together, and carried them to Tamoanchan. As soon as he arrived, the Cihuacóatl, Snake Woman, placed the bones in a precious metate* and ground them into a meal. Then Quetzalcóatl stood over the ground bones and drew blood from his member to drench them. His sacrificial blood gave life to the bones, and they rose up alive as men and women. Then all the gods rejoiced and did penance with Quetzalcóatl. And they said, "Oh gods, rejoice! Human beings, *macehuales,* those we have deserved because of our penance, have been born!"

Near-Death Experience with Dog

Quoted without changes from Jesús Angel Ochoa Zazueta's *La muerte y los muertos: culto, servicio, ofrenda y humor de una comunidad.*

Mi madre estaba ya anciana, tenía como 70 años cuando murió. Le dimos todos los servicios y la teníamos en el ataúd cuando empezó a respirar y despertó echando espuma por nariz y boca. La atendimos cuando pidió café y un cigarro, luego platicó que sintió cómo se desprendió del cuerpo y fue con su misma figura rumbo a un río muy grande con aguas revueltas y terrosas. Ahí estaba el perro que había corrido de su casa muchas veces, flaco y hambriento. El perro la miró con desprecio y no se movió. "Perro—le dijo—, llévame al otro lado porque soy muerta." El perro la miró despectivamente y le dijo: "¿Quieres que te lleve al otro lado? ¿Acaso me diste comida, agua, dulces? ¿No me pateabas?, ¿me bañabas con agua caliente de tu ropa sucia? ¿Qué te hacía para que en vida te portaras mal conmigo? No te puedo llevar, fuiste mala conmigo, te quedas aquí a vagar por tu barrio, a caminar por las chinampas, alma en pena serás." Entonces mi madre respiró profundo y volteó para atrás: su cuerpo se enfriaba pero aún le llegaba el olor del café y de los tamales y pensó: "Si huelo el café y los tamales es que soy ánima, pero si el perro no me pasa y mi cuerpo se enfría seré un cuerpo en pena y mis familiares se disgustarán." Entonces se revolcó en la tierra y vio a Jesucristo y a San Andrecito, y en eso estaba cuando despertó con mucha espuma. Luego nos dijo: "No maltraten a los perros porque los necesitarán." Por eso en Mizquic [sic] hay tantos perros.

Near-Death Experience with Dog (translation)

My mother was old already, she was seventy when she died. We gave her all the services, and we had her in the coffin when she started to breathe, and she woke up foaming at the nose and mouth. We served her when she requested coffee and a cigarette, then she told us that she felt how she became detached from the body and went with her own figure toward a very big river with turbulent and gritty waters. There she saw the dog she had thrown out of her house many times, skinny and hungry. The dog looked at her with scorn and didn't move. "Dog," she said to him, "take me to the other side because I'm dead and the Lord is looking for me." The dog looked at her haughtily and asked: "You want me to take you to the other side? Did you, by chance, give me food, water, sweets? Didn't you used to kick me? Did you bathe me with the hot water from your dirty clothes? What did I do to you in life to make you behave badly toward me? I can't take you, you were mean to me. Stay here to wander through your neighborhood, to walk along the chinampas,* a suffering soul you will be."

Then my mother breathed deep and looked back; her body was getting cold, but the smell of coffee and tamales still reached her, and she thought: "If I smell the coffee and the tamales, it means I'm alive, but if the dog won't take me across and my body gets cold, I'll be a suffering body, and my relatives will be displeased." Then she thrashed around on the ground and saw Jesus and Saint Andrecito, and at that point she woke up with a lot of foam. Later she told us, "Don't mistreat dogs because you'll need them." That's why in Mixquic there are so many dogs.

Fragmento de Coplas por la muerte de su padre
Jorge Manrique

Nuestras vidas son los ríos
que van a dar en la mar,
qu'es el morir;
allí van los señoríos
derecho a se acabar
e consumir;
allí los ríos caudales,
allí los otros medianos
e más chicos,
allegados son yguales
los que viuen por sus manos
e los ricos.

Fragment From Couplets for the Death of His Father
Jorge Manrique

Our lives are the rivers
that travel to the sea,
that is death;
there go the kingdoms
directly to end
and be consumed;
there the rushing rivers,
there the medium rivers
and the small ones,
once there, all are the same,
those who work with their hands
and the wealthy.

Appendix C: Notes on Posada's Engravings

Calaveras* de Posada*

Titles and translations, along with the notes I have transferred from another section of their text, are from Roberto Berdecio and Stanley Appelbaum, *Posada's Mexican Prints: 237 Cuts by José Guadalupe Posada.* Most of the reproductions are in their original size. My comments or paraphrases are between curly brackets ({}), as Berdecio and Appelbaum use both parentheses and square brackets.

1. {Detail of Rivera mural "Sueño de una tarde de domingo en La Alameda" [Dream of a Sunday Afternoon in the Alameda] from left: Diego Rivera as a child, Frida Kahlo, La Catrina, José Guadalupe Posada}— Figure 4.9.

2. "La calavera catrina." Broadside, zinc—Figure 1.27.
   Rivera incorporated this calavera (converting it into a full-length figure arm in arm with Posada himself) in his 1947 Hotel del Prado mural {see Figure 4.9}.

3. No identification, zinc. {"Como nunca se habrá visto en toda esta capital" (As never seen in this entire capital)}.

301

4. "Rebumbio de calaveras" [Skeleton Hubbub]. Broadside, type metal engraving. Newsboys hawking calavera sheets—Figure 4.3.

5. Calavera depicting contemporary newspapers as skeleton cyclists. Broadside, type metal engraving; 1889–1895 —Figure 4.23. {Accompanying literary calavera:}

De este famoso hipódromo en la pista,	In this famous race on the track not
no faltará ni un solo periodista	a single journalist will be missing;
La muerte inexorable no respeta	inexorable death respects not even
ni a los que veis aquí en bicicleta.	those you see here on bicycles.

. . . In the complete broadside each skeleton is labeled with the name of the newspaper he represents: The monk {cut out of this version on the left} is *Voz de México* [Voice of Mexico; a paper supporting the church]; the other skeleton no longer visible . . . is *Raza Latina*. . . . In the top row are, from left to right, *Patria* . . . {Fatherland}, *Universal* (with starry cap), *Tiempo* (Time); with hourglass headpiece and flowing beard), *Partido Liberal* (Liberal Party; with Phrygian cap, symbol of liberty), *Gil Blas* (with plumed Spanish cap), and *Siglo XIX* (nineteenth century, with top hat) . . . in bottom row are, from left to right, *Siglo XX* (twentieth century; this label is still legible), *Quijote* (on the ground with plumed helmet), *Fandango* (with sombrero), and *Casera* (housekeeper with skirt). . . . The bicycle theme . . . was popular during the 1890s in *Punch* and in American humorous publications.

6. "Chispeante y divertida calavera de Doña Tomasa y Simón el aguador" [Witty and Amusing Calavera of Doña Tomasa and Simón, the Water Carrier]; type metal engraving—Figure 1.14.

7. {One} of the thirteen illustrations from a calavera representing market women as skeletons. Broadside; zinc—Figure 1.19.

The main title . . . is: "Una calavera chusca Dedicada á las placeras, Tortilleras, verduleras y toda gente de lucha" (A Merry Calavera Dedicated to Market Women, Tortilla Vendors, Vegetable Vendors, and All Contentious People). {I would translate the last phrase: and all people with fighting spirit.} No. 29, from the recto side of the sheet, represents Agapita, the cheese vendor; No. 30, from the verso, depicts Doña Paz, the tamales seller.

8. "Calavera de los patinadores" (Streetcleaners' Calavera. Broadside, type metal engraving. Criminals convicted of minor offenses were used as street cleaners: hence the police guard and the variety of clothing—Figure 4.16.

9. "Calavera revolucionaria" (Revolutionary Calavera). Broadside, zinc; 1910 or after. Represents one of the *soldaderas* [woman soldiers, camp followers] who rode and marched with the rebel bands—Figure 4.10.

10. "Calavera de un revolucionario zapatista" (Calavera of a Revolutionary Follower of Zapata). Broadside, zinc, 1910–1912—Figure 4.11.

11. "Calaveras del montón" (Skeletons on the Heap) [or "Calavera de Madero" (Calavera of Madero)]. Broadside, zinc; 92 percent of original size—Figure 4.12.

When this broadside was issued (presumably on the occasion of All Souls' Day, 1910—the year is printed on the sheet), Madero had recently been imprisoned (this is alluded to in the verses), and the outbreak of the Revolution was only weeks away. . . . The lengthy verses are really about many types of tradesmen who will all end up as bones in a common pile— the allusions to Madero are clumsily interpolated. Yet the illustration clearly represents the liberal presidential candidate: The style of mustache and beard is his, and the words on the label of the bottle he carries should probably be completed as "Aguardiente de Parras," brandy from Parras— the latter being Madero's native city (in [. . .] Coahuila) and the site of the vineyards that constituted his family's wealth. His calavera is shown dressed in typical lower-class clothes . . . (because Posada thought of Madero as a friend of the people?).

12. "Gran fandango y francachela de todas las calaveras" (Happy Dance and Wild Party of All the Skeletons). Broadside, metal engraving— Figure 1.22.

13. "El gran panteón amoroso" (The Great Pantheon of Love). Broadside, type metal engraving—Figures 4.17–4.22.

14. {English translation of literary calaveras}

15. "El gran panteón amoroso" (The Great Pantheon of Love) {continued}. Broadside, type metal engraving.

16. {English translation of literary calaveras}

17. "El gran panteón amoroso" (The Great Pantheon of Love) {continued}. Broadside, type metal engraving.

18. {English translation of literary calaveras}

19. "Calaveras Mourning the Dead"—Figure 4.14.

20. "Gran calavera eléctrica" (Big Trolley Calavera). Broadside, zinc; 1907. A cemetery, presumably crowded with victims of the then fairly new electrical conveyances—Figure 4.13.

21. "Skeletons' Banquet"—Figure 4.15.

22. "Calavera de Don Quijote." Broadside, type metal engraving; 95 percent of original size—Figure 4.24.

The heading . . . reads: "Esta es la de don Quijote, la primera / la sin par, la gigante calavera" [This is the calavera of Don Quijote, the first-class one, the matchless one, the gigantic one]. The remaining verses say that {Don Quijote} will spare no one, not even the most learned. Here {he} is shown wearing his barber basin helmet.

23. {"La Calavera del Tenorio De la Colonia de la Bolsa" (The Calavera of the Stock Market's Don Juan). {Manilla's illustration of Zorrilla's *Don Juan Tenorio*}—Figure 4.2.

Appendix D:
A Selection of Náhuatl Poems

Contents

---

[1] I refer to the poems by their first line if they are untitled. Numbers preceding titles refer to the poem's position in Garibay K.'s *Poesía náhuatl II Cantares mexicanos: Manuscrito de la Biblioteca Nacional de México.*

En ningún tiempo, en ningún tiempo cesará[2]

En ningún tiempo, en ningún
tiempo cesará
tañer y cantar al sol:[3]
goza, oh príncipe mío,
tú no siempre estarás en la tierra:
hemos de irnos mañana o pasado.
Da deleite a los Aguilas y Tigres:[4]
nuestra gala única son las flores.
Todo el mundo en la tierra piensa:
y brotan a nuestros ojos las
flores.[5]
Oh, tú por quien se vive,[6]
¿cuál es tu riqueza, cuál tu
ramillete?
¡Flores preciosas que a maíz
huelen,
se tomen prestadas en la tierra!
¿Qué? ¿Hemos de llevarlas al
Lugar de los descarnados?
¿Las llevaremos a tu casa?[7]

At No Time, in No Era

At no time, in no era
will making music and singing to
the sun cease:
enjoy yourself, oh my prince,
you will not always be on earth;
we must leave tomorrow or the
following day.
Give pleasure to the Eagles and the
Tigers;
our only regalia is flowers.
Everyone in the world thinks,
and flowers spring to our gaze.
Oh you for whom we live,
what is your wealth, what is your
bouquet?
Precious flowers that smell like corn
be borrowed from the earth!
What? Are we to take them to the
Place of the Fleshless?
Will we take them to your house?

---

[2] From Garibay K., *Historia de la literatura náhuatl,* 187.

[3] The sun is not only the astronomical entity but also the god of the Aztecs, Huitzilopochtli (Hummingbird on the Left, i.e., from the south). He is also the god of war.

[4] Two divisions of warriors.

[5] Flowers for the Nahuas symbolized life, as well as its brevity. By symbolizing the brevity of life, they also signified death. In addition, the diphrasism *in xóchitl, in cuícatl (flor, canto),* (flower, song) means poetry or poem. For the ancient Nahuas, poetry was more than a form of art; it was the only way divinity could be known, through the inspiration of the poet. Poetry was therefore held in high spiritual, as well as aesthetic, esteem. See, for instance, "Song of Sadness, I."

[6] An epithet for the supreme deity.

[7] I translate with an effort to preserve the sense, style, and rhythm of Garibay's translations into Spanish, which do the same for the Náhuatl. In the two Náhuatl original versions I include, the reader can perceive the sound and rhythm Garibay and I attempt to reproduce in Spanish and English, respectively. I respect Garibay's punctuation as much as seems proper for English. He uses exclamation marks in place of exclamatory words that have no counterpart in Spanish or English; I use fewer such marks.

Poemas de la Triple Alianza[8]
(Poems from the Triple Alliance[9])

Xochin Cuahuitl (2)

. . .

Niquitoa ni Nezahualcoyotl Huiya.[10]
¿Cuix oc nelli nemohua oa in tlalticpac? Ihui Ohuaye.
¡An nochipa tlalticpac:
zan achica ye nican! Ohuaye Ohueya.
Tel ca chalchiuitl no xamani,
no teocuitlatl in tlapani,
no quetzalli poztequi Yahui Ohuaya.
¡An nochipa tlalticpac:
zan achica ye nican! Ohuaye Ohuaye.[11]

---

[8] From Garibay K., *Poesía náhuatl II Cantares mexicanos: Manuscrito de la Biblioteca Nacional de México*, 3–4, 41, 53.

[9] That is, México-Tenochtitlan, Texcoco, Tlacopan (Tacuba).

[10] This is one of the best-known Náhuatl poems, and I offer the original, which can be pronounced like Spanish except for the intervocalic "x," which should be pronounced *sh,* and the intervocalic "z," which should be pronounced *ts.* The stress falls on the penultimate syllable.

[11] *Huiya, ihui, ohuaye, ohueya, yahui* are expressions of lament, like sighs.

El árbol florido (fragmento)

. . .

Lo digo yo, Nezahualcóyotl
¿Es que acaso se vive de verdad en
la tierra?
¡No por siempre en la tierra,
sólo breve tiempo aquí!
Aunque sea jade: también se
quiebra,
aunque sea oro, también se hiende,
y aun el plumaje de quetzal se
desgarra:
¡No por siempre en la tierra:
sólo breve tiempo aquí!

21 Canto de tristeza, I[12]

¡No hay más que llamar a ti, dador
de la vida:
sufro, pero sólo tú eres nuestro
amigo!
Hablemos sólo tu bella palabra,
digamos por qué estoy triste:
Busco placer de tus flores,
la alegría de tus cantos, tu riqueza.
Dicen que dentro del cielo hay dicha,
se vive y hay alegría: allí está en pie el
atabal,
es persistente el canto, y con él se
disipa
nuestro llanto y tristeza,
su casa es lugar de vida . . . ¡eso lo
saben vuestros corazones,[13]
oh príncipes!

The Flowering Tree (fragment)

. . .

I say it, I Nezahualcóyotl:
Does one truly live on the earth?
Not forever on the earth,
only a brief time here.
Although it be jade, it will also
fragment,
although it be gold, it will also
break,
and even the quetzal's plumage
tears:
Not forever on the earth,
only a brief time here.

21 Song of Sadness, I

I can but call to you, giver of life;
I suffer, but only you are our friend!
Let us speak only your beautiful
word,
let us say why I am sad:
I seek pleasure from your flowers,
the joy of your songs, your treasure.
They say that in heaven there is
happiness,
one lives, and there is joy. There
stands the drum;
song is persistent, and with it are
dissipated
our weeping and sadness.
His house is the place of life . . .
your hearts know that,
oh princes!

---

[12] The numbers were assigned by Garibay for his anthology.

[13] In Náhuatl discourse, personal character was called *the heart, the face,* and the young were consciously raised to develop strong and compassionate hearts and faces. The heart was considered the seat of courage, wisdom, and integrity, as well as of passion and desire.

28 Canto de guerreros, 4 (Primera parte)

Por mucho que llore yo,
por mucho que yo me aflija,
por mucho que lo ansíe mi
corazón,
¿no habré de ir acaso al Reino del
Misterio?
En la tierra dicen nuestros corazones:
¡Ojalá que no fuéramos mortales,
oh príncipes!
¿Dónde está la región en que no
hay muerte?
¿No habré de ir allá yo?
¿Vive acaso mi madre allá en la
Región del Misterio?
¿Vive acaso mi padre allá en la
Región del Misterio?
Mi corazón trepida . . . ¡no he de
perecer . . .
me siento angustiado!

28 Warriors' Song, 4 (Part One)

No matter how much I weep,
no matter how much I suffer,
no matter how much my heart
desires it,
will I by chance not go to the
Kingdom of Mystery?
On earth our heart says:
Would that we were not mortal, oh
princes!
Where is the region where there is
no death?
Am I not destined to go there?
Does my mother perhaps live there
in the Region of Mystery?
Does my father perchance live there
in the Region of Mystery?
My heart trembles . . . I must not
perish . . .
I feel anguished!

Treinta Poemas de Cuahcuauhtzin
(Thirty Poems by Cuahcuauhtzin)

Que se abra tu corazón como las flores (Segunda parte)

Let Your Heart Open Like a Flower (Part Two)

Que se abra tu corazón como las
flores,
que llegue a entenderlo tu corazón.
Tú vives, tú me aborreces,
tú me preparas la muerte . . .
¡Uno que se va, uno que ha de
perecer!
Puede ser que por mí llores,
que por mí te aflijas, oh amigo mío,
pero yo me voy, yo me voy . . .
No dice más mi corazón:
¡Nunca más vendré,
nunca más habré de pasar por la
tierra,
en tiempo oportuno,
porque yo me voy, yo me voy . . . !

Let your heart open like a flower,
let your heart come to understand it.
You live, you abhor me,
you prepare death for me . . .
One who leaves, one who must
perish!
It may be that you will weep for me,
that for me you will suffer, oh my
friend,
but I am leaving, I am leaving . . .
My heart says no more;
I shall come no more,
I shall never again walk on the earth
in an opportune time,
because I am leaving, I am
leaving . . . !

Tercera parte

Quiere con ansia flores mi corazón.
Sólo sufro con cantos,
sólo ensayo mis cantos,
en la tierra, yo Cuahcuauhtzin.
Con ansia quiero flores,
que estén en mi mano,
¡soy un desdichado!
¿A dónde hemos de ir
que nunca muramos?
Aunque fuera yo jade,
aunque fuera yo oro,
seré fundido, seré perforado
en el crisol:
mi corazón, yo Cuahcuauhtzin,
soy un desdichado! (p. 57f)

Part Three

My heart longs for flowers anxiously.
I only suffer with songs,
I only essay my songs,
on the earth, I Cuauhcuahutzin.
With anxiety I want flowers,
may they rest in my hand,
I am wretched!
Where will we go
that we may never die?
Although I were jade,
although I were gold,
I will be melted, I will be perforated
in the crucible.
My heart, I Cuahcuauhtzin,
am a wretched man!

Poemas de Chalco: Cantos de Guerreros
(Poems from Chalco: Warriors' Songs)

4 En memoria de héroe (Tercera parte)

Ay, oíd aquí la palabra que dejó
dicha
el rey Chichicuepan el pacificador.
"¿Es posible que vengan
del Reino de los muertos los
caudillos
a ver su palabra y su aliento?
Se irán trepidando los plumajes de
quetzal,
allá al dominio de los descarnados,
allá al sitio donde de algún modo
se existe.[14]
Allá están felices nobles y
príncipes:
Tlacatécatl Xocuahuatzin,
Tozmaquetzin, Necuametzin.
Por breve tiempo los tuvo en lista
el que hace vivir todo.
Por tu merecimiento estás allá
tú rey Cuatéotl,
Chalchiuhtlatónac." (p. 65)

4 In Memory of Heroes (Part Three)

Oh, hear here the word that King
Chichicuepan the pacifier said and
left us.
"Is it possible for the leaders to
return
from the Kingdom of the Dead
to see their word and their breath?
Quetzal plumage shall go trembling
there to the domain of the fleshless,
there to the place where somehow
one exists.
There nobles and princes are
happy:
Tlacatécatl Xocuahuatzin,
Tozmaquetzin, Necuametzin.
For a brief time he who makes
everything live
had them on his list.
Because of your deserts you are there,
you King Cuatéotl,
Chalchiutlatónac."

---

[14] Mictlan* is the domain of the fleshless, the place where somehow one exists, the kingdom of mystery, and so on. It has been compared to the Hebrew Sheol or the Greek Hades, a dark place where spirits feed on dust and barely exist. We see in these poems other speculations about it.

17 El enigma de vivir

Lloro, me alfijo, cuando recuerdo
que dejaremos las bellas flores, los
bellos cantos.
Ahora gocemos, ahora cantemos,
del todo nos vamos y
desaparecemos en su casa![15]
¿Quién de vosotros, amigos, no lo
sabe?
Mi corazón sufre, se llena de enojo:
No dos veces se nace, no dos veces
es uno hombre:
sólo una vez pasamos por la tierra!
Si aún por breve tiempo
estuviera con ellos y a su lado . . .
¡Nunca será, o nunca tendré placer,
nunca gozaré!
¿Dónde es el sitio de vivir de mi
corazón?
¿Dónde está mi casa, dónde está mi
hogar durable?
Aquí en la tierra solamente sufro.
¿Sufres, corazón mío?
No te angusties en esta tierra:
ése es mi destino: ¡tenlo por sabido!
¿Dónde merecí yo venir a la vida,
dónde merecí ser hecho hombre?
¡Acción suya fue!
Allá se hacen las cosas ondulando
donde vida no hay.
Es lo que dice mi corazón.
¿Y el dios, qué dice?

17 The Enigma of Living

I weep, I grieve when I remember
that we shall leave the beautiful
flowers, the lovely songs.
Now let us enjoy ourselves, let us sing,
we leave entirely and disappear into
his house!
Who among you, friends, does not
know this?
My heart suffers, it is full of anger;
not twice is one born, not twice is
one a man;
only once do we pass through the
earth!
If yet for a brief time
I were with them and at their side . . .
It will never be, oh never will I take
pleasure or delight!
Where is the place for my heart to
live?
Where is my house, where my lasting
home?
Here on the earth I only suffer.
Do you suffer, heart of mine?
Do not grieve on this earth;
this is my destiny; know it!
Where did I deserve to come into life,
where did I deserve to be made a
man?
It was his deed!
There things are done fluttering
where there is no life.
That is what my heart says.
And what does the god say?

---

[15] That is, the house of the sun.

—No en verdad vivimos aquí,
no hemos venido a durar en la
tierra.
Oh tengo que dejar el bello canto,
la bella flor
y tengo que ir en busca del Lugar
del Misterio.
Él pronto habrá de hastiarse:
prestado tenemos sólo su bello
canto. (p. 82f)[16]

18 Vida fugaz

Inicio el canto, intento tomar
tus flores, autor de la vida.
Tañemos ya nuestros enflorados
tambores.
Éste es nuestro deber en la tierra.
Flores que no se pueden llevar,
cantos que no se pueden llevar al
Reino del Misterio!
Totalmente nos vamos: Nadie
quedará en la tierra.
Un día por lo menos, oh mis
amigos:
tenemos que dejar nuestras flores,
nuestros cantos.
Tenemos que dejar la tierra que
perdura.
Gocémonos, amigos, gocémonos.
(p. 84)

"We do not live here in truth,
we have not come to last on the
earth."
Oh, I must leave the lovely song,
the lovely flower,
and I must go in search of the Place
of Mystery.
He will soon be weary;
only on loan do we have his lovely
song.

18 Fleeting Life

I begin the song, I attempt to take
your flowers, author of life.
We play our flower-decked drums.
This is our duty on earth.
Flowers that cannot be taken,
songs that cannot be taken to the
Kingdom of Mystery!
We leave totally; no one will
remain on earth.
One day at least, oh my friends:
let us leave our flowers, our songs.
We must leave the world that
perdures.
Let us enjoy ourselves, friends, let
us enjoy ourselves.

---

[16] The Náhuatl epistemology held that the only truth one can know comes through the divine revelation that poets experience when their heart is inspired, *yoltéotl,* literally, goddened. Flower, song mean poetry, poem.

20 Incertidumbre del fin

¿A dónde iré, ay?
¿A dónde iré?
Donde está la Dualidad . . .
¡Difícil, ah, difícil!
¡Acaso es la casa de todos allá
donde están los que ya no tienen
cuerpo,
en el interior del cielo,
o acaso aquí en la tierra es el sitio
donde están los que ya no tienen
cuerpo!
Totalmente nos vamos, totalmente
nos vamos.
¡Nadie perdura en la tierra!
¿Quién hay que diga: Dónde están
nuestros amigos?
¡Alegráos! (p. 86)

20 Uncertainty About the End

Where am I to go?
Where Duality is . . .
Difficult, oh, difficult!
Perhaps there lies the house of all
where those who no longer have a
body abide,
within heaven,
or perhaps here on earth is the
place
where abide those who no longer
have a body.
We leave entirely, we leave entirely.
No one lasts on earth.
Who is there who might say: where
are our friends?
Rejoice!

21 Elegía por Ayocuan

Flores de rojo y azul color
mézclense a flores de rojo vivo.
Es tu palabra, tu corazón,
oh mi príncipe, rey de los
chichimecas,
tú, Ayocuan.
Por breve tiempo date a ver en la
tierra.
Lloro porque la muerte
destruye nuestras creaciones,
destruye el bello canto.
Por breve tiempo date a ver en la
tierra. (p. 87)

21 Elegy for Ayocuan

May flowers of red and blue color
mix with flowers of brilliant red.
It is your word, your heart,
oh my prince, king of the
Chichimecas,
you, Ayocuan.
Briefly make yourself visible on
earth.
I weep because death
destroys our creations,
destroys the lovely song.
Briefly make yourself visible on
earth.

Poemas de Huexotzínco

3 Angustía del poeta

Me llega al alma cuanto yo digo,
oh amigos míos:
He andado haciendo vagar mi
corazón en la tierra,
lo he andado tiñendo tal como
vivimos:
lugar de placer, lugar de bienestar,
de dicha junto a otros.
¡No soy aún llevado a la Región del
Misterio!
Bien lo sabe mi corazón,
con verdad lo digo, amigos míos,
Todo el que hace plegarias al dios,
daña su corazón al entregarlo.[17]
¿Es que aún no más en la tierra?
¿Acaso no es posible nacer dos
veces?
¿De verdad se vive allá en la
Region del Misterio,
dentro del cielo?
Se es feliz solamente aquí. (p. 94)

3 The Poet's Grief

Everything I say pierces my soul,
oh my friends.
I have lived making my heart
wander on the earth,
I have been dyeing it just as we live:
place of pleasure, place of well-being,
of pleasure next to others.
I am not yet taken to the Region of
Mystery.
My heart knows it well,
with truth I say it, my friends,
everyone who raises prayers to the
god
harms his heart upon delivering it.
. . .
Is it not possible to be born twice?
Is it true that one lives there in the
Region of Mystery,
inside heaven?
One is happy only here.

---

[17] The Nahuas believed it was important to preserve the integrity of one's "heart" by retaining a certain distance from people and things rather than by losing control of one's feelings. For example, to fall in love and "deliver up one's heart" was to lose some of one's character ("heart") and integrity.

Poeta anónimo (náhuatl)

Ma ciuhtia o in quinequi noyollo
zan chimalli xochitl in ixochiuh in
ipalnemoani.
¿Quen conchihuaz
noyollo?Yehuaya
¿o nen tancico tonquizaco in
tlalticpac?Ohuaya Ohuaya.
Zan ca yuhqui nonyaz in
oompopoliuh xochitl . . .

¿Antle notleyo yez in quenmanian?
¿Antle noitauhca yez in tlalticpac?
Ma nel xochitl, ma nel cuicatl . . . !
¿Quen conchihuaz
noyollo?Yehuaya
¿o nen tacico tonquizaco in
tlalticpac?Ohuaya Ohuaya. (p. 101)

9 Poeta anónimo

Esfuércese en querer mi corazón
sólo flores de escudo: son las flores
del dios.
¿Que hará mi corazón?
¿Es que en vano vinimos, pasamos
por la tierra?
De igual modo me iré
que las flores que han ido
pereciendo.
¿Nada será de mi fama algún día?
¿Nada de mi nombre quedará en la
tierra?
¡Al menos flores, al menos
cantos . . . !
¿Que hará mi corazón?
¿Es que en vano vinimos, pasamos
por la tierra? (p. 101)

9 Anonymous Poet

Let my heart make an effort to love
only shield flowers; they are the
flowers of the god.
What can my heart do?
Is it in vain that we come, that we
pass through the world?
I will leave the same way
as the flowers that have been
perishing.
Will my fame come to nothing one
day?
Will nothing of my name remain in
the world?
At least flowers, at least songs . . . !
What is my heart to do?
Do we come in vain, in vain pass
through the world?

34 Elegía

Yo por mi parte digo:
¡Ay, sólo un breve instante!
¡Sólo cual la magnolia abrimos los
pétalos!
¡Sólo hemos venido, amigos, a
marchitarnos
en esta tierra!
Pero ahora, cese la amargura,
ahora dar recreo a vuestros pechos.
¿Pero cómo comer? ¿Cómo darnos
al placer?
Allá nacen nuestros cantos, donde
nació el atabal.
He sufrido yo en la tierra
en donde vivieron ellos.
Se enlazará la amistad,
se enlazará la corporación junto a
los tambores.
¿Acaso yo aún vendré?
¿Aún habré de entonar un canto?
Pero yo solo estoy aquí: ellos están
ausentes.
Al olvido y a la niebla yo tengo que
entregarme.
Creamos a nuestro corazón:
¿Es nuestra casa la tierra?
En sitio de angustias y de dolor
vivimos.
Por eso solamente canto y pregunto:
¿Cuál flor otra vez plantaré?
¿Cuál maíz otra vez sembraré?
¿Mi madre y mi padre aún habrán
de dar fruto nuevo?
¿Fruto que vaya medrando en la
tierra?

34 Elegy

For my part I say:
Oh, only a brief instant!
Only like the magnolia do we open
our petals.
We have only come, friends, to wilt
on this earth.
But now, let bitterness cease,
now give recreation to your
breasts.
But how to eat? How to deliver
ourselves to pleasure?
There are our songs born, where
the drum was born.
I have suffered in the world
where they lived.
Friendship will be intertwined,
corporation will be intertwined
along with the drums.
And shall I by chance come?
Will I still be able to intone a song?
But I am alone here; they are
absent.
To forgetfulness and fog I must
deliver myself.
Let us believe our heart:
is the world our home?
We live in a place of grief and sorrow.
That is why I only sing and ask,
what flower shall I plant again?
What corn shall I plant again?
Will my mother and my father yet
give new fruit?
Fruit that will go thriving in the
world?

Es la razón por que lloro:
nadie está allí: nos dejaron
huérfanos en la tierra.
¿En dónde está el camino
para bajar al Reino de los
Muertos,[18]
a dónde están los que ya no tienen
cuerpo?[19]
¿Hay vida aún allá en esa región
en que de algún modo se existe?
¿Tienen aun conciencia nuestros
corazones?
En cofre y caja esconde a los
hombres
y los envuelve en ropas el dador de
la vida.
¿Es que allá los veré?
¿He de fijar los ojos en el rostro
de mi madre y mi padre?
¿Han de venir a darme ellos aún
su canto y su palabra?
¡Yo los busco: nadie esta allí:
nos dejaron huérfanos en la tierra!
(p. 129f)

That is my reason for weeping:
no one is here; they left us orphans
in the world.
Where is the path
to descend to the Kingdom of the
Dead,
where are those who no longer
have bodies?
Is there still life in that region
in which somehow one exists?
Are our hearts still conscious there?
In coffer and box the giver of life
hides men
and wraps them in clothes.
Will I see them there?
Will I fix my gaze on the face
of my mother and my father?
Will they still come to give me
their song and their word?
I seek them; no one is there.
They left us orphans in the world!

---

[18] *Itemoyan*, the path by which to descend to Mictlan.*

[19] *Ximohuayan*, form of those who live in Mictlan,* bodiless, but *quenonamican*, they exist somehow, although the living do not know how.

38 Poema de Tochihuitzin[20]

Ya nuestros cantos, ya nuestras
flores elevamos:
son los cantos del dios.
Con ellos hay abrazos de los
amigos,
se da a conocer con ellos la
corporación.
Como solía decir Tochihuitzin,
como lo dejó dicho Coyolchiuhqui:
"Sólo hemos venido a dormir,
sólo hemos venido a soñar:
No es verdad, no es verdad que
vinimos a vivir en la tierra.
Nos vamos haciendo cual hierba
en cada primavera: viene a brotar,
viene a estar verde nuestro
corazón,
es una flor nuestro cuerpo,
abre unas cuantas corolas:
entonces se marchita."
Así solía decir Tochihuitzin.
(p. 135)

38 Tochihuitzin's Poem

Now our songs, now our flowers
do we raise;
they are the songs of the god.
With them there are friends'
embraces,
with them the corporation is made
known.
As Tochihuitzin used to say,
as Coyolchiuhqui said:
"We have only come to sleep,
we have only come to dream.
It is not true, it is not true that we
come to live in the world.
We go along becoming like grass,
our heart becomes green,
our body is a flower,
it opens a few corollas,
then it wilts."
Thus was Tochihuitzin wont to
speak.

[20] Tochihuitzin was king of Mexicatzinco and witnessed the conquest.

Works Consulted

Acosta, Aurea. "De múltiples maneras interpretan los artistas nacionales el engima de la muerte."[1] México, D.F.: *Excélsior,* 31 Oct. 1991.

Anaya, Jorge. "Qué noche—dijo la muerte—." "La Jornada Niños." México, D.F.: *La Jornada,* 2 Nov. 1993.

Anderson Imbert, Enrique. *Historia de la literatura hispanoamericana I.* México, D.F.: Fondo de Cultura Económica, 1965 [1954].

Arellano, Jerónimo. Untitled poem. St. Paul: Unpublished, 1998.

Argüello Sánchez, Jorge. *Boletín informativo sobre el origen de la ofrenda.* México, D.F.: Privately published, 1990.

Ariès, Philippe. *The Hour of Our Death.* New York: Alfred A. Knopf, 1981.

Aviña, José Carlos. "Día de muertos, tradición cristiana; Halloween, fiesta celta pagana." México, D.F.: *Heraldo,* 31 Oct. 1993.

Baker, Nicholson. *Vox.* New York: Random House, 1992.

Bakhtin, Mikhail M. *The Dialogic Imagination.* Austin: U of Texas P, 1981.

———. *Rabelais and His World.* Bloomington: Indiana UP, 1984 [1965].

Barthes, Roland. "Myth Today." *Mythologies.* Trans. Annette Lavers. New York: Farrar, 1972 [1957].

---

[1] For bibliographical references to books published in Mexico, I adhere to MLA conventions of punctuation and to Spanish conventions of capitalization.

————. *Camera Lucida, Reflections on Photography.* Trans. Richard Howard. New York: Hill and Wang, 1981 [1980].

————. "The Photographic Message." *A Barthes Reader.* New York: Hill and Wang, 1982, 194–210.

Beltrán, Alberto. "Muero por que no muero." México, D.F.: *El Día*, 1 Nov. 1992.

Berdecio, Roberto, and Stanley Appelbaum. *Posada's Mexican Prints: 237 Cuts by José Guadalupe Posada.* New York: Dover, 1972.

Boase, T.S.R. *Death in the Middle Ages: Mortality, Judgment and Remembrance.* New York: McGraw, 1972.

Bolaños, Fray Joaquín. *La portentosa vida de la muerte, emperatriz de los sepulcros, vengadora de los agravios del Altísimo, y muy señora de la humana naturaleza cuya célebre Historia encomienda a los Hombres de buen gusto.* México, D.F.: Oficina de los Herederos del Lic. D. Joseph de Jáuregui, 1792.

Bonfil Batalla, Guillermo. *México profundo: una civilización negada.* México, D.F.: Consejo Nacional para la Cultura y las Artes, Grijalbo, 1990 [1987].

————. *Pensar nuestra cultura.* México, D.F.: Alianza, 1992 [1991].

Bourdieu, Pierre. "The Aristocracy of Culture." *Distinction: A Social Critique of the Judgment of Taste.* Cambridge: Harvard UP, 1984.

Brenner, Anita. "The Pyramid Planters," "The Dark Madonna," "Posada the Prophet." *Idols Behind Altars.* Boston: Beacon, 1970 [1920].

Butler, Judith. "Gender Trouble, Feminist Theory, and Psychoanalytic Discourse." *Feminism and Postmodernism.* Ed. Linda Nicholson. New York: Routledge, 1990.

Bynum, Caroline Walker. *Holy Feast and Holy Fast: The Religious Significance of Food to Medieval Women.* Berkeley: University of California Press, 1987.

————. *Fragmentation and Redemption: Essays on Gender and the Human Body in Medieval Religion.* New York: Zone, 1991.

Cáceres Carenzo, Raúl. *La noche de los muertos: Velación en los panteones de Toluca.* Toluca: Gobierno del Edo. de México, 1974.

Camus, Albert. "Le mythe de Sisyphe." *Essais.* Eds. R. Quilliot and L. Faucon. Paris: Bibliothèque de la Pléiade, 1965.

Cardoza y Aragón, Luis. *José Guadalupe Posada.* México, D.F.: Universidad Nacional Autónoma de México, 1963.

Carmichael, Elizabeth, and Chloë Sayer. *The Skeleton at the Feast: The Day of the Dead in Mexico.* Austin: British Museum P and U of Texas P, 1992.

Castillo, Herberto. "Llamar a cuentas." México, D.F.: *Proceso*, 18 July 1994.

Centro de Estudios Históricos de la Sierra Norte de Puebla, A.C. "Cuetzalan: compendio monográfico." Cuetzalan: Presidencia Municipal Constitucional, 1990.

de Certeau, Michel. *The Practice of Everyday Life.* California: U of California P, 1984.

———. *Heterologies: Discourse on the Other.* Minneapolis: U of Minnesota P, 1986.

Charlot, Jean. "José Guadalupe Posada and His Successors." *Posada's Mexico.* Ed. Ron Tyler. Washington D.C.: Library of Congress, 1979.

Cienfuegos, Benito. "Metropoligrama." México, D.F.: *El Día,* 2 Nov. 1993.

Clendinnen, Inga. *Aztecs: An Interpretation.* Cambridge: Cambridge UP, 1993 [1991].

Connerton, Paul. *How Societies Remember.* Cambridge: Cambridge UP, 1989.

Cordry, Donald. *Mexican Masks.* Austin: U of Texas P, 1980.

Cornides, A. "All Souls' Day." *New Catholic Encyclopedia.* Volume I. New York: McGraw Hill, 1967, 319.

Cortés Ruiz, Efraín, Beatriz Oliver Vega, Catalina Rodríguez Lazcano, Dora Sierra Carrillo, and Plácido Villanueva Peredo. *Los Días de muertos, una costumbre mexicana.* México, D.F: G. V. Editores, 1990.

Coy, Peter. "Current Ethnic Profiles and Amerindian Survivals." *Cambridge Encyclopedia of Latin America and the Caribbean,* 2d ed. Eds. Simon Collier, Thomas E. Skidmore, Harold Blakemore. Cambridge: Cambridge UP, 1992.

Cuevas, Simón, and Romualdo Galindo. Untitled news article. Mexico, D.F.: *La Jornada,* 3 Nov. 1995.

Culler, Jonathan. *The Pursuit of Signs, Semiotics, Literature, and Deconstruction.* Ithaca: Cornell UP, 1981.

Durán, Diego. *Historia de las Indias de Nueva España e Islas de la Tierra Firme.* Volume I. México, D.F.: Porrúa, 1967.

Eco, Umberto. *Apostillas a El nombre de la rosa.* Barcelona: Lumen, 1984.

Eliade, Mircea. *The Sacred and the Profane: The Nature of Religion.* New York: Harcourt, 1957.

———. *Cosmos and History: The Myth of the Eternal Return.* New York: Harper, 1959 [1954].

Eliot, T. S. "Burnt Norton." *The Complete Poems and Plays 1909–1950.* New York: Harcourt, 1962 [1952], 117–122.

Estrada Sagaón, Georgina. *Paralelismos rituales de las religiones azteca y católica.* México, D.F.: UNAM, Facultad de Filosofía y Letras, 1959.

"Expresó Clariond Reyes su defensa por las tradiciones de nuestros antepasados." México, D.F.: *Uno más uno,* 3 Nov. 1992.

Fiske, John. *Reading the Popular.* Boston: Unwin Hyman, 1989.

———. *Understanding Popular Culture.* Boston: Unwin Hyman, 1989.

———. *Semiotics of Culture* (unpublished course notes). Minneapolis: U of Minnesota, 1991.

Foucault, Michel. *The History of Sexuality, I.* New York: Vintage, 1990 [1978].

———. *The Foucault Reader.* Ed. Paul Rabinow. New York: Pantheon, 1984.

IV Expo "Culto a la Muerte." México, D.F.: *Excélsior,* 2 Nov. 1991.

Gamiño Espinoza, Juan. *La fiesta de los muertos en San Jerónimo Miacatlán* [Milpa Alta, D.F.]. México, D.F.: Instituto Nacional de Antropología e Historia, 1987.

García Canclini, Néstor. *Las culturas populares en el capitalismo.* México: Nueva Imagen, 1981.

García Márquez, Gabriel. *Cien años de soledad.* Buenos Aires: Editorial Sudamericana, 1971 [1967].

Garduño Espinosa, Roberto. "Ricos y pobres, dispuestos a poner ofrenda a sus muertos." México, D.F.: *Jornada,* 31 Oct. 1993.

———. "Viva la tradición de la noche de muertos; pero va a transformarse." México, D.F.: *La Jornada,* 1 Nov. 1993.

Garibay K., Angel María. *Poesía náhuatl II Cantares mexicanos: Manuscrito de la Biblioteca Nacional de México.* México: UNAM Instituto de Investigaciones Históricas, 1965.

———. *Historia de la literatura náhuatl: Primera parte.* México: Porrúa, 1971.

Gerlero, Elena de. "La escatología en el arte monástico novohispano del siglo XVI." *Arte funerario: coloquio.* N.p.: n.p., n.d.

Godzich, Wlad. "The Further Possibility of Knowledge" (Foreword). In Michel de Certeau. *Heterologies: Discourse on the Other.* Minneapolis: U of Minnesota P, 1986.

González, Raymundo. "Actos conmemorativos del Día de muertos en delegaciones del DF." México, D.F.: *Novedades,* 30 Oct. 1992.

———. "En Mixquic singular ceremonia para recordar a sus difuntos." México, D.F.: *Novedades,* 1 Nov. 1992.

Grimrac, Héctor. *Más allá de la muerte.* México, D.F.: Posada, 1976.

Guarneros, Fabiola. "En fiesta se convierte el Día de muertos en Mixquic." México, D.F.: *Universal,* 2 Nov. 1993.

Guarneros, Fabiola, and Adriana Días. "El culto a los muertos, una tradición que vence a las penurias económicas." México, D.F.: *Universal,* 1 Nov. 1993.

Guillén Peralta, Guillermina. "Mixquic, el pueblo que vive por la muerte." México, D.F.: *Universal,* 30 Oct. 1993.

Guthke, Karl Siegfied. *B. Traven: The Life Behind the Legends.* Trans. Robert Sprung. Chicago: Lawrence Hill, 1991.

Hernández, Juan. Untitled news article. México, D.F.: *Novedades,* 1 Nov. 1992.

———. "El encarecimiento ha disminuido el lujo de las ofrendas a los muertos en Tlaxcala." México, D.F.: *Novedades,* 1 Nov. 1992.

———. "Tlaxcalles y Tlatlapas, los platillos preferidos de los muertos tlaxcaltecas." México, D.F.: *Uno más uno,* 1 Nov. 1992.

Herrera, Joaquín. "Bosque de cirios convirtió a Mixquic en un enorme faro." México, D.F.: *Excélsior,* 3 Nov. 1991.

Hobsbawm, Eric. "Introduction: Inventing Traditions" and "Mass-Produced Traditions: Europe, 1879–1914." Eds. Eric Hobsbawm and Terence Ranger. *The Invention of Tradition*. Cambridge: Cambridge UP, 1983.

Horcasitas, Fernando. *The Aztecs Then and Now*. México, D.F.: Minutiae Mexicana, 1979.

Hubbell, Sue. "'Hopping John' Gets the Year Off to a Flying Start." Washington, D.C.: *Smithsonian*, Vol. 24, Num. 9, Dec. 1993.

Ingham, John M. *Mary, Michael, and Lucifer: Folk Catholicism in Central Mexico*. Austin: U of Texas P, 1986.

Jara, René, and Nicholas Spadaccini, eds. *Amerindian Images and the Legacy of Columbus*. Minneapolis: U of Minnesota P, 1992.

Johansson, Patrick. "Sincretismo evangelizador y muerte precolombina." México, D.F.: *Nacional*, 2 Nov. 1993.

Kandell, Jonathan. "Conquest," "Birth of the Spanish City," and "Megalopolis." *La Capital: The Biography of Mexico City*. New York: Random, 1988.

Kastenbaum, Robert. "Dance of Death (Danse Macabre)." *Encyclopedia of Death*. Eds. Beatrice Kastenbaum and Robert Kastenbaum. Phoenix: Oryx, 1989.

Kent, Rolly, and Heather Valencia. *Queen of Dreams: The Story of a Yaqui Dreaming Woman*. New York: Simon, 1991.

Krauss, Carlos. Personal Interview. México, D.F.: INAH, 16 Jan. 1992.

Lafaye, Jacques. "From Daily Life to Eternity." *Posada's Mexico*. Ed. Ron Tyler. Washington D.C.: Library of Congress, 1979.

León-Portilla, Miguel. *La filosofía náhuatl estudiada en sus fuentes*. México, D.F.: UNAM, 1974 [1956].

——. *Visión de los vencidos: relaciones indígenas de la conquista*. México, D.F.: UNAM, 1980 [1959].

——. *Los antiguos mexicanos*. México, D.F.: Fondo de Cultura Económica, 1985 [1969].

Lévi-Strauss, Claude. *Myth and Meaning*. New York: Schocken, 1977.

López Chiñas, Gabriel. *El concepto de la muerte entre los zapotecas*. México: Vinnigulasa, 1969.

López Soriano, Eliseo. *Míxquic y la conmemoración de los difuntos*. México, D.F.: Privately published, 1990.

Luna Pimentel, Miguel. "Michael Jackson," "Calaveras de La Jornada." México, D.F.: *La Jornada*, 2 Nov. 1993.

Magaña Vázquez, Guillermo. "Hay muertos que no hacen ruido." México, D.F.: *Heraldo*, 31 Oct. 1993.

Malvido, Elsa. "A la muerte en México sólo le quedan sus mil chistes." México, D.F.: *Excélsior*, 2 Nov. 1993.

Mankekar, Purnima. "Television Tales and a Woman's Rage: A Nationalist Recasting of Draupadi's Disrobing." *Public Culture,* Vol. 5, Num. 3, spring 1993, 469–492.

Martel Díaz Cortés, Patricia. *Apuntes sobre la muerte en la poesía infantil de México.* México, D.F.: UNAM, Facultad de Filosofía y Letras, 1970.

Martínez, José Luis. *Nezahualcóyotl, vida y obra.* México, D.F.: Secretaría de Educación Pública, 1984 [1972].

Matos Moctezuma, Eduardo. *Muerte a filo de obsidiana: los nahuas frente a la muerte.* México, D.F.: Sep/Setentas Num. 190, Secretaría de Educación Pública, 1975.

———. *Estudios de cultura popular.* México: Instituto Nacional Indigenista, 1981.

Narr, Michael Cook. "Central America." *Legacy.* PBS. Minneapolis, Feb. 1992.

Natalí. "Reportera del 'Más allá.'" México, D.F.: *Universal,* 2 Nov. 1991.

New English Bible With the Apocrypha. New York: Oxford UP, 1971 [1961].

Nutini, Hugo. *Todos santos in Rural Tlaxcala.* Princeton: Princeton UP, 1988.

Ochoa Zazueta, Jesús Angel. *La muerte y los muertos: culto, servicio, ofrenda y humor de una comunidad.* México, D.F.: Sep/Setentas, 1974.

Olvero, Alfonso (producer). "Celebrating the Day of the Dead" (videotape). Texas: Educational Video Network, 1992.

Palacio Albor, María Estela. "Cementerio de mil colores." México, D.F.: *Heraldo,* 31 Oct. 1993.

Paz, Octavio. *El laberinto de la soledad.* México, D.F.: Fondo de Cultura Económica, 1973 [1950].

Poniatowska, Elena. "El gran Panteón de Dolores." México, D.F.: *Nacional,* 2 Nov. 1993.

Price, Sally. *Primitive Art in Civilized Places.* Chicago: U of Chicago P, 1989.

Reuter, Jas. "The Popular Traditions." *Posada's Mexico.* Ed. Ron Tyler. Washington D.C.: Library of Congress, 1979.

Rey, Agapito. *Cultura y costumbres del s. XVI en la Península ibérica y en la Nueva España.* México, D.F.: Mensaje, 1944.

Reyes, Mathilde. "Creencias y cultos a la muerte en México." Querétaro: *Querétaro,* Num. 52, Anno V, Oct. 1989.

Río García, Eduardo del (Rius). *Posada.* México, D.F.: Editorial Posada, 1989.

———. *El mito guadalupano.* México, D.F.: Editorial Posada, 1990.

Rivera, Candelario. "Siempre exisitirá la duda: ¿después de muertos, adónde vamos?" Puebla, Estado de Puebla: *El Sol de Puebla,* 2 Nov. 1993.

Rosenthal-Urey, Ina. "Contemporary Size and Distribution of Population." *The Cambridge Encyclopedia of Latin America and the Caribbean.* 2d ed. Eds. Simon Collier, Thomas E. Skidmore, and Harold Blakemore. Cambridge: Cambridge UP, 1992, 151–158.

Rosoff Beimler, Rosalind (text), and John Greenleigh (photographs). *The Days of the Dead/Los Días de Muertos: Mexico's Festival of Communion With the Departed/Un Festival de Comunión con los Muertos en México.* San Francisco: Collins, 1991.

Rothenstein, Julian, ed. *Posada: Messenger of Mortality.* London: Redstone, 1989.

Rowe, William, and Vivian Schelling. *Memory and Modernity: Popular Culture in Latin America.* London: Verso, 1991.

Rubin, Miri. *Corpus Christi: The Eucharist in Late Medieval Culture.* Cambridge: Cambridge UP, 1991.

Rulfo, Juan. "Puntos de partida hacia el poema" (audiotape). México, D.F.: N.p., n.d.

Sahagún, Fray Bernardino de. *Historia general de las cosas de la Nueva España.* México, D.F.: Porrúa, 1969 [1956].

Sahlins, Marshall. "La Pensée Bourgeoise: Western Society as Culture." *Culture and Practical Reason.* Chicago: U of Chicago P, 1976.

Santana Rebollar, Antonio. Personal Interview. 21 Jan. 1992.

Sayer, Chloë, ed. *Mexico: The Day of the Dead.* Boston: Shambala, 1993.

Sepúlveda, María Teresa. "Días de muertos en Iguala, Guerrero." México, D.F.: *Boletín INAH,* Num. 7, 1973, 3–12.

Shakespeare, William. *Hamlet. Major Plays and the Sonnets.* Ed. G. B. Harrison. New York: Harcourt, 1948.

Sierra Martínez, Luis. "Con el Miquixtli reciben a los muertos en Morelos; el mucbilpollo, listo en Yucatán." México, D.F.: *El Nacional,* 2 Nov. 1993.

Smith, C. "All Saints, Feast of." *New Catholic Encyclopedia.* Volume I. New York: McGraw Hill, 1967, p. 318f.

Sontag, Susan. "The Image-World" in *A Susan Sontag Reader.* New York: Farrar, Straus and Giroux, 1982, 349–367.

Soustelle, Jacques. *La vida cotidiana de los aztecas en vísperas de la conquista.* México, D.F.: Fondo de Cultura Económica, 1994 [1955].

Stallybrass, Peter, and Allon White. *The Politics and Poetics of Transgression.* Ithaca: Cornell UP, 1986.

Suárez Farías, Francisco. "Poesía funeraria en la Ciudad de Mexico: siglos XVIII, XIX y XX." México, D.F.: *Reforma,* Sección D Cultura, 31 Oct. 1994.

Tovar, General Remigio (alias "un católico"). *La fiesta de Todos los Santos en la iglesia Católica.* Guadalajara: N. T. Pratga, 1883.

Turner, Victor. *The Ritual Process: Structure and Anti-Structure.* Ithaca: Cornell UP, 1969.

Turok, Marta. *Cómo acercarse a la artesanía.* México, D.F.: Plaza y Valdés, 1988.

Tyler, Ron. *Posada's Mexico.* Washington D.C.: Library of Congress, 1979.

Vanegas Arroyo, Antonio, ed. *Celebración del Día de los Muertos en México*. México, D.F.: Antonio Vanegas Arroyo, 1990.

Verti, Sebastián. *Tradiciones mexicanas*. México, D.F.: Diana, 1991.

Villarruel Velasco, Bulmaro. "Mixquic: lugar de los muertos." México, D.F.: *Uno más uno*, 1 Nov. 1992.

Villaurrutia, Xavier. *Nostalgia de la muerte*. México: Ediciones Mictlan, 1946.

Weckmann, Luis. *The Medieval Heritage of Mexico*. Trans. Frances M. López-Morillas. New York: Fordham UP, 1992 [1984 Colegio de México].

Westheim, Paul. *La calavera*. Trans. Mariana Frenk. México, D.F.: Antigua Librería Robredo, Colección México y lo mexicano, 1953.

———. *Arte antiguo de México*. México, D.F.: Fondo de Cultura Económica, 1963 [1950].

Williamson, Judith. "Cooking Nature." *Decoding Advertisements*. London: Marion Boyers, 1978.

Wollen, Peter. *Posada: Messenger of Mortality*. Ed. Julian Rothenstein. London: Redstone, 1989.

Index

[Index does not include citations to figures and plates. Informants who are quoted from published texts are not cited; rather, the editors/authors of the texts are. Terms that appear here are also indexed for their entries in the glossary. Appendices are also indexed.]